THE
BRILLIANT
BEAN

THE BRILLIANT
B·E·A·N

SALLY AND MARTIN STONE

BANTAM BOOKS
TORONTO · NEW YORK · LONDON · SYDNEY · AUCKLAND

For Abby, Matt, our
friends and family

THE BRILLIANT BEAN
A Bantam Book / February 1988

BOMC offers recordings and compact discs, cassettes
and records. For information and catalog write to
BOMR, Camp Hill, PA 17012.

LIBRARY OF CONGRESS CATALOGING-IN-PUBLICATION DATA
Stone, Sally.
The brilliant bean.
Includes index.
1. Cookery (Beans)   I. Stone, Martin.   II. Title.
TX803.B4S76   1988   641.6'565   87-19609
ISBN 0-553-34483-8

Published simultaneously in the United States and Canada

Bantam Books are published by Bantam Books, a division of Bantam Doubleday
Dell Publishing Group, Inc. Its trademark, consisting of the words "Bantam
Books" and the portrayal of a rooster, is Registered in U.S. Patent and
Trademark Office and in other countries. Marca Registrada. Bantam Books, 666
Fifth Avenue, New York, New York 10103.

PRINTED IN THE UNITED STATES OF AMERICA

CONTENTS

THE
BRILLIANT
BEAN

INTRODUCTION

Beans have never been chic. They have always been peasant food, to be eaten when meat was unavailable, hard to come by, or, more to the point, too expensive. But today, as we rediscover the delights and satisfactions of peasant food (a.k.a. home cooking), we're confirming what most of us already knew or suspected: that although inexpensive, beans taste very good indeed and are one of the most nutritious of all foods on the hoof or off the vine.

To give beans more panache, food writers and aficionados lump them together with the new American cuisine—most of which arrived with its practitioners on Ellis Island. Most beans are not naturalized, however: they are indigenous. Like the Indians, beans, with four or five exceptions, were here to begin with, or were growing in Central or South America long before Columbus postulated that the world was round. They are reverse immigrants. They emigrated from the Western Hemisphere to Europe and then came back disguised—as though they had never set root here before. And they have most of us fooled.

All the cuisines of the world have in their repertoires intoxicating dishes based on beans and peas. You'll think at once of the cassoulet of France, the *dal* of India, the feijoada of Brazil, the black bean soup of Spain, the *frijoles refritos* of Mexico, the *hummus* of the Middle East, the *pasta e fagioli* of Italy, the stir-fried tofu and peapods of China, the bean paste of Japan, and, of course, the baked beans of New England and the black-eyed peas of the South.

On these pages we've taken these dishes and scores of others, turned them inside out and upside down, changed them, adapted them, invented and reinvented them to make beans right for the new American cooking: lighter, healthier, and quicker to prepare.

WHAT *IS* A BEAN?

Did you know that kidney beans are the mature, dried seeds of the vegetable that, when picked young, we eat pods and all as green beans? Or that alfalfa is a legume?

A legume, according to the dictionary, is a vegetable that is the seed of a plant having pods. A peanut is really a legume, not a nut.

Because all legumes absorb nitrogen from the air, they are rich sources of protein and are useful in maintaining the fertility of the soil. It is this, also, that makes them legumes and distinguishes them from other vegetables.

Beans have a long and interesting history going back millennia. They were one of the first wild plants to be domesticated. Their use as a life-sustaining nourishment before the advent of domesticated animals is well known but little exploited in our affluent, carnivorous society.

TODAY'S HEALTH FOOD

It is only recently that medical research has proclaimed beans a near-perfect food, touting them especially as a preventive of many modern ills. They are superior to bread, cereals, potatoes, and pasta as a source of carbohydrates for diabetics and joggers. They are an excellent source of dietary fiber (promoting regularity and keeping colon cancer at bay). They help control blood cholesterol and blood glucose while being free of cholesterol themselves. They help control weight by retaining water in the digestive tract, thus promoting a feeling of fullness and delaying the return of hunger.

Most of the calories in beans and peas come from complex carbohydrates (starches), which, unlike fats, have no history of risk to health. Beans derive only a minuscule percentage of their calories from fat, 2 to 6 percent, as contrasted with meat or cheese, which derive 80 percent and 75 percent of their calories from fat respectively. Soybeans are an exception (they're used as a commercial source for oil, remember) with 34 percent fat calories. However, as is the case with all beans, the fat in soybeans is polyunsaturated.

Besides being cholesterol-free, beans have, according to recent research, a chemical that helps fight the deposit of platelets (fat globules) in veins and arteries.

Although the protein in beans and peas may not be complete, as is that in animal foods (soybeans do provide complete protein), it can, with the addition of small amounts of grain foods or animal protein such as milk, cheese, bits of meat, poultry, or fish, offer protein as useable and total as that of meat alone. At the same time they are providing this protein at a fraction of the cost. *Useable* is the key word here. The recent release of a new set of federal dietary guidelines and changes in recommended daily dietary allowances under review by the National Academy of Sciences point to new theories that may prove the protein content of beans and peas complete enough to replace animal protein.

Mature legumes (in addition to peas and green beans, which are really picked before they are allowed to develop fully) are chock-full of vitamins and minerals. They're well endowed with the B vitamins: thiamine, niacin, B_6, and folic acid. About a cup of cooked beans provides as much as 40 percent of adult daily needs for thiamine and B_6.

Women especially can benefit from eating beans. A cup of lentils, for instance, offers a quarter of the daily recommended requirement of iron. The body is helped to absorb this high iron content when the lentils are eaten with foods high in vitamin E such as tomatoes, peppers, broccoli, and citrus fruits or juices. Luckily, lentils are compatible with all these foods.

Other important minerals plentiful in peas and beans include calcium, phosphorus, and potassium.

Beans are a boon to diabetics and hypoglycemics because eating them doesn't trigger a rise in blood sugar or require that the pancreas pour out extra quantities of insulin to readjust the glucose level in the blood. Carbohydrate foods like bread, cereals, potatoes, and pasta cause the body to release insulin. The release of insulin promotes the storage of body fat. Since beans do not trigger outpourings of insulin, eating them actually helps to flush away fats rather than allowing the body to store them away for future use as fuel. Thus it is important for those on weight-loss diets to avoid most carbohydrate foods and switch to beans.

Beans also give you more volume and weight of food for the number of calories ingested (2½ to 4 times the volume for the calorie equivalent of meat or cheese). What's more, their fiber content sends them on a clean sweep through the digestive system. As a result, you feel you've eaten more (which in fact you have); you feel full and satisfied because the beans absorb moisture and increase in bulk as they travel through the intestines.

But one of the best things about beans and weight control is that the body uses up more calories digesting beans and peas than most other foods. So some of the calories you eat by choosing beans don't really count!

Lest you misunderstand, this is neither a diet book nor a health-food book; it is certainly not a vegetarian cookbook, even though it has many recipes vegetarians can use. This is a cookbook for people who like to eat elegant, delicious, interesting food. It just so happens that the subject of the book is good for what ails you.

RUNNING HOT AND COLD

There are over 14,000 species in the leguminosae family although only 22 are grown in any quantity for human consumption. They thrive today in a wide range of climatic conditions. Because it was native to the cold uplands of Peru, the lima bean can tolerate colder, temperate latitudes. The soybean likes the warmth of summers in Mongolia and our own plains states. The haricot thrives in the Mediterranean climates (who doesn't!) and pigeon peas prefer the hot, humid tropics. Anywhere they are grown—and they can be grown even in relatively poor soil— the yield per acre is high and the soil becomes more fertile than it was before (they play an important role in the farming practice of crop rotation, absorbing nitrogen from the air through their root systems and passing it on into the soil).

BEAN BASICS

IF YOU DON'T KNOW
BEANS ABOUT BEANS

It is not easy to identify by sight all the different kinds of beans available in the market. What we describe here are the more familiar varieties, including as many names in common use as we could discover (some beans have as many as fifteen different colloquial names depending upon the region of the country or the ethnic group. We also describe their distinguishing features, including special nutritional qualities; we give suggestions for their uses in cooking and mention some of their traditional culinary partners and seasonings; and we indicate which are best fresh, dried, or frozen. Some by-products are also given.

The more you know about the many varieties of beans available—their colors, sizes, and flavors—the more versatile and useful you'll find them in the kitchen. The beans described here belong to the legume family, the third largest group of flowering plants (the other two being the orchid and the daisy). After grains, beans are the second most important food in fueling the human body. Some are eaten in the pod: snow peas, string beans, yard-long beans, among many. Some are shelled fresh: lima beans, black-eyed peas, green peas. Others are dried to be stored and reconstituted by soaking: chick-peas, Great Northerns, kidney and navy beans are in this group. Many are used in all three ways as well as being canned and frozen.

ADZUKI (*Phaseolus angularis*)
a.k.a. Azuki, Aduki, Adsuki, Asuki, Feijao

The adzuki is a small (¼-inch long), oval, reddish-brown bean with a thin white keel, or ridge. It has been grown and eaten in China and Japan for thousands of years. It even looks Asian, as though it had been designed by a contemporary Japanese graphic artist. Adzukis are bush beans (they grow on bushes rather than vines) and are eaten fresh, dried, sprouted, and ground into flour. The adzuki is so versatile and delicious with its light, nutty flavor that is it known in Asia as the "king of beans" and is used for both savory and sweet dishes. In Japan these beans are steamed with rice to give the grain a pink blush as in the festival wedding dish, Sekihan. They are also made into candied bean cakes and other confections and served with green tea at the end of a meal. These beans are wonderful simply boiled and served with butter or in salads. Because their skin is quite thick, they need long soaking and should be cooked for about 2 hours. Adzukis are an excellent source of protein (25 percent), iron and other minerals, calcium, thiamine, and other B-group vitamins. They are available from health-food, Chinese, Japanese, Indian, and yoga stores.

BLACK BEANS (*Phaseolus vulgaris*)
a.k.a. Turtle Beans, Frijoles Negros, Mexican Blacks, Spanish Black Beans

A large (⅝-inch long), kidney-shaped bean, shiny black in color with a white keel, it is a native of South America and is used throughout South and Central America and the Caribbean, where it is a staple to be boiled, fried, spiced, and mixed with rice and other foods. The black bean has a slightly mushroomy flavor and is traditionally made into black bean soup in Cuba, Puerto Rico, and Spain. In Brazil it is the basis of feijoada, the national dish. In the West Indies it is a major source of protein in the rice and bean combination that in Cuba is called *Moros y Christianos* (Moors and Christians). Black beans take about 1 hour to cook after soaking for 4 hours. (See quick soak method, p. 22.) They contain about 23 percent protein and good quantities of iron, calcium, and the B vitamins. They are available in most supermarkets, health-food stores, and Hispanic markets.

BLACK-EYED PEAS
(*Vigna unguiculata*)
a.k.a. Brown-eyed Peas, Black-eyed Beans, Cowpeas, Oea Beans, China Beans, Marble Beans, Black-eyed Suzies

A creamy-colored, kidney-shaped bean, medium-sized (½ inch), with a purplish black keel that distinguishes it from other beans and, of course, suggested the popular name. Probably a native of China (a relative of the mung bean and other Asian legumes), the black-eyed pea no doubt traveled the Silk Route, ended up in Arab hands, and found its way to Africa. From there it was brought to the Western Hemisphere by slaves and became established in the plantation diet early in the eighteenth century. These beans are still used in many African dishes, and in Indian cooking as well. Black-eyed peas have a light, smooth texture and a subtly savory flavor. Because they have a thin skin, the beans may be cooked without presoaking. They should be checked for doneness after 30 minutes. Overcooking makes them disintegrate, as does too many turns of the mixing spoon.

The young pod of the fresh beans may be eaten as a vegetable and its leafy shoot is said to taste like Swiss chard. The beans add texture to salads, take easily to seasoning, can be made into fritters, and go well with yogurt. They are superlative with rice, as in the southern dish Hoppin' John (originally made with pigeon peas, called in the French-speaking islands of the Caribbean *pois à pigeon* and pronounced ah-pee-jon, hence "Hoppin' John"). Black-eyed peas contain about 22 percent protein, some iron, calcium, phosphorus, potassium, vitamin B complex—and some vitamin A, unlike most beans. They are available in supermarkets all over the country. Dried black-eyed peas can be bought loose and in plastic bags (90 percent of these are from California). The cooked peas are sold both canned and frozen.

BROAD BEANS (*see* Fava Beans)

BROWN BEANS (*Phaseolus vulgaris*)
a.k.a. Swedish Beans

These small (⅓ inch) oval brown beans take their nickname from the people who use them the most. In Scandinavia they are used for sweetened purees to be served with smoked pork or ham, and for other lusty dishes. They are not widely available here. Try Scandinavian specialty food shops, gourmet sections of department stores, or simply substitute small white beans.

CANNELLINI BEANS
(*Phaseolus vulgaris*)
a.k.a. Fasolia

This member of the haricot bean family was originally cultivated in Argentina. Cannellini beans are now associated with Italian cuisine and are grown commercially in Italy. They are white, oval in shape, medium-sized (about ½ inch), with a tough seed coat. Their texture is smooth and they have a subtly nutty flavor. These are the favored beans for *pasta e fagioli* (recipe page 88) and other Tuscan dishes. You will find them canned in most supermarkets. They have the same protein and nutritive value as others of the genus *Phaseolus*.

CHANNA DAL (*Pisum stivum*)
a.k.a. Chenna, Chanai, Arhar Dal, Toor Dal, Tur, Toer, Toovar Dal, Ooloonthoo, Pigeon Peas

These are yellow split peas grown and eaten in India and parts of Southeast Asia. Small (¼ inch) and round, they come hulled and split and are rather soft, so they cook quickly. *Channa dal* is used alone, in rice, meat, and vegetable dishes and as a puree. When ground, they are sometimes substituted for chick-pea flour because they are easier to grind at home. When packed in castor oil, *channa dal* are known as *toer, tur, arhar, or toovar dal*. The oil is used as a preservative and to discourage insects. It should be washed off in several changes of water. The taste of these *dal* is a little different from that of *channa dal* because of the oil, but they may be used for the same purposes. Substitute American yellow split peas for the same texture, but don't expect the flavor to be nearly so nutty. These are a source of iron, vitamin B—and protein, of course. They are available in Indian and Asian markets.

CHICK-PEAS (*Cicer arietinum*)
a.k.a. Garbanzos, Ceci, Hummus

The Romans named this bean *arietinum* (ramlike) because it looked like a ram's head with horns curling over the sides. *Cicer* is the bean itself. The venerable Roman family name of Cicero is derived from this bean, which was a staple of the ancients' diet. Round, beige, medium-sized (³⁄₈ inches in diameter), with a beaklike sprout, chick-peas are among the most versatile of all the legumes. They have a nutty taste and a firm texture. It is almost impossible to overcook them. Chick-peas originated in North Africa and the Middle East, where they were first cultivated around 5000 B.C. The Carthaginians introduced the chick-pea into Europe through Spain, where they are called *garbanzos* (derived from Greek), and where they still play an important part in regional cooking.

Chick-peas are widely grown in India and Burma, where they rival wheat in acreage under cultivation (more than three-quarters the acreage of wheat). They are India's most important legume, finding their way to the table boiled, fried, roasted, in fritters, sprouted, made into soups, and ground into flour to use as a thickener for stews and sauces and for making dumplings and pancakes. We have found the puree useful for replacing flour in several classic and improvised cake recipes. Perhaps the most popular dish made from chick-peas is the Middle Eastern *hummus,* a paste with many variations but whose principal ingredients are the puree to which garlic, tahini (sesame paste), oil, a bit of paprika, and lemon juice are added. The rich, full flavor of the bean makes it perfect for pâtés, pies, casseroles, and soups. The chick-pea is one of the most nutritious members of the bean family, rich in protein, calcium, iron, and the B group of vitamins. Extremely hard, these legumes usually need long soaking. They are widely available both dried and canned.

DAL (*Dhal*)

Dal is the generic name the Indians give to legumes—lentils, peas, and beans. *Dal* are used hulled or unhulled, roasted or unroasted, and are basic to Indian cooking because they are a good source of protein, iron, and the B vitamins.

FAVA BEANS (*Vicia faba*)
a.k.a. Faba, Broad Bean, Horse Bean

The fava (it appears here in its Italian guise) was the only bean known to Europeans before the discovery of the New World and the subsequent introduction into Europe of the common bean (the kidney and all its relatives). The fava is a large bean (¾ inch) that, in this country, is sometimes confused with the lima, which it resembles slightly in appearance but not at all in flavor. The thick, bright green pod holds the bean in an inner layer that looks like Styrofoam and feels like down. The bean, nestled in its velvety bed, is an intense, pale green without a trace of yellow. In its dried form it is creamy brown in color with a wrinkled brown skin that is often tough even after cooking. For this reason, the dried form is most successfully used as a puree. Fava beans are virtually never to be found on the American table unless the family happens to be Italian, Greek, or Spanish. They have an earthy flavor in contrast to the nuttiness of most beans. Their pedigree goes back to ancient Egypt, where they are said to have been a staple, along with garlic and onions, in the diet of the builders of the pyramids. They are still a staple of the Eygptian diet.

In other countries around the Mediterranean, favas are cultivated for both human and animal food. Falafel, a Greek and Middle Eastern street food and a familiar fast food in many American cities, is traditionally made with dried, ground fava beans—although in this country you are more likely to find it made with chick-peas.

In Italy the first crop of tiny, tender new beans, the first green vegetable to appear in the spring, is greeted with enormous enthusiasm. Romans love them raw in an antipasto along with sharp pecorino cheese. Elsewhere on the boot they may be slowly simmered with ham and scallions until they almost melt.

If you are not familiar with the fresh variety of the fava, open a pod at the market and look inside. If the beans are a gleaming, clear green, take them home. If they are fat, with a yellowish-green skin, forget them, they're old and not worth the trouble of shelling. The pods of fresh fava beans are also edible but tough.

Favas are hardy and are easily grown in temperate climates. Dried favas need long soaking, sometimes a day and a half, plus an hour's cooking. Some prefer to skin them after cooking (British cookbooks suggest this, but it's only the old beans that need skinning; puree them instead). The philosopher Pythagoras forbade his followers to eat favas because, according to legend, they contained the souls of the dead. More likely, behind this proscription was the blood disorder favism, a serious anemic condition suffered, although rarely, by people of Mediterranean extraction, the result of eating undercooked favas or inhaling their pollen. Only eight cases of the disease have been recorded in this country.

Traces of the fava's cultivation have been found in Bronze Age sites in Switzerland and in Iron Age remains in Great Britain.

Available fresh in early spring at some specialty greengrocers, health-food stores, and ethnic markets; favas are available dried and in cans at some supermarkets.

FLAGEOLETS (*Phaseolus vulgaris*)

Flageolets are immature kidney beans that have been removed from their pods when very young. They are to beans as veal is to beef—a delicacy in the bean world. They are very tender, of course, and have a light, fresh taste and a pale, pastel green color. Cultivated mainly in France and in Italy, flageolets are traditionally tossed in an herbed vinaigrette and served cold in an *hors d'oeuvre varié* or an antipasto. Available fresh at specialty greengrocers and some gourmet shops, they can also be found canned at these same outlets.

GARBANZOS (*see Chick-peas*)

GREAT NORTHERN BEANS (*see* Haricot Beans)

HARICOT BEANS (*Phaseolus vulgaris*) a.k.a. Great Northern Beans, Small Whites, Navy Beans, Soissons, Cannellini, White Kidney Beans

Haricot beans come in many varieties and colors, but the most common are ivory-white small (⅜ inch) ovals, slightly kidney-shaped and with a tough skin. They are the mature, dried white seeds of the green bean (string bean, known as *haricot vert* in France). They are probably the most widely used of all the common beans. Because of them the people of Tuscany are known as *mangia fagioli* (bean-eaters); France has a class-erasing dish called cassoulet and Boston is known as Beantown. Haricots are the beans in Boston Baked beans, which gave rise to the turn-of-the-century doggerel:

> And this is good old Boston,
> The home of the bean and the cod,
> Where the Lowells talk to the Cabots
> And the Cabots talk only to God.

An old Bostonian recalls that "everyone in Boston ate baked beans and brown bread on Saturday night, it was almost a ritual." Rituals die easy in affluent societies—especially when they recall less palmy days of eating beans because they were cheap and filling. No matter that they were delicious and had an illustrious history dating back to the Sunday dinners of the Puritans. In 1620 the Pilgrims saw Indian squaws baking beans with deer fat and onions overnight in clay pots resting on hot stones lining a hole. They adapted the tradition, replacing the deer fat with pork and adding brown sugar and seasonings.

Buy baked beans in cans (B&M brand) if you must, but try them from scratch with mustard and molasses or maple sugar to know just why they were so popular. Your supermarket has dried haricots in plastic bags under the generic name Great Northern. They contain 23 percent protein, 61 percent carbohydrate, as well as iron, calcium, and B vitamins, among other nutrients.

KIDNEY BEANS (*Phaseolus vulgaris*) a.k.a. Habichuelas, Chili Beans, Mexican Beans

Kidney beans are a deep liver-red bean of average size (½ inch long) and are, of course, shaped like a kidney. They also come in brown, black, and white varieties. Kidney beans are all good sources of protein, iron, and the B-group vitamins. The red kidney bean is enjoyed throughout the world for its rich flavor and color and turns up in one guise or another in all types of cuisines. In this country, the kidney is most famous as the red bean of New Orleans's Red Beans and Rice and the Southwest's *chili*, with or without the *carne*. Red Beans and Rice made properly requires time and attention and so restaurant versions usually fall short. There are also several schools of thought as to what should be added to the pot along with the beans—garlic, bay leaf, onion, carrot, sweet pepper, thyme, red pepper or Tabasco—and whether it should be cracked hambone, pickled pork, or spicy sausage. Whatever the choice, the whole is simmered gently for at least 3 hours, until the beans melt into a rich, thick red gravy seasoned with generous amounts of garlic, to be served over fluffy white rice.

Kidney beans, because of their color and texture, can add eye appeal and a pleasant "mouth feel" to many standard recipes. You can be inventive with them and at the same time contribute to nutrition. The kidney bean is one of those common beans that have been developed in hundreds of varieties since coming under cultivation 7000 years ago in southwestern Mexico. They were not to be exported to Europe (by Spanish explorers) until several thousand years later.

LENTILS (*Lens esculenta*)

The lentil is most probably the oldest cultivated legume, dating from 8000 to 7000 B.C. Its place of origin is southwestern Asia, what are now the fertile lands bordering the Indus River. From there it was dispersed first to the rest of the Middle East and to northeastern Africa, then to India and eastern Europe. *Lens* is the Latin word for lentil, hence its coinage in the seventeenth century as the word for a doubly convex piece of glass, shaped like a lentil. This legume is mentioned in the Old Testament. Esau sold his birthright for a mess of "pottage of lentils" (thought to be an ancient Middle Eastern dish of lentils and onions simmered slowly in sesame oil). The French word for lentil soup is *potage Esau,* and in classic French cuisine the word *Esau* usually signifies a dish whose main ingredient is lentils (Eggs Esau: poached eggs served in a nest of pureed lentils). Lentils are the seed of a small shrub. They were eaten by the Egyptians, the Greeks, and the Romans, and have been eaten ever since.

Lentils are enormously important to the diet of people in many of the underdeveloped countries, and they play a vital role in providing protein for the North African and Asian populations. Despite the fact that they are featured in many an elegant repast, lentils are looked down upon by some because of their link with the poor. Even in ancient times, foods were sometimes disdained because of their association with poverty. Aristophanes used this idea in his play *Ploutos,* in which a character remarks of a *nouveau riche* acquaintance, "Now he doesn't eat lentils anymore." The line became a proverb that was applied to anyone who had risen from rags to riches and denied his background.

Lentils need no soaking and they cook relatively quickly. They must be watched, however, because they soften easily and can lose their texture. This is fine if they are to be pureed, but a disaster otherwise. Lentils are 25 percent protein and are rich in other nutrients, including iron and vitamin B.

- BROWN LENTILS. Gray-brown in color, shiny and flat (1/4 inch round). They are France's *lentilles blondes* and are known as the most flavorful of the three lentils. In France they are often served simply with butter. In the Middle East olive oil is substituted for the butter, and when the lentils are served with rice, they can constitute a meal. Be careful when cooking them as they can disintegrate if not watched. Check for tenderness after 18 to 20 minutes. The smaller Chinese brown lentil has an earthy taste and is the one found in supermarkets here.
- BROWN MASOOR LENTILS. Used in Indian and Middle Eastern dishes, these are the red lentils in their seed coats. They should *not* be used in place of brown lentils in continental recipes (they are too tender).
- GREEN LENTILS, a.k.a. Egyptian Lentils. A dull olive, flat lentil similar in size to the brown lentil. These have a light, fresh flavor and are tastiest dressed simply with an herbed vinaigrette and served cold. The best are from France and the best in France are from Le Puy. They have a nice firm texture and take a little longer to cook, from 20 to 30 minutes. Ask for them at gourmet counters in department stores and at imported food specialty shops.
- RED LENTILS, a.k.a. Egyptian Lentils as above. Ads Majroosh. An orange-pink lentil, 1/4 inch round. These are best when cooked to a smooth puree. If you want to serve them whole, check them after only 10 minutes for tenderness.
- MASOOR DAL, a.k.a. Masar Dal, Malika Masoor, Mysor Dal. Smaller than the European red lentil, this is the brown *Masoor* with its seed coat removed. It should not be substituted for the European varieties because it cooks even more quickly and rapidly disintegrates into a puree. For this reason it should be used in soups and stews and Indian and Middle Eastern recipes calling for purees.

LIMA BEANS (*Phaseolus lunatus*)
a.k.a. Butter, Madagascar, Curry, Pole, Sieva Beans

These are flattish, creamy white to pale pastel green-colored beans that have two main species: the large lima (1-1/4 inches long), which is native to Central America but reached Peru several millennia ago, taking its name from that country's capital; and a smaller variety (1/2 inch long) from Mexico called the baby lima or sieva. The Spanish explorers brought both varieties to Europe, where they thrived in the temperate climate. The slave trade brought the lima to Africa, where it is now the most important bean on the continent. Whether large or small, the lima tastes pretty much the same. The smaller lima cooks in less time, however, and has a thinner, tenderer skin. The lima dispersed quickly early on and became a staple of the American Indian diet. Succotash, of Algonquin origin, which the Indians called *musicickquatash*, was a combination of corn and limas stewed together. Lima beans are available everywhere, in fresh, dried, canned, and frozen form. They contain 23 percent protein and are a source of B vitamins, iron, calcium, phosphorus, potassium, and the trace minerals.

MUNG BEANS (*Vigna radiata*)
a.k.a. Moong Dal, Mung Dal, Green Gram, Golden Gram, Lou Teou

Mungs are small (1/4 inch), round beans with a yellow interior wrapped in an olive green seed coat. They are sold and used either whole or without their husk, hulled or unhulled, or split (*Moong dal*). The pods of the young beans are eaten as a green vegetable when tender. Although native to India, they spread to China in early times. They were first cultivated about 1500 B.C.

Mung Beans are the beans the Chinese and Indians use as bean sprouts. While the whole bean is quite rich in vitamins A and B, it is fivefold richer in food value after it is sprouted. In sprouting it even forms vitamins not found in the bean, the elusive vitamins C and B_{12}. Bean sprouts are the only source of these two crucial vitamins in the whole bean family. They are also much easier to digest than the whole bean, because while they are sprouting the starches are broken down into simple sugars, the proteins into amino acids and what fats there are, into fatty acids. Sprouts may be cooked along with other ingredients or used raw in salads or as a garnish for sandwiches. The whole bean is eaten with butter and/or spices, pureed, or ground into flour. Mung bean flour is that used for bean threads or cellophane noodles by the Chinese (a hot-water bath turns the brittle threads into flexible, translucent, edible strands in minutes).

There are also brown and black varieties of the mung bean. The black gram, called *urad*, is indigenous to Africa, Asia, and the West Indies.

Mung beans can be soaked for an hour, but it's really not necessary. The whole bean contains 24 percent protein and 60 percent carbohydrate; the sprout contains 4 percent protein and 7 percent carbohydrate. Both bean and sprout are available in Chinese and Indian markets. The sprouts are found fresh and in plastic bags at many produce stands and canned in supermarkets.

NAVY BEANS (see Haricot Beans)
a.k.a. Pea Beans

These require long, slow cooking and are often used for baked beans and soups. Navy beans are small, oval, white beans and are interchangeable with haricot beans.

PEAS (*Pisum sativum*)

The flavor of fresh peas is so heavenly to some that they are said to have originated in the Garden of Eden. They did in fact originate in the Middle East, where they were domesticated before 6000 B.C., and from which they spread throughout the Mediterranean, India, and China. By the time Athens was flourishing, dried peas were already a staple, the Greeks having learned of them from the Aryans of the East. After the Greeks, the Romans ate them, but, again, dried. (The Chinese were the first to eat peas fresh.) The Elizabethans, too, ate dried peas. In 1555 the wild pea helped the peasants of England survive a famine. Peas, it seems, were not cultivated there until late in the sixteenth century and were unknown, it is said, before 1509, the beginning of the reign of Henry VIII. They had, however, been in use in Europe throughout the Middle Ages, dried and stored for eating during the long, lean winters in such dishes as soups, stews, and puddings. The "pease porridge" of the nursery rhyme was made with dried peas, served hot or cold, even nine days old. It was not until the seventeenth century that fresh garden green peas were eaten in Europe—but they were still strange to most.

The manner in which the aristocrats of the French court of the Sun King, Louis XIV, ate peas seems odd to us now: the peas in their pods were dipped in a sauce, the peas then stripped from their shells with the upper front teeth, much the way artichokes are eaten, and the pods discarded. Some ladies of the court had peas waiting for them in their bed chambers to eat before going to sleep—natural green sleeping pills. By the end of the seventeenth century, peas were so popular that, according to Madame de Maintenon, the anticipation and pleasure of eating fresh peas provided the main topic of conversation for some courtiers over a four-day weekend. It's a wonder the French Revolution didn't start a hundred years sooner!

The green pea is one of the few vegetables that can withstand freezing and still taste fresh. Look for the tiny frozen peas called "petite." Thanks to modern food technology, green peas can be eaten all year long, fresh or frozen. Canning peas still confounds the technologists. The peas turn grayish, are mushy, and taste

like a completely different vegetable. They are unworthy of the name *pea*.

The dried marrowfat garden pea is gray-green, small (3/8 inch) and has a wrinkled skin. It is good for soups and purees, but if soaked and cooked till just tender (*al dente*), it can be used as a vegetable. These peas have an affinity for smoked pork products and can be turned into hearty winter stews. They have a good share of iron, protein, calcium, and some vitamin A and B. They were the dried pea of the Middle Ages.

Dried green split peas, husked and split, go back in history to ancient Egypt, Greece, and Rome. They're still cheap, nourishing, and filling, and they make delicious soups.

Dried yellow split peas, husked and split, need no soaking and cook in just half an hour. They are used by the Germans and Scandinavians for thick, stick-to-the-ribs soups with ham, sausage, bacon, and pork. The yellow split pea is the pea of pease porridge.

All split peas cook quickly without soaking and have an earthy flavor different from that of fresh peas.

Sugar Snap Peas

Crisp and flavorful, the comparatively new sugar snap is a cross between the English garden pea and the Chinese snow pea. Like the snow pea, they are eaten pod and all. Sugar snaps have yet to enter the mass market mainly because they are difficult for commercial farmers to grow and harvest—they grow larger and bear later than either of their parents, and their vines grow tall and need good support. The pod, not flat or pale green like the snow pea, but round, fat, and deeply colored like the green bean, is quite juicy. The peas inside appear as mere ripples on the surface of the pod.

The snap pea's sweetness is best preserved by quick cooking—steaming, stir-frying, or blanching until just heated through. If overcooked these peas become limp and taste bland. They can replace snow peas in a recipe. To prepare for cooking or eating raw, simply remove the string that runs down the spine of the pod. To freeze, blanch briefly (about 2 minutes), refresh in ice water immediately, drain, dry with paper towels, and pack in freezer bags sealed as airtight as possible. To cook frozen snap peas, allow them to thaw slowly at a cool temperature (refrigerator is fine), pat dry with paper towels, and cook until just heated through or, when adding to a dish, put them in just before serving. Do not cook them directly from the freezer or they will be limp and tasteless. Home gardeners can make the early summer pea season last longer by planting sugar snaps. They mature just when the last of the garden peas have been picked.

PIGEON PEAS (*Vigna sinensis*)
a.k.a. Gandules, Congo Peas, Goongoo Beans

Brought by slaves from Africa, these are the peas used in many of the rice and peas dishes of Jamaica and other Caribbean islands such as "Hoppin' John." They are rumored to have a slightly narcotic effect, but the kind of stupor they are said to induce usually results from overeating rather than any chemical content. Pigeon peas were cultivated by the Egyptians 4000 years ago. They are found canned (and sometimes dried) in Hispanic sections of the supermarket and at health-food stores.

PINK BEANS (*Phaseolus vulgaris*)

This is a pale pinkish-beige version of the red kidney bean. It is used in South American dishes. The red kidney bean, dark or light, or the pinto bean can stand in for it.

PINTO BEANS (*Phaseolus vulgaris*)

A small (3/8 inch) kidney bean, oval in shape, from South America. It is beige in color and

has streaks of brownish pink on the skin. Its name is from the Spanish word for *painted*. The horse of the same name (sometimes called Old Paint) has similar markings. The pinto is used in South American and Mexican dishes. When cooked, it loses its mottled appearance and turns a uniform pink. Pintos are widely available dried and canned.

ROSECOCO BEANS
(*Phaseolus vulgaris*)
a.k.a. Cranberry, Roman, Borlotti, Saluggia, Crab-eye Beans

Like the pinto but reversed in color. These have beige markings on a pink skin. The shape, texture, and taste are almost identical. Rosecoco and pinto beans are also interchangeable in recipes, especially when called for in Italian cookbooks, where they may be referred to as borlotti or saluggia beans. Although their colors are different, these beans taste exactly the same as pintos. Anyway they both turn pink in the cooking.

SOYBEANS (*Glycine max*)
a.k.a. Soya Beans

Soybeans are round in shape, about the size of a pea (3/8 inch) and are usually a pale ivory-yellow in color (but they also come in black, green, and brown). It is the hardest of all the beans and consequently needs the longest soaking and cooking.

The ancient Chinese called the soybean "the miracle bean." It still deserves this appellation. Before the end of World War II, hardly anyone in this country who wasn't of Asian heritage knew what a soybean was. Soybeans still aren't used much in American cooking, but 2 billion bushels (55 million tons) are produced here annually by farmers on 68 million acres of land. Half that enormous harvest is exported.

What does a country that hardly ever picks up a soybean from a plate do with the rest of this harvest? The soybean has an enormous variety of uses. Since the bean is 34 percent oil, much of the crop is turned into salad oil, margarine, and oils used in industry. It is a principal ingredient in livestock feed (38 percent of its edible weight is protein). It has found its way into soaps, glue, bottle caps, pencils, paint, disinfectants, face powders and creams, linoleum, nitroglycerin, cement, varnish, diesel fuel, and more. It is used to make plastics, detergents, and fiberboard. If we do not use soybeans themselves much in our diets, they creep in anyway in the form of lecithin emulsifiers, the substance that holds chocolate bars and other foods together. As insurance against starvation, the Nazis had hoarded a 2-million-ton cache of soybeans by the time World War II broke out. But, as of now, only 2 percent of the soybeans grown in this country are used for human food. What have been discovered by a relative few are the products Asians have been subsisting on for thousands of years: tofu (soybean curd), miso (soybean paste), soy sauce, soy milk, soy flour, tempeh, and hundreds of other incarnations of the bean.

What the rest of the population doesn't know is that many of the supermarket brands they (and their pets) eat every day contain soybean products—extenders, emulsifiers, fortifiers, extracts, and proteins. Soybeans are also made into imitation (analogue) salami, meatloaf, chicken breasts, shrimp, crabmeat, spareribs, chocolate drinks, cheese, hot dogs, and so on. These are almost indistinguishable in taste and texture from the real thing; most of the time they are superior nutritionally to the real thing, as well as being easier to digest. But because processing costs are high, so, often, are the prices.

Where did the single largest cash crop (75 percent of the world's supply of soybeans) in this country get its start? In northern China, probably Manchuria, where the soybean has been cultivated for over 5000 years. There it is known as "the meat of the soil." The soybean was introduced to Europe in the seventeenth century and wasn't even bothered with in the United States until 1900. Henry Ford was a promoter of the bean not only for food but for industrial use. He had one of his cars clad in a soybean compound that he said was tougher than steel. He even had material woven from soybean thread and made into two suits.

It is only in the Far East that the soybean is an important human food crop. In fact, in China and Japan soybean products are so numerous that just to list them would fill this book. However, soybean products have seen a tremendous increase in popularity in the West recently. One, tofu, has reached almost cult status in the vegetarian world. This cheese-like product is made by grinding the beans, blending them with water, boiling the mixture, and cooking and straining out the solids. Miso, used primarily to make soups, is fermented bean paste that is mixed with rice, barley, and other grains to create many forms with distinctive flavor and color. Miso, besides being protein-rich like tofu, also has vitamin B and bacteria, which are good for the digestive system.

Soy milk, made from ground beans boiled with water and strained, has been consumed at breakfast in Japan for hundreds of years. It is richer than cow's milk in iron, calcium, and phosphorus and can be used as a milk substitute in baking and dessert recipes. It is because of soy milk that the soybean is called the "cow of China." Tempeh, an Asian food made by treating soybeans with a fungus, has just recently started to become popular here in certain health-food circles. In Indonesia tempeh is so popular that 41,000 shops make and sell 169,000 tons of it a year to satisfy a populace that literally gobbles it up—mostly seasoned and fried. It has a meaty texture and good "mouth feel."

Soy sauce is the principal seasoning used in Asian cooking. The soy sauce that is naturally fermented from soybeans, wheat, and sea salt has a better flavor than do the commercial brands. You can check for authenticity by shaking the bottle until the liquid fizzes. If it does and the bubbles persist for a minute, it's the fermented kind. This soy sauce is also sold under the generic names *shoyu* and *tamari*. *Tamari* is the richer, thicker, and more concentrated of the two. British doctors have attributed the generally good teeth, good dental health, and absence of rickets among the Chinese to soybeans. The Chinese eat soybeans fresh, sprouted, and, when very young, in the pod. And so can we. The sprouts are not as tender as mung bean sprouts, but they're larger and crisper.

TEPARI BEANS (*Phaseolus vulgaris*)

Teparies are Mexican haricot beans and are similar to them in appearance. They are used in many regional dishes there. Use haricot beans as a substitute.

WINGED BEANS
(*Psophocarpus tetragonolobus*)

Distantly related to the soybean, the winged bean has been touted as the soybean of the tropics. It is said that the flowers of this 12- to 14-foot-high vine have the look and texture of mushrooms; leaves that taste like spinach; edible tubers with 8 times the protein of cassava or potatoes; and edible pods and beans. Oil can be processed from the bean, as it can from the soy; winged beans can be made into tofu, milk, and tempeh; and the vines can be used for fodder. These beans thrive in hot, humid climes (unlike the soybean, which needs a temperate climate), so it can be grown in places like the East Indies, Equatorial Africa, Indonesia, the Philippines, southern India and Sri Lanka. The winged bean could become a home-grown protein factory for these undernourished areas.

AN END TO THE GAS GLUT

Beans, beans the musical fruit,
The more you eat, the more you toot,
The more you toot, the better you feel.
So eat some beans at every meal.

There is a second verse that begins, "Beans, beans they're good for the heart . . ." and goes on to say pretty much the same as the first.

Beans and peas do tend to create gas in the lower intestine, but no more so than broccoli, cabbage, turnips, cauliflower, and many other vegetables and fruits such as grapes and melons. (Then there are seeds and nuts.) Gas from beans can be controlled, however.

You see, when you eat beans, you ingest complex sugars called oligosaccharides, which can't be digested by human digestive enzymes. You might think that these complex sugars, like the fiber in beans, would then pass through the intestinal tract and be excreted. No such luck. When these molecules leave the upper intestine and enter the lower they are met by a large, ravenous resident bacteria population. These bacteria eat the oligosaccharides and in the process give off various gases, mostly carbon dioxide, as waste products. It is these bacteria and their hunger, therefore, that produce flatulence after eating beans.

Oligosaccharides exist in greater quantities in more mature legumes like dried beans. Green beans and young, fresh peas are much less bothersome. Navy beans and limas are the most offensive. And peanuts, considering that they are also legumes, are the least.

Flatulence is more likely to be a problem for people who eat beans infrequently. For those who are regular consumers of dried beans (the Mexicans and most South Americans, for example) the intestinal tract seems to have adapted, and gas is less of a problem. Maybe the bacteria eat themselves into oblivion and no longer create gases. Or maybe they eat so much that they become sluggish, suffer fatigue, and just give up. In any case, if beans are a regular part of the diet, flatulence seems to be less of a problem.

The body and its digestive system normally produce gases—about a pint a day. Half of this is the result of swallowing air along with food and drink. The other half is a product of those intestinal bacteria. Each individual is different: the population of bacteria varies (even from day to day); the ways people swallow are different; the idiosyncratic activity of the gastrointestinal tract and the various foods eaten all contribute, adding to or detracting from the quantities of gas produced.

Here are some tested methods for reducing the flatulence factor. Cooking beans thoroughly can reduce the possibility of flatulence. The reason for this is that uncooked starch is harder to digest. Those bacteria get to feast on the undigested starch and create gas. If beans are cooked until they are soft and mash easily when pressed between the tongue and the palate—not al dente the way other vegetables should be cooked—starches will have been cooked completely and can be easily digested, leaving the bacteria to go hungry.

To reduce flatulence by 60 percent, the Center for Science in the Public Interest suggests a solution devised by the Department of Agriculture: use 9 cups of water for each cup of beans; soak for 4 or 5 hours, discard the water and add 9 cups of fresh water; cook for ½ hour and drain; if beans are not completely cooked (most beans won't be), add fresh

water, cook again and drain once more. There are a couple of disadvantages to this method, neither of them serious. First, it's time and labor intensive. It's tedious and you have to think too far ahead. Second, you lose some of the water soluble B vitamins and proteins. The loss is negligible when you consider that there are enough nutrients left behind to make beans one of the most nutritionally rich foods around.

One of the easiest and best antiflatulence techniques is to change the soaking water as often as you think of it (2 or 3 times is thinking enough), adding fresh tap water in the same quantity each time. *Always* drain and then cook in fresh water or cooking liquid. *Do not cook in the soaking liquid.* The oligosaccharides which have been leached out of the beans are in the soaking water. Why allow them to be reabsorbed in the cooking? Especially if you're worried about gas.

Another good idea is to rinse the beans thoroughly *after* they've been soaked. Do this in a colander under running water, gently moving the beans around with your hands so that any sugars clinging to the skins will be washed away.

If you are adding cooked beans to another dish for further cooking and melding of flavors, try rinsing the separately cooked beans before they are added. Again, you'll be rinsing away some of the gas-promoting substances.

Drain canned beans of their liquid and rinse well before adding to other ingredients.

When you are using any of the quick-soak methods for softening and reconstituting dried legumes, rinse after allowing to stand in the hot water for the required time and before proceeding to add them to a recipe.

Do *not* add baking soda (sodium bicarbonate) to the cooking water as some cookbooks recommend. It does not work on the offending sugars and therefore does not solve the problem. Baking soda can actually toughen beans—as does salt—if added to soaking or cooking water. It also destroys some valuable nutrients.

Any of these methods for reducing flatulence can be discontinued, of course, as soon as the body and its bacteria adjust to the *frequent* intake of beans and one develops a "Mexican stomach." Gas then becomes a minor or nonexistent problem.

BEAN PREPARATION

This section deals almost exclusively with the techniques used to reconstitute dried beans.

First, we should talk about quantities. Most dried beans double in volume and weight after being soaked and cooked. Soybeans and chick-peas can usually be counted on to triple their size. As a general rule, 1 cup (8 ounces) of dried beans increases to 2 to 2½ cups (1 to 1¼ pounds) of cooked beans. One cup of dried beans is usually enough to serve four as a side dish. One cup for four people is a good guide whether the beans are to be served as a side dish or are combined with other foods in salads, main dishes, or appetizers (the other ingredients, needless to say, flesh out the portions).

The recipes in this book give specific quantities to serve four or six diners. You may adjust up or down according to the appetites involved (Note: When dieting for weight loss, watch the size of servings—they should be adjusted to the body weight of the dieter. Don't serve the same amount to a 5-foot 3-inch woman as you would to a 6-foot adolescent boy. Restaurant eating is a big problem for dieters partly because portions are the same no matter what the size of the patron. Just as it takes less fuel to run a compact car than it does a big, luxury sedan, small people need less food than big people. Diet books almost never discuss this subject. It's important and something to remember when training children to eat properly.)

SORTING AND
WASHING DRIED BEANS
Packaged dried beans bought in groceries and supermarkets usually just need to be rinsed lightly before soaking and cooking to remove dust and any tiny bits of broken beans. Loose beans, more economical, the kind bought from a sack or bin at health-food and discount food stores, may not have been presorted and can contain pebbles, grit, seed pods, leaves, and twigs. Beans bought loose should be carefully picked over to remove any visible debris. Special care should be taken with chick-peas and lentils bought loose. They have particularly nasty reputations for concealing pebbles. It's not easy and takes a sharp eye to find the rubble in the beans because the tiny stones and the beans look so much alike. It's better to find them with your eyes and fingers beforehand than with your teeth during a meal.

SOAKING DRIED BEANS
Beans are soaked before cooking for two reasons: (1) to soften and return moisture to them and thus reduce cooking time; and (2) to break down the oligosaccharides (the indigestible sugars that cause flatulence.) Lentils, split peas, and black-eyed peas generally do not need soaking and may be cooked from their dry state.

Soaking beans reduces cooking time by about one half and saves vitamins, minerals, and proteins, which can be lost during prolonged heating. Returning moisture to the beans will have been accomplished during soaking and just the cooking and heating remains to be done.

Beans should be soaked in plenty of water (generally use three or four times as much water as beans) for about four hours. Soaking overnight is called for in many recipes. Except for a few tough kinds of beans (and for beans that have been stored for long periods), soaking overnight is done merely for convenience.

Tests show that beans absorb all the soaking water they can hold in the four-hour period. Old beans, fava, and *ful nabeds* (another form of fava or broad bean) have very tough seed coats and *should* be soaked overnight or even for 24 hours. When soaking beans for long periods, change the water every so often to prevent them from fermenting, and to cut down on the flatulence problem.

Do not add salt to the soaking water, or to the cooking liquid, for that matter, until the beans are as soft as you want them. Salt reacts with the seed coat, forming a barrier which prevents absorption of liquids.

There are ways to cut down soaking time from 4 hours or more to ½ to 1 hour. We use one of these methods when we don't have time for a long soak or haven't thought ahead (more likely). Fewer nutrients are lost in the long soak because of the lower temperature of the soaking water. This is one reason some cooks prefer the long soak. The loss is negligible, however. Eating an extra forkful or two makes up for it.

Quick Soaking Method 1
1. Place washed and picked-over beans in a large saucepan and cover with 2 inches of fresh water (unsalted).
2. Bring to the boil and boil for 2 minutes.
3. Remove from heat and allow to soak covered for 1 hour.
4. Discard soaking water, rinse beans, and they are ready for use.

Quick Soaking Method 2
1. Place the washed and picked-over beans in a large saucepan. Cover with 2 inches of fresh water (unsalted) or three times their volume.
2. Bring to the boil. Reduce heat to medium and boil for 10 minutes.
3. Drain the beans and cover with 2 inches or three times their volume of fresh, cool water.

4. Allow to soak for 30 minutes. Discard soaking water, rinse and the beans are reconstituted and ready for further cooking.

There is some controversy about cooking beans in their soaking water versus draining and cooking them in fresh water. The controversy concerns nutrition and digestibility. Discarding the soaking water means that some of the water-soluble B vitamins and bean protein are discarded with it. But the amount is so little (1 percent to 3 percent) that in the long run it's not worth worrying about. Remember, you're also draining off the oligosaccharides that produce gas and we think the trade-off is worth it.

If you are worried about nutrition, do forget all the friendly advice you hear about adding baking soda to the soaking water or cooking liquid to hasten soaking or cooking time. Don't do it. Baking soda adds so much alkalinity to the water that it affects both flavor and nutrient content adversely. Cell wall hemicelluloses are more soluble in heavily alkaline water. The resulting loss of cell wall material allows nutrients to be leached out of the beans and to escape in steam or when the soaking or cooking water is discarded.

Soybeans take longer to cook than any other beans. You can shorten cooking time by freezing them after soaking right in the soaking water. When ready to cook, thaw, discard soaking water, cover with fresh water, and cook until tender. (The freezing method can be used for other beans as well.)

Of course, you can cook beans without soaking them first, if you do it in a pressure cooker. In the chart on page 23 we state the extra cooking time necessary for unsoaked beans. It usually amounts to from 5 to 20 minutes in the pressure cooker.

COOKING BEANS
The recipes in this book call for either soaked dried beans or precooked beans. If the recipe

specifies precooked beans use the table below to discover how long the type of bean indicated should be cooked. The preliminary cooking required for the beans in most recipes is done either with some seasonings or alone; the beans are then combined with other ingredients. *Do not add salt* until the beans are tender. If added too soon, the tenderizing process is halted. The beans just will not get any softer. This phenomenon, which can ruin a pot of beans in one case, can be put to good use in another. When the texture of the beans is just right for your taste, add the salt (or add the beans to an acidic or salted sauce). They then can be kept warm, reheated, or cooked further with other ingredients, and their texture won't change. If you add only partially cooked beans to an acidic sauce or to an already salted soup, for instance, they will not get any softer no matter how long you cook them. It's the cell wall of the bean that's the culprit. It becomes less soluble in a salted or acidic environment. The seed coat can actually toughen and resist any further efforts at tenderization. So remember to add salt (and acidic ingredients like tomato, vinegar, or lemon juice)

TABLE OF SOAKING AND COOKING TIMES (approximate)

Type	Soaking (Hours)	Cooking	Pressure Cooker (Soaked Beans)	Pressure Cooker (Unsoaked Beans)
Adzuki	4	1 hour	15 minutes	20 minutes
Black Beans	4	1½ hours	15 minutes	20 minutes
Black-eyed Peas	-	45 minutes to 1 hour	-	10 minutes
Lima Beans	4	1 to 1½ hours	20 minutes	25-30 minutes
Cannellini Beans	4	1 to 1½ hours	15 minutes	20 minutes
Chick-Peas	4	2 to 2½ hours	25 minutes	35 minutes
Dals	-	30 minutes	-	8 minutes
Fava (Broad Beans)	12	3 hours	40 minutes	1 hour
Ful Nabed (Broad Beans)	12	3 hours	40 minutes	1 hour
Great Northern Beans	4	1 hour	20 minutes	25 minutes
Brown Lentils	-	35 minutes	-	12 minutes
Green Lentils	-	40 minutes	-	12 minutes
Red Lentils	-	30 minutes	-	8 minutes
Mung Beans	4	45 minutes to 1 hour		
Split Peas	-	30 minutes	-	10 minutes
Whole Peas	4	40 minutes	15 minutes	20 minutes
Pigeon Peas	-	30 minutes	-	10 minutes
Pink, Calico, Red Mexican Beans	4	1 hour	20 minutes	25 minutes
Pinto Beans	4	1 to 1½ hours	20 minutes	25 minutes
Red Kidney Beans	4	1 hour	20 minutes	25 minutes
White Kidney Beans (Cannellini)	4	1 hour	20 minutes	25 minutes
Small White (Navy) Beans	4	2 hours	25 minutes	30 minutes
Soybeans	12	3 to 3½ hours	30 minutes	35 minutes

only *after* the beans are as tender as you like them. Don't add beans that need additional cooking to other salted or acidic ingredients until you have cooked them completely.

You may season beans with onions, garlic, bay leaf, herbs and spices, celery, and parsley. You may simmer them in chicken, beef, or vegetable broth that is unsalted or very *lightly* salted. Beans should not be cooked in tomato juice, or tomato sauce, with vinegar, lemon juice, or molasses; nor should they be cooked in salted or acidic liquids—add these later, when the beans are cooked.

The simplest method for cooking presoaked and drained beans is to place them in a pot, cover them with fresh, cold water, bring to the boil, reduce heat, partially cover, and simmer them for the indicated length of time until they are soft and tender.

Very old beans may take longer to become tender than the times listed. Taste for doneness by pressing the cooked bean against the roof of your mouth with your tongue. If it mashes easily, it is done. If not, cook it a little longer. Pressure from a fork on a flat surface accomplishes the same test without the chance of burning your palate.

Cooking Beans in a Pressure Cooker

When using a pressure cooker be sure the pot is no more than half full of ingredients, including water or cooking liquid.

Cook at 15 pounds pressure for the required time. Reduce pressure at the end of the cooking time by running cold water over the lid of the pressure cooker. The cooker can also be removed from the heat and allowed to gradually reduce in pressure. If this method is used, remember that the beans continue cooking so you must cut the cooking time shown on the table by 2 to 3 minutes.

Some beans, soybeans especially, have a tendency to froth or bubble up through the pressure valve during cooking. This can be stopped by adding one tablespoonful of vegeta-

ble oil per cup of beans to the ingredients before cooking. The oil not only stops the frothing but also keeps any bean skins that might come loose from rising up and clogging the steam escape valve.

Cooking Beans in Hard Water

Hard water can lengthen cooking time appreciably. Hard water, containing an abundance of calcium and magnesium, can act like salt and acidic ingredients to interfere with the tenderizing process of cooking by toughening the seed coat of the beans before the starches can be completely gelatinized, the texture altered, and the flavor improved. If the water is extremely hard the beans may be completely uncookable. This is the one case where baking soda can help. Adding 1/8 teaspoon per cup of beans to the soaking and cooking water will shorten the cooking time; there is no loss of thiamine and other nutrients, and the quality of flavor and texture is almost as good as beans cooked in soft water. Don't use more than the 1/8 teaspoon of soda per cup or the beans will turn dark and mushy and their nutritive value will be lowered.

Another way of rendering beans cookable in extremely hard water is to stir-fry presoaked beans in oil for 10 minutes, then cook them in the usual manner. This shortens the cooking time—especially for soybeans—even better than the addition of soda. More nutrients are retained and the flavor of the beans is better as well. You're just taking in a few more calories because of the oil.

Miscellaneous Cooking Notes

Do not try to save time by cooking beans in the sauce, trying to soften and flavor them at the same time. Beans soften and get tender in an alkaline environment; the acid in tomato sauce for example, will keep the beans from softening even if you leave them on the flame for hours. So don't put uncooked or partially cooked beans into the chili and expect them to soften. The calcium in molasses has the same effect on baking beans. Be sure the beans are nearly tender before adding the molasses, or you'll use up a lot of gas or electricity waiting for them to get done.

We have recommended that you use a tablespoon of oil per cup of beans when pressure-cooking them. You can add oil to beans cooked in a conventional saucepan, too, in order to reduce foaming. Keep the lid loose for the first few minutes of cooking anyway, just as an added precaution.

The temperature of the water in which beans are soaked affects their cooking time. The warmer the soaking water, the shorter the cooking time. Don't listen, though, when someone recommends soaking beans in an oven that has a pilot light. The loss of nutrients and certain other chemical reactions are detrimental to flavor and texture as well as digestibility. Use one of the Quick Soaking Methods instead.

Don't be in a hurry to shorten the cooking process. The slower you cook beans the easier they are to digest. In other words, don't boil them unless you're using a Quick Soak method. Simmer them over low heat.

When planning a meal remember that beans swell up with soaking and cooking. They will measure at least twice as much after cooking as they did dry. Keep these approximate equivalents in mind so you will know just how much to cook and serve:

1 cup of dry beans = 2 to 3 cups of cooked beans
1 cup of dry beans = 1 to 1¼ pounds of cooked beans
1 cup of dry beans = 4 servings
2 cups of dry beans = 1 pound (dry weight)

Keep an eye on beans as they cook. Add water as it is absorbed or steams away. Always keep cooking beans moist.

Microwave Cooking
Do not use microwave for cooking dry beans. Dry beans need to be simmered slowly in plenty of water to soften, tenderize, and rehydrate properly.

Microwave ovens are fine for reheating *cooked* beans or for the final stages of blending already cooked beans and other ingredients and for heating dishes like soups, stews, and casseroles.

Crockpot Cooking
If you have a crockpot, by all means use it for cooking beans. Slow cooking over very low heat is perfect for dried legumes. Follow the manufacturer's directions, or cook them at the lowest setting all day, or until done.

Sprouting Beans
Almost all dry beans can be sprouted. The best-known are the mung bean sprouts used extensively in Chinese cooking; but adzukis, lentils, chick-peas, and soybeans also yield delicious, crunchy sprouts. 2 to 3 tablespoons of dry beans will yield 6 to 8 ounces (1½ to 2 cups lightly packed sprouts).

Sprouting Beans.
1. Pick through beans and discard any broken or discolored ones that may have a tendency to go moldy.
2. Soak beans 4 to 6 hours or overnight in plenty of lukewarm water.
3. Drain the soaked beans and place in a clean clay plant pot (cover the hole in the bottom with blotting paper or wadded cheesecloth) or any clean jar. Set the container in a warm place (80° F/27° C). If the sprouting place is cooler, it doesn't matter—they'll take longer to sprout, that's all. As low as 65° F/18° C is fine.
4. Tie a piece of clean sheeting or a double layer of cheesecloth over the top of the jar or pot.
5. Rinse the sprouts with fresh, lukewarm water every morning and evening to keep them moist. Drain off excess water through

the cloth cover. Drain well to prevent the beans from molding or rotting.

6. Check after 4 days and remove any beans that have not sprouted. By now—or by the next day—the sprouts should be ready to eat. Rinse them thoroughly to remove any loose skins and drain well.

7. Sprouts may be stored for several days in the refrigerator. But they are best (and most nutritious) fresh.

It is unnecessary to place sprouting beans in a light spot. As a matter of fact, most are grown commercially in the dark. Darkness gives them a washed-out color and a more delicate flavor. As the sprout uses the cotyledons for energy, it also uses up carbohydrates or calories. Protein content, although rearranged to form new amino acids, does not change. In soybean sprouts the oils also diminish. One nutrient that increases significantly is ascorbic acid or vitamin C—from 3 to 5 times the levels in the dry bean. Ascorbic acid is especially concentrated in growing tissue and, other than the obvious difference in flavor and texture, is the most important advantage eating sprouts has over eating cooked beans. Vitamin A and thiamine decline in the sprout; niacin and riboflavin increase slightly. Minerals decline because of the wet environment.

Eating sprouts instead of cooked beans for greater nutritional value is hardly valid. Eating them as a fresh vegetable during a season when most greens are unavailable, or because they have a crisp texture and a fresh, nutty taste is another story.

Because they are higher in proteins, B vitamins, and iron than most other vegetables (and lower in calories than the dry bean); and because the oligosaccharides have been consumed in the germinating process, thus minimizing the problem of flatulence, sprouts offer simply another attractive alternative to the dry bean.

LEFTOVER BEANS: WHAT DO YOU DO WITH THEM?

Sometimes, either by miscalculation or by design, you may have an excess of beans when dinner is over. Don't despair. Be overjoyed. It means you can have them at another meal or two without time-consuming soaking or slow cooking. Cooked beans keep well in the refrigerator and freeze even better.

To freeze, just pack in plastic containers in portions to feed as many as you anticipate at a future meal. Actually, if you freeze in 1- or 2-cup containers you can always defrost additional portions as you need them for a recipe. The reverse doesn't work. You don't want to defrost a gallon of beans just to get a cup's worth, nor do you want to hack off part of a large block of frozen beans. Freezing recipe-sized portions is best. Beans also can be frozen in plastic sandwich bags. These are perfect for freezing one cup. *Beans keep in the freezer for over a year.*

Treat leftover cooked beans out of the refrigerator or defrosted from the freezer exactly as you would freshly cooked beans. If they should be added to a recipe warm or hot, simmer them for 10 to 15 minutes with a little additional liquid (tap water is fine) so they don't burn or stick to the pot. Drain and add.

Leftover beans usually mean small quantities, which are just right for adding to soups, stews, salads, sandwich spreads, other vegetables, casseroles, wherever you want extra body, another texture, and more nutritional value.

Don't forget, too, that a small quantity of leftover beans can be used to thicken soups and sauces. Just mash or puree the beans in a blender or food processor. If you want a smoother consistency, press the puree through a fine sieve to remove any bits of skin—or puree with a little of the soup or sauce in a processor or blender until smooth.

You can also puree large quantities of beans ahead. Puree in a blender or processor, then freeze the puree in ice cube trays; dump them frozen into a plastic bag and pull out a few at a time to add to and thicken soups, sauces, and main dishes; return the rest to the freezer. Thawing isn't necessary. The cubes are small, have a large surface area, and will melt quickly in hot liquid.

Leftover cooked beans are not really leftovers in the true sense: they should be thought of as a staple that keeps well. Even if added to a salted or acidic soup or sauce (or if salted at the end of the cooking time), leftover cooked beans will not change texture with further cooking and, therefore, are exactly the same as freshly cooked beans.

When cooking beans for freezing or storage be sure to label them "seasoned" or "unseasoned." It's also a good idea to list on the label which seasonings you've used. It's no fun to bake brownies (p. 253) with beans that have been cooked with onions and garlic.

BEAN BASICS AT A GLANCE

Some Do's and Don'ts to Remember.

1. Before soaking, nonpackaged, loose dried beans should be carefully picked over and rinsed thoroughly to remove pebbles, dust, and other debris.
2. The reason dried beans are soaked before cooking is to return moisture, reduce cooking time, and remove the complex sugars (oligosaccharides) that cause flatulence (gas).
3. Dried beans double in volume and in weight after soaking and cooking. Soybeans and chick-peas triple. *Rule of thumb:* 1 cup (8 ounces) dried beans equals 2 to 2½ cups (1 to 1¼ pounds) soaked and cooked.
4. No-soak beans: dried lentils, split peas, and black-eyed peas can be rinsed and then cooked without soaking.
5. Soak dried beans in at least three or four times their volume of water.
6. Almost all beans (except the very old or those with tough skins) absorb all the water they can in 4 hours of soaking or less.
7. Changing soaking water several times (2 or 3) cuts down the flatulence problem.

For the same reason *don't* cook beans in the soaking water or the complex sugars leached out will be reabsorbed.
8. 1 cup of dried beans serves four, when soaked and cooked, as a side dish or when combined with other ingredients in a main dish.
9. *Never* add salt to the soaking water—salt toughens the seed coat and prevents water absorption.
10. Don't add salt to cooking beans *until they are tender.* Again, the skin becomes impermeable and liquids will not be absorbed.
11. Don't add acidic ingredients—including tomato, lemon, or pineapple—before beans are the texture you like. If you do, they will not be any softer no matter how long you cook them.
12. Add partially cooked beans to unsalted soups or sauces. Wait until they are tender before salting.
13. Baking soda added to soaking water destroys nutrients and affects flavor and texture (beans become mushy). *Don't* do it. (Add baking soda *only* in extremely hard water and then a scant ⅛ teaspoon per cup of beans.)

14. Unsoaked beans may be cooked in a pressure cooker—add from 5 to 20 minutes to cooking time (see chart p. 22).

15. Cook beans in a pressure cooker at 15 pounds pressure.

16. Add a tablespoon of vegetable oil per cup of beans before pressure cooking to prevent frothing and bubbling up through the valve.

17. Cooked, tenderized beans can be kept warm, reheated, or cooked again with other ingredients *after* salt has been added without changing their texture.

18. Cook beans partially covered to prevent foaming.

19. Don't boil beans, simmer them slowly over low heat. Speeding the cooking makes them less digestible.

20. Always keep cooking beans moist, adding liquid a little at a time as it boils or steams away.

21. Frozen cooked beans will keep in the freezer for at least a year, sometimes longer.

22. Drain canned beans of their liquid and rinse in a sieve or colander before adding to other ingredients.

23. Soaking beans reduces cooking time by about half and saves nutrients that prolonged heating can destroy.

24. Beans are soaked overnight for convenience only. (Except for old beans and those with tough seed coats.)

25. In a hurry? Use one of the Quick Soaking Methods (p. 22) to cut soaking time to ½ or 1 hour.

26. Shorten the cooking time of soybeans by freezing them in the soaking water, then thawing them and discarding the soaking water. Cover beans with fresh water and cook. This method works with very old beans, too.

27. Taste for doneness by pressing a cooked bean against the roof of your mouth to see if it mashes easily. Or press with a fork against a flat surface.

28. In hard-water areas you can cut cooking time by stir-frying presoaked beans in a little oil for 10 minutes, then cooking in the usual manner.

29. Don't cook beans in a microwave. Even presoaked beans need slow cooking in plenty of water. Use microwave only for reheating cooked beans.

30. Treat leftover or frozen beans just as you would freshly cooked beans.

31. Use small quantities of leftover beans, mashed or pureed, to thicken soups or sauces.

32. Freeze pureed beans in individual ice cube trays, store in plastic freezer bags, and use 1 or 2 cubes to add to soups, sauces, gravies, and main dishes.

33. Store dried beans in a dry, cool place. Do not store in the refrigerator.

34. Read the labels of canned beans and pass up those that list lots of preservatives, additives, salt, and sugar.

BUYING AND STORING BEANS

Beans come in so many different varieties, in so many shapes, colors, and sizes, in so many forms—fresh, dry, frozen, canned, and hydrastable—that no recipe will taste exactly the same if the type of bean is changed. This is because each kind of bean has its own elusive flavor and texture, which can range from beany to nutty to bland. Some are fragrant, some are not. Some are crisp, some chewy, some mealy, some soft. Even color can change the perception of taste—bright colors seem to intensify flavor, dark colors make them dusky and exotic, pale colors make flavors seem bland and subtle. We can only urge you to try as many varieties of beans as possible. Interchange them in recipes where color is not important. Learn which you prefer and use them often. Nowhere is it written that you must switch beans with each meal. However, it is always wise to try a recipe as written, with the bean variety suggested, because there may be a good textural, taste, or visual reason for its specification.

Try to learn to identify the common varieties and find out the colloquial name for them in your area (the names for beans, like those for chilies, change with the territory).

Beans should be bought at shops or markets where the turnover is high. Old beans that have been resting on a shelf for months will take longer to cook and sometimes never get soft. The best place to buy beans, therefore, is at ethnic stores—Chinese, Indian, West Indian, Hispanic—where the prices are competitive and the dried beans younger because they are used often in these ethnic cuisines. Try to avoid buying beans in health-food stores unless you've compared prices. Health-food stores, we've discovered, often charge two or three times as much as supermarkets and ethnic grocers.

If you buy loose beans, inspect them for holes (this may be an indication that there are little bugs inside called bean weevils, rare in commercial varieties) and for an inordinate quantity of stones and debris.

If you buy packaged beans, be sure the packages (usually plastic bags) are well sealed. Look through the transparent plastic to check if there are many broken or cracked beans. If there are, choose another bag. Do the same with beans packaged in boxes. They usually have a cellophane window so with a few shakes of the box you can check the contents.

When you get the beans home you can transfer them to glass jars with tight-fitting lids. You can also store them on a cool pantry shelf right in the plastic bag or box. We like to put them in jars on open shelves because their warm, earthy colors lend a country look to our city kitchen.

All beans take longer to cook if stored at high temperatures and/or in moist, humid conditions. If you buy beans in large, economy-sized quantities, by all means transfer them to air tight glass containers and store in a dry, cool place—but *not* in the refrigerator.

These days, unless you live in a completely inaccessible area, most grocers and supermarkets in your neighborhood carry a variety of dried beans either boxed or bagged. If you can't find a specific bean that you simply can't live without, check your library for lists of mail order outlets, ask for a rundown on beans and bean products, or write for a catalog.

Dried beans, along with their frequent companion rice, are the most stable foods in the pantry. Even very old beans are still good, though they may need longer cooking.

CANNED BEANS AND PEAS

Canned limas and string beans can be found in most food stores and along with canned peas should be left there. As far as we're concerned they have absolutely no relationship in flavor to the fresh, dried, or frozen varieties. Fed to children—which they often are—they can produce an army of lifelong bean haters. The only canned beans worth using (and we use them often) are various kinds of kidney beans, fava beans, lentils, and chick-peas usually found in the ethnic sections of markets with Italian, Hispanic, or French labels. Most are canned here in this country but are packaged primarily for these ethnic groups. They are usually softer than home-cooked, but if drained and rinsed, then seasoned or mixed with other ingredients, they can save a lot of time. Buy the house brands if available, or the generics—they're more economical. There's no need to choose the more expensive brands unless you are looking for seasoned or sauced beans.

Canned beans are a wise investment, especially if you are trying a variety you've never had before. You're buying in smaller quantity and if you don't like them, you can go on to another kind.

Just remember, when buying canned beans, to read the label. If there are lots of preservatives, additives, salt and/or sugar listed in the ingredients, choose another brand.

Almost all the recipes in this book calling for cooked dried beans can be made with canned. Drain and rinse first.

Keep a supply of a variety of canned beans on hand for those times when you want to whip up something quickly. They're some of the best, most successful fast foods around.

FROZEN BEANS AND PEAS

Limas, black-eyed peas, fava beans, snow peas, string beans (in various cuts), and peas all are available in your grocer's freezer compartment. We are especially partial to the tiny peas (*petit pois*), which are frozen so soon after they are harvested that they taste fresher than the days-old fresh peas in the pod at the produce stand. Snow peas are not so successfully frozen—they lose their crisp, crackling attractive quality. Other beans are fine. Even frozen green beans will do in a pinch. Packaged frozen beans may be stored in the home freezer for months. Home-frozen beans keep for more than a year.

BEAN PASTAS
a.k.a. Cellophane Noodles, Bean Threads, Saifun, Fansee

The Chinese make these transparent noodles out of mung bean flour. They can be found in most Asian markets packaged in cellophane bags. The noodles are thin, brittle, and white and are reconstituted simply by placing them in a bowl and pouring boiling water over them. Let them sit for about 15 or 20 minutes to soften and become transparent; cut them into smaller lengths with kitchen shears, drain, and they are ready to be sauced or stir-fried with other ingredients.

BEAN FLAKES

These are partially cooked and rolled beans that have been developed to shorten cooking time. They may be used in place of beans to provide a more interesting texture. They are sold in health food stores.

THE BEAN FACTOR: GOURMET PREVENTIVE MEDICINE

Adding beans to your diet is easy and good for you.

But that's just it: promoting beans as preventive medicine, we're afraid, can be a real turn-off if you like to cook, like to eat, are tempted by delicious-sounding recipes, start salivating as soon as you pick up a cookbook, or always look at the dessert side of the menu first.

Our advice is to read this section, then forget that beans are good for what ails you. It's just nice to know that a food that tastes so good and is so versatile an ingredient can help keep you in better shape and make you healthier in general.

Underdeveloped societies have neither the medical facilities nor the technology to prevent their populations from succumbing to infectious diseases. Yet degenerative diseases are almost unheard of among these peoples. The reason? Their diets contain huge quantities of fiber such as that found in beans. In fact, most of these populations receive a good proportion of their daily protein and calorie supply from legumes, which contain other substances as well that keep degenerative diseases at bay.

As these countries increase in wealth, they can afford to replace large amounts of healthful complex carbohydrates in their diets with meat and other foods loaded with fats and cholesterol. As they do, there is an increase in the incidence of degenerative diseases, along with a general decline in health.

Somewhere there is a happy medium. Perhaps the recipes in this book can help change the way we eat. With the proliferation of Tex-Mex restaurants that serve beans (although heavily laced with fat) even fast food establishments may find beans a profitable and enjoyable alternative to hamburgers and fried chicken. Our giant food conglomerates could put their research departments to work developing a bean breakfast food, soon to be followed by instant beans, bean dessert mixes, bean refrigerator cookies, and all manner of bean-based prepared foods. All we can hope is that they leave what's good about beans intact and don't mill, reconstitute, manufacture, and overprocess it all away.

Meanwhile, you'd do well to think of beans just as food that tastes great and has the added bonus of good nutrition. Eat beans often. As often as possible, in as many ways as possible, and you'll live a more healthy life. And probably live it longer.

Researchers are only beginning to plumb the complex biochemical reasons for the relatively few cases of cancer of the digestive system, diverticulosis, hiatus hernia, hemorrhoids, appendicitis, gallstones, varicose veins, diabetes, intestinal ailments, and cardiovascular diseases in the third world and nonindustrialized nations and their relationship to the large quantity of beans and other fiber foods in the diet. But there is more than just a lot of fiber to beans. There are other complex compounds, proteins, vitamins, minerals, and chemicals that interreact to form a preventive phalanx in the battle against certain degenerative maladies.

THE BEAN FACTOR: FIBER AND THE DIGESTIVE SYSTEM

Fiber—spelled *fibre* in botanical usage—is the cell walls of plants—and only plants—that give them their strength, rigidity, and unyielding structure. It also consists of the composition of nonstructural substances and plant starches associated with those cell walls. Fiber is almost exclusively polysaccharides, that is, complex carbohydrates, cellulose. Dietary fibers are those components of foods that cannot be broken down, cannot be digested by enzymes in the human alimentary canal. In other words, fiber cannot be absorbed or assimilated into the system (which is an advantage when you are on a slimming diet. What you can't digest can't be turned into body fat. But more about that later).

There are bacteria living in our colons that *can* process—by fermentation—about half the fiber that passes through the intestines. This operation produces gases (which are discussed in another section of this book) and volatile fatty acids, some of which may be absorbed into the body through the walls of the intestine. The rest, however, passes through—and out—unmolested.

Not all fiber is exactly the same. Different kinds have different properties. Some absorb large amounts of liquids, mainly water, others just a little. Some are completely fermented by intestinal bacteria, others go on their merry way unscathed and end up flushed down the toilet.

Fiber can appear very unfiberlike. It rarely bears any visible similarity to hairs or threads except for cellulose, which, under a microscope, seems filamentous. Although called roughage in previous generations, fiber isn't necessarily coarse, tough, and irregular in shape (like some of those little pellets of bran cereal). It can be smooth and soft. As we said, it just has to be made up of mostly indigestible material.

The fiber found most often in human foods are cellulose, hemicelluloses, lignin, pectins (in ripe fruits), gums (especially guar gum, an important health component of beans), and mucilages.

As you have probably deduced, plants have different fibers or combinations of fibers with different properties, and in differing quantities. Just as the calorie counts of various foods differ enormously, so the fiber content varies to a great degree. Some have generous quantities, such as grains and cereal-based foods—that is, if their fiber hasn't been milled and stripped away in the refining process. Fruits and vegetables differ so much even in their raw, unprocessed state that they can't all be counted on to offer really useful quantities.

Happily, beans, raw, dried, canned, frozen, or cooked, don't have the chance to lose any useable fiber because they don't change at all from the field to the market to your table. They enter your stomach with no processing beforehand except that done by your teeth. And chewing doesn't break down fiber into anything else but what it is.

High fiber beans force you to chew more to allow comfortable swallowing. The more you chew, the slower you eat. The slower you eat, the more time you give your body to feel full. The more you chew, the more substantial the meal seems psychologically. This is especially true when beans are on the menu because of their initial bulk, the saliva added from chewing, which adds more bulk, and the beans' absorption of water as they pass through the digestive system, which adds even more mass.

THE BEAN FACTOR:
IN WEIGHT CONTROL

Beans, despite their bad press in the past (they've been misrepresented as fattening), are a great diet food.

Prepared without excessive amounts of fat and sugar, beans compare more than favorably with their animal competitors. Just look at the calorie counts in a few dishes common to the average diet as compared with beans: one cup of cooked lentils has 212 calories, kidney beans about 218, split peas 230. In contrast a small 3-ounce hamburger (just lying there on the plate without dressing or bun) has 243 calories. Two ounces of cheddar cheese has 225 calories. Besides giving more volume and weight for the number of calories ingested (2½ to 4 times the volume for the calorie equivalent of meat or cheese), the fiber content of beans moves them through the digestive system cleanly. Therefore, you feel you've eaten more (which in fact you have). You get

full faster because the beans absorb moisture and increase further in bulk as they travel through the intestines. In addition, they give you more food for the amount of calories consumed. Two further bonuses: the fiber in the beans has caught up bits of fat and protein and carried them away (these have calories, too); and the body has actually used up more calories digesting the legumes than it would have digesting other foods. So the 212 to 230 calories in a cupful is not what it seems at all. The fattening image can be expunged—and quickly.

You rarely see fat people in areas of the world where a good deal of starchy carbohydrates with their natural fibers intact are the mainstay of the daily diet. But in this country, where low fiber diets are the norm, so is obesity. The more beans and other fiber foods you eat the better your body's ability to control its weight—even if your fat and sugar consumption is on the high side, as is the average American's. Note that we said "your body's ability," not your brain's. Once you get into the habit of eating beans regularly (and we hope the recipes in this book will help you do that), your body will regulate itself by consuming fewer calories and often more "food." Your body, therefore, will feel satisfied and full before you overdose on calories.

Don't misunderstand, the recipes we offer are not for weight loss per se (especially not cassoulet or feijoada), but adding several of the moderate ones to your repertoire and eating them regularly can help change your eating habits and offer a more satisfying diet. If you look through them, you'll find many of them contain meat, chicken, butter, cheese, and other "fattening" ingredients. But *not* in large quantities, and not, usually, as the main ingredient. A lentil soup, for example, may call for a ham bone or bits of ham. The ham is there for flavor and texture (and color) and, unless you are on a restricted diet that precludes eating high cholesterol foods, adds fewer calories to a meal than if the ham were the star of the meal and the lentils only a bit player. Part of our theory of dieting for weight loss is not giving up your favorite foods but giving them a minor role instead of a major role in a recipe.

When you want to slim down but don't have the willpower to give up flavor while doing it, you'll take in fewer calories with a meal of lentil soup with ham than you will with a meal of roast ham and all the trimmings. Besides, it's better for you, better for your heart, your stomach, your intestines, and your circulatory system. But don't necessarily think about these beneficial side effects. Just enjoy.

Going on a diet that includes many of the recipes in this book doesn't mean quick weight loss. You probably won't even be aware that you're slimming down to normal—but you won't be aware that you're dieting either! Give

it time. Have patience. You'll certainly never feel a sense of denial.

USING THE OLD BEAN TO DIET

No one would advocate a strictly bean diet. Especially us. Just a glance at some of the recipes in this book will tell you that. But if you are interested in weight control, just pick and choose among those recipes that feature beans in greater proportion to any other ingredient. Use our chapter on substitutions to change these recipes and make them less fattening.

There is a simple way to diet without changing the menus you are fond of: add cooked beans to a dish so it out-proportions the calorie-laden ingredients. Let's say you like pot roast. Pot roast is made with meat cooked to falling-apart tenderness. It's easy to eat. There are no bones. You don't have to chew much. It's tasty, too. So you have an extra helping. Maybe more after that, what the hell. *But,* if you had added a few cups of cooked beans to the pot roast ten minutes or so before it finished cooking, they would have added bulk that would fill you up, absorb some of the natural fats, and stop you from having too much of the meat—that second portion.

Just adding beans to a menu can do the same thing. You can't toss beans on the barbecue with the steak, but you can give them a lot of room on the plate, and room in the stomach so you don't go back for more sirloin. Try it. You won't be changing your diet, you'll just be changing the quantities of high calorie foods you consume.

Studies show that vegetarians suffer less from obesity than the rest of the population. Pure vegetarians weigh from 10 to 30 pounds less than the rest of us. But you needn't become a pure vegetarian to lose weight and keep it off. You just have to adjust your diet to *include* foods like beans so that your body has the protein it needs for replacement, reconstruction, and renovation (see p. 44); it has the help it needs to prevent certain diseases and body dysfunctions; it has the pleasure and satisfaction it wants from a tasty, textured, and colorful diet; and it is provided with necessary vitamins and minerals. Beans really are a diet superfood, and not just because of their high protein and fiber content. Other high fiber foods like bran don't do anything to lower and regulate cholesterol. Beans do!

THE BEAN FACTOR: IN RELIEVING HEART AND CIRCULATORY PROBLEMS

As you now know, beans are a high fiber food. But so is bean (wheat fiber). Bran is more than 90 percent cellulose, the most fibrous of fibers. Yet bran has *no* known beneficial effect on cholesterol levels other than removing some bits of fat as it courses through the intestines.

Dietary fiber of certain types *can* lower cholesterol levels in the blood. If lower cholesterol levels truly reduce the risk of heart and circulatory disease, then bean eaters may rejoice and converts may look forward to lower counts. It is known that in countries where the diet contains large quantities of fiber (and very little fat), rates of heart disease are significantly lower than in the United States and other highly industrialized countries.

Most beans and peas are naturally low in fats. The fats that do occur—mainly in soybeans—are polyunsaturated, and it is only the saturated fats (animal and palm oils and some hydrogenated vegetable fats) that should be avoided. Beans, besides being absolutely cholesterol-free, have a chemical, according to recent research, that helps fight the deposit of platelets (fat globules) in the veins and arteries much the way aspirin does. There are strong implications that a diet rich in beans has a therapeutic effect on blood clotting and other circulatory problems like atherosclerosis.

So it is the *type* of fiber you eat that is important in controlling cholesterol. Bran, while good for digestion, has no effect on lowering cholesterol. But the pectins in most fruit fiber, the fiber in rolled oats and carrots, and the guar gum found in our favorite, beans, *can* bring about significant lowering of cholesterol levels.

Recent studies have shown that guar gum especially has the ability to reduce the percentage of serum cholesterol by 36 milligrams. Pectin, a runner-up, reduced levels by 29 milligrams. Bran, on the other hand, almost pure cellulose, *raised* cholesterol levels by almost 7 milligrams. (Eating a lot of bran to help your digestion, as a lot of people are doing these days, doesn't do a thing for your circulatory system. Beans can be counted on to do both.)

When patients in another study, who were taking cholesterol-lowering drugs, were given 5 grams of guar gum before each meal, their cholesterol levels dropped an average of 10.6 percent in addition to the reduction caused by the drugs.

The cholesterol-lowering effects of the fiber in beans are obvious and may be due in part to beans' ability to increase the excretion of bile acids, which are manufactured from cholesterol, and partly from fiber's ability to bind cholesterol to itself and be excreted in feces.

Triglycerides, another substance in the blood closely related to heart disease, according to a study done by Veterans Administration Hospital researchers in Kentucky, are reduced by fiber in the diet. Triglycerides usually go up with a high carbohydrate diet. But when vegetable and plant fiber is consumed along with the carbohydrates, there is no consequent rise in triglyceride levels. On the contrary, patients who had higher than normal triglyceride levels given a high fiber, high carbohydrate diet, lowered their triglyceride levels significantly.

Of course, you should not expect the fiber in beans to be complete protection against coronary heart disease—the environment, heredity, smoking, obesity, stress, overdosing on animal fats, eggs, and refined sugar along with other factors contribute heavily. But you can expect beans to help lower cholesterol and triglyceride levels if you eat enough of them and regularly. And, of course, are careful about the rest of your diet. How much is enough?

No one is sure. But normal portions, eaten several times a week, seem to do the trick. Anyway, they can't hurt in helping to keep the heart healthy. Absolute, conclusive evidence is not in as yet, but research to date points to a clear and important relationship.

If you have coronary and circulatory problems, please don't change your diet expecting prevention, control, and remission without consulting your doctor.

THE BEAN FACTOR: IN THE CONTROL OF DIABETES

Diabetes is a disorder in which the body cannot control the levels of sugar in the blood. It can threaten the heart, eyes, brain, kidneys, and life itself.

Insulin is a control hormone, a stabilizing substance. As blood sugar levels go up with the digestion of food, insulin is secreted to reduce the quantities of blood sugar by helping these sugars to be absorbed by the cells. If a person's insulin production is faulty, his blood sugar levels can rise dangerously high and he is said to be a diabetic.

Carbohydrates along with fat are the body's major source of fuel. Carbohydrate foods like bread, cereals, rice, potatoes, and pasta offer lots of energy but require the pancreas to pour out quantities of insulin to readjust and stabilize the glucose level in the blood. Beans offer the same kind of energy as the foods just listed but are a boon to diabetics and hypoglycemics: eating them does not trigger a rise in blood sugar and the consequent necessity for production and release of insulin into the blood by the pancreas.

If some diabetics include the dietary fiber in beans and fruit in their diets, medical studies have shown that they (85 percent of them, anyway) can often get by (under supervision) without daily shots of insulin or other anti-diabetes drugs. The effective dietary plant fibers, again, are guar gum (in beans) and pectin (in fruit).

Researchers have proved that in both the healthy and the diabetic, the consumption of these dietary plant fibers *along with* carbohydrates regulate and keep in check the levels of blood sugar and insulin. These don't rise as high as when carbohydrates are eaten alone.

Legumes supply carbohydrate fuel in the form of starch. Unlike the starch in white flour and other processed foods, the starch in beans comes beautifully packaged in a nutrient envelope which helps supply a good deal of nutritional requirements while satisfying the body's energy needs. You see, starch, consisting entirely of chains of glucose (a simple sugar) is easily transformed by digestion into this most efficient fuel that is the *primary* fuel carried by the blood to every cell in the body. The nutrient envelope surrounding the carbohydrates in beans has not been processed away (as it has in white flour) so the B vitamins necessary to metabolize the carbohydrates into fuel are right there helping to burn the glucose as energy.

Besides, the fat and protein also contained within this indigestible fiber "package" slow down the digestive process and give the glucose sugars created from carbohydrate metabolism a longer time to enter the blood stream.

This time factor has an extra benefit: it prevents *rebound hypoglycemia*, or the feeling of hunger only an hour or two after you've eaten. When glucose enters the blood rapidly, as it does when you eat highly refined foods and sugars, the insulin sent out by the pancreas to suppress unhealthy levels of blood sugars keeps on working even after it has done its job. Consequently, an hour or two after eating, blood sugar levels have gone past the "normal" point, lowering them to the point that the body signals that it is hungry again (hungry for glucose). The fiber in beans lengthens the absorption time, staves off hunger signals, and regulates the production of insulin so that there isn't an excess amount to keep working past the stabilization point.

The Importance of Insulin for Nondiabetics

For nondiabetics and those interested in controlling their weight, stopping the pancreas from overproduction of insulin is highly desirable. Insulin regulates blood sugars by forcing cells to absorb the excess. This in turn promotes the storage of body fat.

Simplified, this means that if you can keep the release of insulin in check, you can keep your weight in check.

Diabetes and obesity are strongly linked. It is thought that they are both the result of the same metabolic problem. When one suffers from diabetes there is a relative *lack* of insulin and consequently higher than normal levels of glucose in the blood. But some diabetics, paradoxically, have higher than normal levels of insulin—a condition called hyperinsulinism. How can excess insulin and diabetes coexist? Because of insulin resistance. These diabetics produce insulin that is unuseable to metabolize the glucose—the cells of the body gradually become unresponsive to it, immune to it. In such cases the insulin produced is ineffective and allows the blood sugar levels to rise precipitously. The pancreas spews out an excess of insulin in an attempt to override this insensitivity, but it can't.

An excessive supply of insulin is related to obesity. In theory this would seem to be the opposite of diabetes, yet diabetes mellitus (maturity onset diabetes, the most prevalent form) takes many years to develop, thus its name, and can result from just such a chronic overproduction of insulin and resultant insulin fatigue. In effect the pancreas has had to manufacture so much insulin for so long just to keep the blood sugar levels normal that its assembly line is sabotaged, slows down, or gives up in exhaustion. This is the reason chronically overweight people are more likely to develop diabetes or what is known as a "diabetic condition"—less serious than diabetes but serious nonetheless.

These very same people, if prescribed a high carbohydrate, high natural fiber diet (based on beans) can often reverse their insulin resistance dramatically and even be weaned from their dependence on insulin therapy and overeating. The results are startling and can be accompanied by a remarkable weight loss.

Fiber in beans moderates insulin response by taking longer to digest, metabolizing into glucose very gradually. Sugar on the other hand enters the bloodstream almost instantly and a lot of insulin is needed to deal with it.

Insulin not only metabolizes glucose but is used to stimulate (1) the production of fats by the liver; (2) the production of lipoproteins (three types of fatty proteins important in the transport of cholesterol through the blood); and (3) the growth of adipose or fatty tissue for storage fat. Do you wonder then that the obese usually are found to have too much insulin in their blood? Diabetic patients, those treated with insulin, often have a tendency toward obesity unless their diets are carefully restricted. The close association of hyperinsulinism and overweight is borne out by laboratory animals who, when injected with long-lasting insulins, uncharacteristically gorge themselves into obesity.

THE BEAN FACTOR:
LOWERING THE RISK OF COLON CANCER

No other cancer is more directly related to the Western diet than cancer of the colon or large intestine—that from which President Reagan suffered. The diets of the economically developed countries may appear to be right in almost all respects but may still lead to an intestinal environment that promotes the production or the concentration of carcinogens, cancer-inducing substances.

It all comes down to fiber and the way fiber cleans out the gut. Rural Finns eat twice as much fiber as New Yorkers do. Cancer of the colon is rare in the Finnish countryside. It is far from rare among New Yorkers. Studies have tracked Japanese who have moved from Japan to Hawaii or California and adopted a Western style diet. As in rural Finland, colon cancer is rare among the Japanese at home or among those who stick to their traditional diet here. But Japanese who adopt the American way of eating also run a risk of colon cancer equal to that of their American neighbors within only one generation. The proliferation of American fast-food outlets in Japan and their success in romancing the Japanese market into a new way of eating could change the relative immunity of the Japanese to large bowel cancer and other intestinal disorders.

Of course, genetic susceptibility also plays a role here. But even among the genetically susceptible it makes more sense to eat a diet containing fewer fats and more dietary fiber like that in beans. The fiber in beans provides a protective edge against this type of cancer as does a high fiber diet in general. We happen to be talking about beans, however, and beans offer not only fiber but proteins, vitamins, and minerals in abundance—and a bare minimum of fat. Beans are a sensible and tasty alternative to a high meat diet, or to tasteless bran cereal supplements.

The National Cancer Institute's first dietary guide recommending a food regimen to protect against cancers of several different types was issued in 1979. It suggested changing the American diet to emphasize larger amounts of natural carbohydrate foods and far smaller amounts of animal foods. The guidelines also restricted the intake of fats of all kinds. The more fats and cholesterol in the diet, the guide suggests, the more likely the production and presence of cancer-causing agents in the bowel. Fiber acts as a protector against colon cancer by retaining water and forming bulk in the intestines. It dilutes the toxins that come in contact with intestinal walls and hurries them through so that they are in the bowels for a shorter period of time, thus having less time to do damage. A high fat, low fiber diet such as that of most Americans is also implicated in breast, uterine, ovarian, and prostate cancer. The greater sex hormone production resulting from such a diet and the consequent bile breakdown in the intestine is said to be ultimately perilous in many vulnerable people.

Eating beans regularly along with other fiber foods and cutting down the amounts of animal fat and protein in the diet can reduce the vulnerability to these forms of cancer.

THE BEAN FACTOR:
PREVENTING CONSTIPATION

Laxatives are big business in this country. You can hardly watch your favorite daytime or prime time television show without being bombarded by expensive pitches for scores of over-the-counter purges. Many of these so-called natural laxatives are fiber, processed and expensively packaged. We suggest you save your money and switch to our brand, packaged by that consummate designer, Mother Nature, in your choice of color and size, and at a price you can afford. And we guarantee that our brand is more fun to ingest. Besides that, the natural product has scores of other attributes an advertising copywriter would love to turn his or her skills loose on.

Forgive us if we repeat ourselves but in economically underprivileged countries where the diet consists of great percentages of fiber-laden beans, vegetables, and whole grains, there may not even be a word for our national curse in the language.

Industrialized countries like ours consider constipation an annoying but harmless condition that comes with the territory. It needn't. And it needn't lead to more serious problems related to constipation such as hemorrhoids, diverticulitis, varicose veins, and other intestinal complaints.

Some women believe constipation is a cross they have to bear. Don't you believe it. It's our high animal protein, high fat, low carbohydrate diet that's to blame.

The effect of a change in diet that puts more emphasis on beans and vegetables and salads can save you money, and give you more space in your medicine chest.

We recommend that you promote "regularity" by eating more beans. They're *really* one of nature's laxatives.

THE BEAN FACTOR: HELPING THOSE WITH DIVERTICULOSIS

Have you heard of diverticulosis? Chances are you've not only heard of it, you have it or know someone who does. It's quite common, afflicting 10 percent of those over the age of 40 and 1/3 of those over 70. It has only become a widespread problem in the Western world in the past 70 years, ever since the passion for fiber-free foods has skewed our national diet. Chronic constipation is one cause of diverticulosis: it forces the colon to work harder to push the small compact stools through its passageway. The terrific pressure can cause part of the mucous membrane to be pushed through the thickened muscular wall of the colon, creating a pocket, the diverticulum, where bits of waste matter can be trapped and cause inflammation. Then diverticulosis becomes diverticulitis, which can be quite discomforting and even painful.

A high fiber diet and beans in particular is very effective in treating the painful symptoms of diverticulitis. Studies of sufferers from the malady who were advised to eat a fiber-filled diet show that many of the symptoms were relieved (36 percent) or completely eliminated (52 percent). Among those who switched, only about 14 percent continued to rely on laxatives. Putting fiber back in the diet undoubtedly helped a majority of these patients cope with the condition without the use of drugs.

Hemorrhoids are another affliction of those on "civilized" diets; in all likelihood they are brought on by constipation. Appendicitis, too, is encouraged by low-fiber diets. It is the most frequent emergency operation performed in the United States.

The kind of physical suffering caused by diverticulitis, hemorrhoids, and appendicitis is largely unnecessary and is brought about by a diet too high in animal fats and proteins and too low in fiber. A diet with its emphasis on the fiber found in foods such as beans could greatly reduce the incidence of these diseases.

THE BEAN FACTOR: FORGETTING GALLSTONES

Gallstones are made up mostly of cholesterol and sometimes calcium. They occur chiefly in economically developed nations. Gallstones are manufactured when concentrations of blood cholesterol are abnormally high, for instance in people suffering from obesity, diabetes, and high serum triglycerides. Reduce weight, reduce cholesterol with a bean-fiber highlighted diet and you can reduce your chances of getting gallstones.

THE BEAN FACTOR: IF YOU'RE THE SENSITIVE TYPE

Millions of people in this country are sensitive to all kinds of foods. Food allergies are as common as runny noses and headaches and are often the cause of these annoying ailments—and countless others.

Many who have food allergies must give up not only foods they like but the nutrition they need that these foods supply.

Allergy sufferers will be happy to learn that the United States Department of Health and Human Services classifies the common bean as one of the five *least* allergenic foods. Beans are hardly ever associated with allergic reactions. Yet they are packed with an abundance of the very nutrients allergy sufferers are denied unless they supplement their diets with vitamin pills, protein additives, and the like. But even these supplements can contain sugar, starch, artificial dyes, food colorings, and preservatives, which in themselves can cause allergic reactions.

Beans are simple. They come to you as nature made them. And because there are so many different kinds of peas, beans, and lentils, they have a great variety of flavors, colors, and textures. They don't get or need a lot of processing or additives by their producers to make them interesting. You and only you do the processing to make them pleasant to your palate. You cook them, season them, add other foods to them, or add them to other foods. Then you chew and swallow them. You have control over them. There's no artificial anything in them unless you put it there. If you have allergic reactions to specific flavorings, colorings, and spices—and to certain chemical preservatives used to give a longer shelf life to even some "fresh" vegetables and fruits—you will not find them present in dried beans. Chemical preservatives are rarely used on fresh beans and peas and it is only with frozen and canned beans that you should read the labels carefully and proceed accordingly. If the label doesn't tell you what you want to know, don't buy the product, especially if you are at all sensitive to the "normal" additives in processed foods. Play it safe. Don't use the product. Or switch to another brand with an informative label.

THE BEAN FACTOR:
PROTEIN, THE SOURCE

"The proteins in beans aren't as good or as good for you as the proteins in meat."

Don't you believe it!

The inferiority of vegetable protein is a myth even some vegetarians continue to believe. It's hogwash.

All living tissue, both plant and animal, contains protein. Proteins are essential for the formation, maintenance, repair, rehabilitation, and growth of your muscle, connective tissue, blood plasma and hemoglobin, your skin, its keratin, your finger and toe nails, the hair on your head, the enzymes, hormones, and antibodies that regulate many of your body's most important functions, the very substances in every cell that carry your genetic code (DNA and RNA) and that tell your cells how to replicate themselves—they all require protein enzymes for their structure and composition.

The proteins in our diets are needed to help maintain the variety of proteins in our bodies. The more than twenty-two amino acids, chains of carbon, hydrogen, oxygen, and nitrogen, resident in our bodies combine in countless ways to form the proteins that are the complex building blocks of life.

It is necessary for the body to be supplied with a certain amount of protein from the outside in order to form tissue on the inside. But what kind of outside protein? Animal or vegetable? Actually it doesn't matter. Most of the twenty-two amino acids needed for protein synthesis can be manufactured inside. Eight must come from the outside. All eight of these so-called essential amino acids must be present to synthesize protein. Every single one. If only one is missing, the manufacturing process cannot go on and the other seven are useless. Each food has a unique amino acid pattern—a little more of one, a little less of another. This does not mean that one food's protein is better than another's, it simply means that the amino acid *pattern* is different. Animal or vegetable, they *all* contain the essential amino acids—but in varying quantities.

Animal protein is no better than vegetable protein. Each can keep the body in nitrogen balance. And nitrogen is one of the leading substances from which the body builds protein. The body loses nitrogen through sweat, urine, and feces. If you take in more nitrogen than you lose, or an amount equal to that which you lose, you are said to be in nitrogen balance and getting enough protein from your diet.

Numerous studies have been done showing that protein, even when derived from only one source in the diet (such as potatoes, rice, corn, or wheat) can maintain the body in nitrogen balance as well as does milk protein (the food with the most appropriate amino acid pattern for humans). The amino acid pattern in these plant foods is completely different from that of milk, yet it does not seem to matter. Body chemistry adjusts. If it didn't, or couldn't, there might not be a human race. Early man often subsisted on one kind of plant or animal food for long periods of time. There were no nutritionists around to tell him he must practice protein complementarity, eat a balanced diet, include green vegetables and fruit, drink his milk, have an apple a day, eat animal protein, a certain percentage of fat, roots, nuts, grains, seeds, legumes. He ate what he could *find* or scavenge, what was at hand, what he could kill. Sometimes he was a vegetarian, sometimes he ate meat. If his body had not been able to adjust to the vagaries of nature and the food supply (or lack of it), he wouldn't have survived. He'd have had no descendants and we wouldn't be writing about him today.

No matter that some of the great ancient civilizations unconsciously practiced protein complementarity, mixing approximately 80 percent grain with 20 percent legumes in their diets. Maybe they just enjoyed the combinations of tastes and textures. Maybe they instinctively found this combination the most *efficient* way to fuel and maintain the body. (The 80/20 ratio according to nutritionists allows a balanced amino acid pattern. Better still is 60 percent grain, 35 percent legumes, and 5 percent dark green leafy vegetables.) It was certainly not the *only* way. It couldn't be. However, it worked and worked well and was used by the Chinese, the Aztec, the Mayan, the Sumerians, and other intelligent humans of their day.

All we're saying is that you'll get your vitamins, minerals, and proteins *in adequate supply* if you choose wisely from the variety of foods available to you in the market. The most important thing to keep in mind when preparing a diet is to eat enough of the foods that help prevent degenerative diseases (those not caused by germs or viruses). And one of the best of these is beans, because beans also provide *an adequate supply* of fiber along with an abundance of other nutrients necessary to the body chemistry.

How much protein is necessary to keep the body going? There is great fluctuation from one person to another and even within the same person. The body is able to satisfy the need for different amounts of protein at different times. Even when you take in a very low level of protein, your body, through complex regulatory checks and balances, keeps its internal environment pretty constant, accustoming itself to the amount of protein you usually give it. Extreme variations can throw it off, but only temporarily. It adapts quickly, adjusting the way it uses the nitrogen in protein foods.

The body cannot store protein. It can store fat. So the excess protein is broken down and turned into fat to be burned off or stored. Even protein's nitrogen is tossed aside as waste when there is excess. When there is not enough protein, however, nitrogen is carefully hoarded to build tissue—as long as there are enough calories to burn as fuel. Low calorie diets require additional protein intake to make up for what will be burned off as fuel.

THE BEAN FACTOR: CONCLUSION

While beans may not offer complete immunity to the degenerative diseases discussed in this chapter, they have been shown to slow progression of these diseases or enhance a sufferer's ability to withstand their effects. Experts and scientific studies agree that the regular consumption of beans can promote health and prolong life by helping the body protect itself against disease, lessen the risks of sudden death due to heart attack, resist colon cancer, keep the veins and arteries free-flowing, combat obesity, diabetes, and nutritional deficiencies caused by food allergies—and probably a host of other benefits we don't even know about yet.

Although we haven't tried it, beans in their pureed state would probably make an excellent facial mask (because of their heavy moisture content) and so could add a cosmetic value to their other attributes. But maybe this use should be left to cucumbers, avocados, and mud. Beans have enough going for them as it is.

SUBSTITUTIONS

There are many recipes in which the substitution of one food product for another would be disastrous—to the flavor and texture of a finished dish. However, many recipes don't suffer at all.

A recipe that calls for butter as the medium in which to sauté onions and garlic is only slightly affected by the use of vegetable oil instead. Changing ingredients such as these are the very essence of creative cooking.

Use comparable quantities. For example if a recipe calls for ½ cup butter, in most cases you may substitute ½ cup of oil.

The chemistry of some recipes won't allow for substitution. Eggs are a good example of this kind of ingredient. Eggs coagulate, emulsify, amalgamate, and solidify other ingredients in the cooking. Without them other ingredients might fall apart. If a recipe calls for eggs and you don't want to risk the cholesterol intake, don't make it. Sometimes reading a recipe is satisfying enough—well, not really, but it *can* be healthier.

When we specify chicken or beef stock in a recipe, you may always feel confident that it is perfectly all right to substitute vegetable stock. As a matter of fact, beef stock may be substituted for chicken stock if that's all you have in the larder. And vice versa, naturally.

Olive oil was once thought of as a no-no for those of us with high cholesterol. Recent research has changed that way of thinking. It has shown that olive oil contains *monosaturated* fats, which don't raise cholesterol levels at all.

They may not *lower* them like polyunsaturated fats are said to, but they don't *raise* levels as do saturated fats.

Even though new research indicates that olive oil may *lower* cholesterol levels, we have indicated in our recipes that peanut, corn, soybean, or safflower oils may be substituted. You will notice that we always call for "light Tuscan olive oil" when a recipe specifies olive oil—Bertolli and Berio are good brands. This is a personal bias against the strong olive oils of Spain and Greece and most of those from France. We don't like the taste. If you do, by all means use the olive oil of your choice. (Just don't expect us to ask for seconds.)

A less rich substitute for sour cream is yogurt cheese, or *laban*, as it's called in the Middle East. Just let yogurt rest overnight in cheesecloth over a strainer, with a bowl to catch the whey that runs off. In the morning a delicious fresh creamy cheese will be waiting for you.

As for salt, our recipes say "to taste," even when an actual measurement is given. This means you can use more or less or none. The specified amount is to *our* taste, the amount used when testing the recipe.

If a recipe specifies smoked salmon and you have a particular aversion to it, try smoked turkey breast, or smoked oysters or clams. The taste of the recipe will not be affected noticeably if you substitute one smoked food for another. The texture will be, however.

OTHER SUBSTITUTIONS TO KEEP IN MIND

1 tablespoon fresh herbs = ½ to 1 teaspoon dried herbs

1 cup sugar = ½ cup honey or maple syrup (substitute only for sweetening, not in baking)

1 cup dairy milk = 1 cup soy milk

1 tablespoon grated or minced fresh gingerroot = ¼ teaspoon ground ginger

½ teaspoon salt = 2 teaspoons soy sauce

½ teaspoon salt = 1 tablespoon miso

In our recipes you may substitute low fat or skim milk for whole milk. And, if you like the taste, soy milk for whole or skim.

For recipes substituting tofu for meat, poultry, fish, or shellfish, we suggest the comprehensive source book *The Book of Tofu* by William Shurtleff and Akiko Aoyagi—or several Asian and vegetarian cookbooks covering this subject.

You may substitute canned beans for homecooked dried beans whenever the recipe calls for precooked beans. If the beans should be cooked with certain herbs, spices, and other flavorings before being added to a recipe, we usually will say so in the recipe. Otherwise recipes for cooking beans found in the chapter on basic preparation will do.

When pureeing canned beans for baking recipes, it is especially important to rinse them after draining. This not only insures the flushing away of offending oligosaccharides but salt used in their preparation as well. By all means, use pureed canned beans in our cake recipes, if you don't have homemade on hand.

Frozen homecooked beans can, of course, be substituted for cooked or canned beans in a recipe. Just be sure they are labeled clearly as to the ingredients used when cooking them originally. If you have any doubts and don't have the time to thaw them and taste or to soak and cook them from scratch, you usually won't go wrong if you reach instead for a can of the variety specified.

STALKING THE WILD BEAN

American Indians used their own style of technology to grow beans which the Pilgrims admired and adopted. The Indians planted beans between corn rows, training the vines up the tall corn stalks to seek the sun. The corn stalks became natural stakes for the bean vines and the synergistic combination even found its way into the Indian dish succotash—originally made from corn and kidney beans (today's recipes usually call for lima beans) and, likely, dog meat or deer, all cooked in bear grease. The Pilgrims adopted and adapted it as they did baked beans, which, being Indian, predates clam chowder, another New England historic mainstay. The Indian squaws soaked beans just as we do to make them swell and soften their skins, then baked them in a clay pot with onions and deer fat, the pot set in a hole lined with hot stones. Because the Pilgrims could not cook on Sundays for religious reasons, baked beans put up for dinner the night before seemed the perfect dish to serve on Sunday as well and became a Sunday tradition. By the time it switched days and became the Saturday night meal (after the religious restrictions were lifted) New Englanders had added brown sugar, pork fat, and spices, changing the original to suit their own European trained tastes.

APPETIZERS, SANDWICH SPREADS, AND FILLINGS

BEAN AND CHEESE GNOCCHI

Gnocchi are Italian, of course. The Italians are known as prodigious bean-eaters. Oddly enough, in our research we found no recipes for gnocchi made with beans. The standards all call for semolina, corn meal, or potatoes. The following two recipes are our own invention, using bean puree. And they are delicious. We hope the Italians don't mind our recreating their classic.

SERVES 4

1 small onion chopped fine
2 tablespoons unsalted butter
2 tablespoons minced boiled ham
1½ cups sieved cannellini bean puree*
1 cup all-purpose flour
½ cup freshly grated Parmesan cheese
½ cup shredded Italian fontina cheese
½ teaspoon white pepper
¼ teaspoon nutmeg, preferably freshly grated
1 egg yolk
Salt to taste

FOR BAKING GNOCCHI:
4 tablespoons butter
½ cup grated Parmesan cheese

*Use 1 can of beans; drain, rinse, and puree in blender or food processor. Or cook ¾ cup dried cannellini beans and puree as above.

1. In a skillet sauté the onion in butter until golden, add the ham, and continue cooking, stirring, for 2 minutes.

2. Add the bean puree to the skillet, stirring, and cook until combined and heated through.

3. Transfer mixture to a mixing bowl and add the flour, mixing with a wooden spoon. When combined thoroughly, add the Parmesan, the fontina, pepper, nutmeg, egg yolk, and salt to taste and incorporate into mixture.

4. Pick up some of the mixture with a teaspoon and shape quickly into a ball between the palms of your hands. Continue until all the mixture is used. If the gnocchi begin to stick to your hands, dust your hands very lightly with flour. Make the balls as small as possible so that they cook quickly.

5. Preheat oven to 375°.

6. Bring 3 quarts of salted water to the boil in a saucepan and drop in the gnocchi several at a time. Let the water return to a boil and cook the gnocchi 2 or 3 minutes. Remove them with a slotted spoon and transfer them to a buttered baking dish. Repeat until all the gnocchi are cooked.

7. In a small saucepan melt the butter and drizzle it over the gnocchi. Sprinkle evenly with the grated cheese and bake on the highest rack in the oven for 5 minutes or until the

cheese has melted. Serve from baking dish and pass additional Parmesan at the table.

These gnocchi may be served as a first course or as a main dish accompanied by a vegetable and salad. They are also nice as a side dish with grilled or roast meat or chicken, or even better with a dish that has a sauce or gravy.

VARIATION: Spread gnocchi with 1½ to 2 cups Tomato or Marinara Sauce (p. 121) before sprinkling with Parmesan and baking.

Substitute 1 cup of fine-ground corn meal for the flour for a change of taste and texture.

SIMPLE BAKED WHITE BEAN GNOCCHI

SERVES 6

2 cups sieved cannellini or white navy bean puree*
1 teaspoon minced garlic
Salt and freshly ground pepper to taste
¼ teaspoon nutmeg (preferably freshly grated)
¼ cup flour
1 stick (½ cup) melted unsalted butter
½ cup grated Parmesan
Chopped fresh parsley

*See statement regarding puree in preceding recipe.

1. Place bean puree in a saucepan over very low heat to dry out, beating constantly with a wooden spoon. Beat in the garlic, salt and pepper, nutmeg, and flour. Continue to beat until mixture comes away from the sides of the saucepan and is very smooth and fluffy.

2. Preheat oven to 425°.

3. Using two tablespoons dipped in the melted butter, scoop up and shape the mixture into egg-shaped dumplings. Place the gnocchi side by side and/or over each other in a buttered baking/serving dish. Sprinkle with remaining melted butter and Parmesan and bake 20 to 30 minutes or until Parmesan is golden. Remove from oven, sprinkle with parsley, and serve.

SCALLION WHITE BEAN PANCAKES FLECKED WITH BACON

This is a perfect luncheon dish, especially when served with steamed asparagus or a robust salad of endive, arugula, tomatoes, and yellow peppers. The pancakes also go well with roasts, broiled fish or chicken, or a casserole of vegetables.

SERVES 8

THE PANCAKES
- 4 slices bacon or 2 tablespoons peanut, corn, or safflower oil
- ½ pound dried Great Northern beans, cooked and drained or 3 cups canned cannellini beans, drained and rinsed
- 1 teaspoon white wine vinegar
- 2 large egg yolks
- 4 scallions (both white and green parts), sliced very thin

DRIZZLING SAUCE
- 1 teaspoon white wine or rice vinegar
- 4 tablespoons melted unsalted butter
- 2 tablespoons minced fresh parsley
- 1 teaspoon dry mustard
- 2 tablespoons soy sauce

1. In a skillet cook the bacon until crisp and brown. Drain on paper towels, reserving the fat in the pan. (If omitting bacon, pour oil in pan.) Set aside.

2. In a food processor or blender, puree the cooked or canned beans with the vinegar and egg yolks. Pour into a mixing bowl.

3. Crumble bacon. Add it and the scallions to the puree.

4. Pour off all but 2 tablespoons of bacon fat from the skillet. Heat the fat (or oil, if bacon is omitted) over moderately high heat and drop the batter by tablespoonsful into the skillet. Fry for 2 or 3 minutes or until undersides are golden brown. Flip pancakes and fry until second side is nicely browned. Keep cooked pancakes warm in a 200° oven until you use all the batter.

5. In a bowl combine Drizzling Sauce ingredients and whisk to blend.

6. Arrange pancakes on a serving platter and drizzle the sauce evenly over all. Serve as a side dish or first course.

These pancakes can be fried ahead of time if you'd like to serve them as a late snack after theater or the movies. Allow them to stand at room temperature until near serving time. Mix up the drizzling sauce. Fry the pancakes a second time in just enough oil to coat the pan and heat them through without sticking. This second frying gives them an appealing crispness. Drizzle with sauce and serve.

GREEN BEAN-STUFFED CHICK-PEA CREPES WITH GARLIC BUTTER

You may be unfamiliar with chick-pea flour but it is a staple of Indian cooking. Try it. The flavor is nuttier than that of wheat flour.

MAKES 1 DOZEN 6-INCH CREPES
SERVES 6

THE CREPES

⅔ cup chick-pea flour (available in health-food, Middle Eastern, and Indian stores)
½ teaspoon salt or to taste
1 pinch sugar
½ cup milk
2 eggs, lightly beaten
2 tablespoons peanut, corn, or safflower oil
1 tablespoon warm water

1. Sift chick-pea flour, salt, and sugar into a bowl. Make a well in center and pour in milk, eggs, and oil. Stir just enough to combine ingredients. Add water and stir through. Allow to stand at least 10 minutes, preferably longer.

2. With a small wad of waxed paper moistened with oil, spread a thin film over bottom of crepe pan or small skillet.

3. Heat pan over medium heat until a drop of water sizzles on the surface. Pour or ladle about 2 tablespoons of batter into pan. Tip and rotate quickly to coat bottom evenly. Pour any excess batter back into bowl.

4. Cook until edges of crepe begin to curl and brown and surface turns from shiny to matte, about 30 seconds.

5. Have a clean dish towel spread on a work surface. Turn pan upside down over cloth and tap lightly, releasing crepe and allowing it to fall on cloth. The first crepe may stick or tear. Don't worry, the next one will be perfect.

6. Continue to make crepes in the same manner until all the batter is used.

7. Stack crepes until ready to fill.

THE GREEN BEANS

1½ pounds green beans, trimmed and cut diagonally into ½-inch pieces

1. Bring a saucepan half-filled with water to a rolling boil.

2. Drop in all the green beans at once. Return to the boil and cook from 5 to 10 minutes or until beans are crisp tender.

2 tablespoons melted unsalted
butter
½ cup chopped pecans, walnuts,
or cashews
Salt, if desired
Freshly ground pepper

3. Drain and refresh under cold running water.

4. Drain and return to stove over low heat. Pour melted butter over beans, stir to coat evenly and heat through.

5. Sprinkle nuts, salt, and pepper over beans and stir. Remove from heat.

THE SAUCE
6 tablespoons unsalted butter
2 teaspoons minced garlic

1. Melt butter in a small skillet over moderately low heat. When foam subsides, add garlic and sauté, stirring, for 30 seconds or until garlic is lightly golden.

2. Remove from heat and keep warm.

ASSEMBLING CREPES
AND SERVING
Crepes
Cooked green beans
Garlic butter sauce

1. Preheat oven to 350°.

2. Spoon 2 tablespoons of beans on bottom third of crepe (browned side up).

3. Roll crepe, folding in sides to form a package, and place in greased baking pan.

4. Continue with each of the crepes until all 12 are filled.

5. Drizzle half the garlic butter sauce over crepes and place in center of oven. Bake for 15 minutes. Keep remaining garlic butter warm.

6. Remove from oven and place 2 crepes per person on serving dishes. Pour a little more garlic butter sauce over the crepes.

SUGGESTION: As a luncheon dish for 4, serve 3 crepes per person and garnish with strips of roasted Italian peppers (either freshly prepared or bottled in oil) or strips of boiled ham.

ASIAN PICKLED SQUID WITH VEGETABLES AND WHITE BEANS

Some people turn up their noses at squid and won't even try them. We happen to love them, for their flavor, chewy texture, and their versatility in the kitchen. If you've never tasted them, a good introduction would be the fried rings served in most Italian and some Chinese restaurants or in assorted sashimi (where squid would be only one of several fish served). Be adventurous. It can pay off—especially in this dish, which is both cooling and piquant.

SERVES 4 TO 6

4 cups water
⅔ cup rice vinegar
1 3-inch piece of fresh gingerroot, pared and sliced thin
1 bunch scallions (both white and green parts), cut into 2-inch lengths
8 garlic cloves, halved
4 teaspoons salt if desired
½ teaspoon red pepper flakes
½ teaspoon freshly ground pepper
1 large carrot, pared, cut into ¼-inch slices
2 stalks celery, cut into ½-inch slices
1 medium onion, sliced thin
1 pound squid, cleaned and cut into ½-inch rings by the fishmonger
1 small zucchini, halved lengthwise, and cut into ½-inch semicircles

1. Combine water, vinegar, ginger, scallions, garlic, salt, and red and black peppers in a saucepan. Place over high heat and bring to the boil. Reduce heat to moderate and boil for 15 minutes uncovered.

2. Reduce heat to simmer and add carrots, celery, and onion. Cook 5 minutes more, uncovered.

3. Add squid and simmer 2 minutes more or until squid turns opaque white.

4. Add zucchini and simmer until just crisp-tender, about 2 minutes more.

5. Add beans and cook until just heated through.

6. Remove from heat. Allow to cool to room temperature. With a slotted spoon transfer solids to a 2-quart jar with lid. Pour cooking liquid into jar to fill.

7. Cover tightly and refrigerate for 1 to 2 days.

8. To serve, arrange watercress around edge of serving platter, drain liquid from jar, and pour or spoon contents into center.

1 cup canned cannellini beans, drained and rinsed

1 bunch watercress for garnish

When we were researching our *Mustard Cookbook* we discovered mustard sprouts, called mustard cress in England. White mustard seeds (also called yellow mustard seeds) can be sprouted just like beans. They're a refreshing, delicate substitution for watercress in a salad or in sandwiches. Try them. Just use our directions for sprouting beans (page 25), using mustard seeds instead of the beans.

NONCLASSIC TARAMASALATA WITH PINK BEANS

MAKES 4½ TO 5 CUPS

1 jar (8 ounces) tarama (fish roe available at Greek and Middle Eastern stores, specialty food stores, and some supermarkets)

1 can (16 ounces) pink beans, rinsed and drained

1 medium onion, cut into eighths

⅓ cup fresh lemon juice

½ teaspoon white pepper

1 to 1½ cups light Tuscan olive oil

1. Place tarama, beans, onion, lemon juice, and pepper in a food processor. With machine running add 1 cup of olive oil through the feed tube in a slow, steady stream and process until smooth, stopping processor and scraping down sides if necessary. Blend in more oil only if too thick.

2. Scrape into serving bowl and serve with pita wedges, unsalted crackers, or thin slices of French or Italian bread.

A garnish of lemon, radish and cucumber slices makes a nice contrast to this taramasalata's rich orange-pink glow.

SOCCA OR NIÇOISE CHICK-PEA FLOUR PANCAKE

In Cannes or Nice you'll often see vendors offering socca to queues of Frenchmen on street corners. It is also a favorite in many Italian port towns. We guess you could call it a savory pastry—although sprinkled with sugar and perhaps a little cinnamon it could go well with coffee instead of a danish.

SERVES 4 TO 6

Oil for quiche dish
½ teaspoon salt
1 cup hot water
1 cup chick-pea flour (available in Indian, health-food, or specialty food stores)
4 tablespoons light Tuscan olive oil
Salt and pepper or sugar for sprinkling

1. Preheat oven to 350°. Lightly oil a 10-inch quiche dish.

2. Stir together the salt and hot water until salt is dissolved. Sift the chick-pea flour into a medium saucepan, make a well in the center and, with a wooden spoon, stir salt water mixture into the flour until smooth. Turn heat to low and whisk mixture for 4 to 5 minutes. Batter will still look wet.

3. Spread the batter, smoothing it evenly in the prepared quiche dish. Drizzle about a tablespoon of olive oil over the top and, using a brush or the back of a spoon, spread it lightly over the entire surface. Bake for 30 to 35 minutes or until the surface is golden brown and cracked. Remove dish to a wire rack to cool to room temperature.

4. Pour the remaining 3 tablespoons olive oil into a skillet and heat over moderately high heat until rippling. Cut the socca into 2-inch pieces and fry in batches, until golden brown, about 1 minute. Sprinkle with salt and pepper and serve as a snack or with drinks.

ARMENIAN GRAPE LEAVES STUFFED WITH LENTILS AND BULGUR

MAKES 50

¼ cup light Tuscan olive oil

⅓ cup pine nuts or unroasted cashews, chopped coarse

2 medium onions, minced

⅓ cup dried apricots, chopped fine

½ cup dried currants

¼ cup minced fresh mint or 1 teaspoon dried

1 tablespoon minced fresh savory or 1 teaspoon dried

½ cup lentils, cooked for 25 minutes, until just tender

⅔ cup coarse bulgur (cracked wheat), soaked in hot water for 30 minutes and drained in a fine sieve

⅓ cup lemon juice
Salt and freshly ground pepper to taste
1-pound jar grape leaves, drained (available at specialty food stores and some supermarkets)

1. In a heavy skillet heat the oil over high heat until rippling, turn heat down to moderate, and cook the nuts, stirring, until golden. Transfer with a slotted spoon to a plate. Add the onions to the skillet. Cook, stirring, until translucent and soft.

2. Remove the skillet from the heat and add the nuts, apricots, currants, mint, savory, lentils, bulgur, ½ the lemon juice, and salt and pepper to taste. Combine well.

3. Soak the grape leaves in cold water to cover for 15 minutes. Separate them gently and drain. Place them in one layer on paper towels and pat dry.

4. Line the bottom of a saucepan (do not use aluminum) with about 10 of the leaves.

5. Place a tablespoon of the stuffing on the stem end of one of the remaining leaves. Trim off the stem. Fold in the sides of the leaf and roll it up. Do the same with the remaining stuffing and leaves. Layer the rolls in the saucepan seam side down. Drizzle the remaining lemon juice over them.

6. Put a heatproof plate or Pyrex pie pan just a little smaller than the circumference of the saucepan on top of the rolls to prevent their unrolling. Pour in 1½ cups of boiling water, turn heat down to simmer, and cook the rolls, covered, for 45 minutes.

7. Remove from heat, uncover, and allow to cool. Remove the plate and transfer the rolls to paper towels to drain. Arrange on a platter and refrigerate, covered, for 3 hours or more.

BOMBAY PAKORAS (VEGETABLE FRITTERS)

T hese pakoras are great with ice-cold beer or cocktails.

SERVES 12

THE BATTER

1 cup chick-pea flour (available at specialty stores and Indian markets)
1/4 teaspoon baking powder
1 teaspoon salt
1/2 teaspoon turmeric
1/2 teaspoon ground cumin
1/2 teaspoon freshly ground pepper
1 tablespoon chopped fresh coriander (cilantro)
1/8 teaspoon cayenne pepper
3/4 cup warm water
Peanut oil for deep frying

THE FILLINGS

1 small head cauliflower broken into 1-inch florets
or
3 medium onions, sliced thin
or
3 medium potatoes, skin left on, scrubbed, sliced in thin rounds
or
3/4 pound green beans, trimmed, cut in half

1. Place one of the suggested fillings in a small bowl. Salt and pepper to taste.

2. Or: with a 1/4-cup measure or ice cream scoop, scoop up the split pea, carrot and turnip mixture and form into 2-inch balls. Set balls aside.

TO FRY PAKORAS

1. Make the batter by sifting together the flour, baking powder, and salt. Mix in the spices. Gradually add about 3/4 cup of warm water in a stream (use just enough water to make a batter thick enough to coat the vegetables). Beat until smooth. Let the batter stand, covered, in a warm place for about 30 minutes. (The batter may be made 1 day in advance, covered, and kept chilled. Allow to return to room temperature before using.)

2. Heat 2 inches of oil in a deep fryer or deep heavy skillet or saucepan until hot (350°) but not smoking. Whisk the batter and dip the vegetables or vegetable balls into it to coat and fry them in one layer, slowly, for 2 to 3 minutes, turning them several times, or until they are golden brown.

or
½ to ¾ pound Anaheim or
Italian green chili peppers,
halved, seeded, and deveined,
rinsed and patted dry
or a combination of
1 cup yellow split peas,
simmered 20 minutes,
drained and mashed
1½ cups mashed cooked carrots
1 cup mashed cooked turnips

3. Transfer the pakoras with a slotted spoon to paper towels to drain. Sprinkle with salt and pepper and serve immediately with any of the following: bottled chili sauce; tomato catsup laced with Worcestershire sauce; chutney; yogurt spiced with fresh pepper and minced garlic; or soy sauce mixed with dry mustard and rice vinegar.

PEPERONATA CASALINGA

SERVES 4 TO 6

2 medium eggplants, rinsed
¼ cup light Tuscan olive oil
1 medium onion, sliced thin (1 cup)
1 teaspoon minced garlic
2 medium to large sweet red peppers, cored, seeded, and cut into ½-inch dice
4 ripe medium tomatoes, peeled, seeded, and chopped coarse
1 cup cooked or canned cannellini beans, drained and rinsed
½ teaspoon red pepper flakes
Salt and freshly ground pepper to taste

1. Pare the skin from eggplants in long ½-inch-wide strips; cut strips into ½-inch pieces and set aside; reserve rest of eggplant for another use.

2. Heat the oil in a sauté pan or medium saucepan until rippling. Add onion and sauté about 7 minutes, stirring frequently. Add garlic and continue to sauté until both are golden, about 10 minutes altogether.

3. Add peppers and sauté about 2 minutes more. Add eggplant skin. Cook, stirring occasionally, for about 5 minutes.

4. Stir in tomatoes, beans, and red pepper flakes; cook uncovered until tomato liquid has evaporated, approximately 15 minutes.

5. Remove from heat and taste for seasoning. Add salt to taste and a good amount of freshly ground pepper. Allow to cool slightly and serve warm.

KIDNEY BEAN AND FRESH CORIANDER SPREAD

MAKES ABOUT 1 CUP

1¼ cups canned kidney beans, drained and rinsed
½ teaspoon ground cumin
1 teaspoon minced garlic
½ teaspoon Tabasco sauce
2 tablespoons peanut, corn, or safflower oil
1½ tablespoons wine vinegar
1 heaping tablespoon chopped fresh coriander leaves (cilantro)
Salt and freshly ground pepper to taste

1. In a food processor or blender puree the ingredients to a coarse spread.

2. Serve on pieces of toasted pita bread or on toasted French bread rounds with thinly sliced avocado or hard-boiled egg slices for garnish. Also good as a base for thinly sliced chicken or roast beef sandwiches.

THE FIRST LENTIL TILLERS

The lentil is probably the oldest of all the cultivated legumes. Its origins were somewhere in southwest Asia—around Pakistan, Afghanistan, Syria, Iran, and Iraq—and the year, about 7000 B.C. Along with wheat and barley, it was one of the first crops that the formerly nomadic tribes of this area planted. It is, it seems, on every menu now, part of every meal in India. It has been eaten continuously for the past 10,000 years in the Middle East; and quickly, meaning thousands of years ago, became a staple in eastern Europe. By the time of the Greeks lentils were eaten in and out of season (early on the drying process as preservative was discovered).

LENTIL
AND BULGUR CIGARS

This recipe is of Middle Eastern origin and a little hearty as a first course. Something simple and delicate should follow, such as broiled salmon, grilled baby lamb chops, veal scallopini, or an assortment of sautéed or steamed vegetables.

SERVES 4

1 cup lentils, cooked about 35 minutes until soft, drained
½ stick unsalted butter, cut in pieces
Salt and pepper to taste
¾ cup fine bulgur (cracked wheat)
1 medium onion, chopped fine
¼ cup light Tuscan olive oil
¼ cup sweet green or red pepper, chopped fine
2 scallions (both green and white parts), sliced thin
⅓ cup minced fresh parsley
Paprika

1. Return the lentils to the saucepan in which they were cooked and over low heat stir in the butter, the salt and pepper, and the bulgur. Turn the heat down to simmer and cook the mixture, stirring, for 2 minutes. Turn off the heat and allow to cool while you sauté the onions.

2. In a small skillet, sauté the onion in the oil until it is soft and golden. Transfer to a bowl along with the lentil mixture and, when cool enough to handle, knead with moistened hands until blended very well. Add 3 tablespoons of the pepper, 3 tablespoons of the scallions, and 3 tablespoons of the parsley, and knead again until well combined.

3. Form into 2-inch long cigar shapes and arrange on a platter. Sprinkle with remaining pepper, scallion, and parsley. Dust with paprika, if desired, and serve with a salad of tomato, onion, and basil dressed with mustard vinaigrette.

HUMMUS BI TAHINI OR CHICK-PEAS WITH SESAME PASTE

SERVES 8

¾ cup tahini
1 tablespoon Tuscan olive oil
¾ cup freshly squeezed lemon juice or more to taste
1 tablespoon chopped garlic
1 teaspoon salt or to taste
½ teaspoon freshly ground black pepper
1 can (19 ounces) chick-peas, drained and rinsed
Pinch of hot paprika

1. Combine tahini with the olive oil in a small bowl. Stir until well blended.

2. In a food processor or blender puree the lemon juice, garlic, and salt and pepper, and with the motor running add the chick-peas a handful at a time, alternating with some of the tahini–oil mixture and a tablespoon or two of water. When the puree is smooth and has a creamy texture, taste for seasoning, adding more salt, pepper, or lemon juice if necessary.

3. Transfer to a serving dish and garnish with a sprinkling of paprika. Serve with toasted pita bread wedges or sesame crackers.

There seem to be as many recipes for hummus as there are cooks. Some substitute cayenne for the black pepper or don't use pepper at all. Some like it less garlicky. Some, like us, find garlic almost its reason for being. The garnishes are endless as well—chopped parsley, chopped scallions, chopped mint. We think this dish should remain simple in keeping with its peasant origins.

TA'AMIA OR FALAFEL (EGYPTIAN FAVA BEAN PATTIES)

This is the falafel served from street stands in Egyptian cities the same way its cousin is served here—with tomato slices and lettuce shreds inside Arab bread.

SERVES 4

1 can (19 ounces) fava beans (preferably white favas)
2 teaspoons minced garlic
1 teaspoon ground cumin
2 tablespoons ground coriander
4 scallions (both white and green parts), sliced very thin
½ teaspoon baking powder
1 teaspoon freshly ground pepper
Salt to taste
¼ teaspoon cayenne
Flour for dredging
Oil for deep frying

1. In a food processor process the beans with the garlic, cumin, coriander, scallions, baking powder, pepper, salt, and cayenne until a coarse puree. Transfer to a bowl, cover, and chill in the refrigerator for 30 minutes or more.

2. Shape with moistened hands into small balls, dredge with flour, and set aside to dry for at least 15 minutes.

3. In a skillet over high heat bring 1 inch of oil to rippling; do not let it smoke. Drop in several *ta'amia* at a time, turning occasionally, until they are dark golden brown on all sides. Leave to drain on paper towels while you are frying the remainder in batches. This recipe should yield about 32 patties. Serve hot with drinks or as a first course with Tomato Sauce (p. 121) or in pita bread pockets with fresh tomatoes, shredded lettuce, and vinaigrette dressing.

TWO-TASTE CECI NUTS

Serve these with cocktails or wine before dinner. It's really one dish with two separate and distinct tastes.

MAKES 2 TO 3 CUPS

1 can (19 ounces) chick-peas, drained and rinsed
½ cup (1 stick) unsalted butter
2 teaspoons minced garlic
1 teaspoon dry mustard
1 teaspoon chili powder
¼ teaspoon cayenne
1 teaspoon cumin
2 teaspoons salt or to taste
1 teaspoon onion salt
1 teaspoon ground ginger
1 teaspoon ground coriander
½ teaspoon turmeric
1 tablespoon soy sauce or Maggi Seasoning

1. Divide chick-peas into two parts. Melt ¼ cup of the butter in each of two skillets over moderately low heat. Add 1 teaspoon of garlic to each skillet and sauté for 1 minute.

2. Add half the chick-peas to each skillet and sauté very slowly, shaking the pans and stirring often until beans start to sizzle. You want them to turn a dark golden brown. Taste for doneness—they should take 10 to 12 minutes. Turn off heat.

3. In a small bowl mix together the mustard, chili powder, cayenne, cumin, salt, and onion salt.

4. In another small bowl mix together the ginger, coriander, turmeric, and soy sauce.

5. Sprinkle one mixture over one pan of chick-peas and one over the other pan. Toss to coat them well. Transfer to separate bowls and serve hot. Ceci Nuts may be made ahead and reheated in a 350° oven for 5 minutes or until hot.

SOYBEAN NUTS

MAKES 2 TO 3 CUPS

1 cup dried soybeans, cooked until just tender and drained
½ cup unsalted butter
1 teaspoon minced garlic
1 teaspoon salt
1 tablespoon soy sauce or more to taste

1. Preheat oven to 350°.

2. Spread beans in one layer in a jelly-roll pan or any shallow pan. Roast in the oven for 30 minutes or until browned, stirring occasionally so they brown evenly.

3. Meanwhile, in a small saucepan over moderate heat, melt the butter and add the garlic, salt, and soy sauce. Cook for 3 minutes or until garlic just begins to brown. Remove immediately from heat and set aside.

4. Transfer soybeans to a heatproof bowl and drizzle butter mixture over. Toss gently to coat. Serve warm or at room temperature as a snack with drinks.

THE CHICHI CECI

Chick-peas, known to Romans as cicer arietinum, and which gave Cicero's family its name, were first cultivated in the Tigris and Euphrates area at least 5000 B.C. Today, in Spain, the chick-pea is by far the most popular of the legumes having reached there through two cultures; first the Roman legions brought it as they did so many plants, vegetables, and spices, and then the North Africans. Some Spanish chick-pea dishes have all the exoticism of both sides of the Mediterranean. The Spaniards call them garbanzos, a name derived from the Greek.

In the Middle East and the Eastern Mediterranean countries a puree of chick-peas, garlic, paprika, and lemon called hummus, with all its regional variations is as common as refried beans in Mexico and our own Southwest. In India the chick-pea vies with wheat for acreage devoted to its cultivation and is the most important of the legumes. The variety and ingenuity Indians have used to devise methods for its preparation is rivaled only by the Chinese and Japanese in their use of the soybean. It is boiled, roasted, fried, sprouted; its flour is turned into breads, fritters, and pancakes; it finds its way into salads, stews, and uncountable vegetable dishes; it's eaten at breakfast, lunch, dinner, and for snacks.

DILLED PICKLED GREEN BEANS

Serve these with drinks or use in place of pickles on a deli platter. Cut into ½-inch lengths, the green beans add zesty flavor to salads. Use them in place of olives in a martini or to garnish a Bloody Mary.

SERVES 4

½ pound green beans, trimmed
1 teaspoon minced garlic
1 teaspoon red pepper flakes
8 sprigs fresh dill
¼ teaspoon dill seeds
¼ teaspoon mustard seeds
3 tablespoons sugar
1 cup cider vinegar
1 tablespoon salt

1. Plunge the beans into a saucepan of boiling salted water, turn heat down to simmer, and cook for 5 minutes. Refresh under cold running water, drain well, and transfer to a shallow baking dish.

2. Sprinkle beans with garlic, pepper flakes, dill sprigs, dill seeds, and the mustard seeds.

3. In a saucepan over high heat, boil the sugar, vinegar, salt, and 1 cup of water for 1 minute. Pour hot mixture over beans. Allow the beans to cool, then chill in the refrigerator, covered, at least 24 hours before serving. Or transfer to a plastic or glass storage bowl. Keeps, refrigerated, 10 days or more.

TERRINES
AND PÂTÉS

CURRIED LIMA BEAN PÂTÉ WITH CRYSTALLIZED GINGER

This pâté has a lot going for it; the crunch of peanuts, the exotic flavor of curry, and the special zing of crystallized ginger.

SERVES 4 TO 8

1 cup dried lima beans, cooked and drained
¼ cup (½ stick) butter
1 medium onion, chopped fine
1 cup thin-sliced celery
⅓ cup unbleached flour
1 cup skim milk
1 egg, beaten
1 cup fine, soft bread crumbs
1½ cups grated raw carrots
1 teaspoon salt or to taste
½ teaspoon freshly ground pepper
1 teaspoon *garam masala* or curry powder
1½ cups chopped, unsalted dry-roasted peanuts
½ cup chopped crystallized ginger

1. Mash beans well by hand or process to a coarse puree in a food processor fitted with the steel blade.

2. Melt butter in a sauté pan over moderate heat and add onion. Sauté until wilted and transparent, about 3 to 5 minutes. Add celery, cover, and cook until tender, about 7 to 10 minutes.

3. Add flour to onion-celery mixture and cook 2 minutes more. Add milk and stir until thickened.

4. Preheat oven to 375°.

5. Remove pan from heat and stir in beaten egg, bread crumbs, carrots, salt, pepper, *garam masala*, and peanuts. Mix in mashed lima beans.

6. Spoon mixture into a greased 8-by-4-inch loaf pan and swirl chopped ginger (optional) into batter with a fork. Bake on center rack of oven for 35 to 45 minutes or until a knife inserted into the center of the pâté comes out dry.

7. Run a sharp knife around the edge of pan and turn loaf onto serving platter. Serve hot or at room temperature in 1-inch slices as a first course, side dish, or luncheon main dish.

SUGGESTION: When serving 4 as a luncheon main dish, arrange servings on a baking sheet, top with thin slices of Brie or Camembert and bake until cheese bubbles. Transfer with spatula to serving plates. Accompany with a green salad tossed with a mustard-vinaigrette dressing, along with crusty Italian whole wheat bread and sweet butter.

CURRIED VEGETABLE PIE WITH CHICK-PEA CRUST

SERVES 4

THE FILLING
(Make this the day before)

2 tablespoons peanut, corn, or safflower oil

4 carrots, pared, cut into ¼-inch dice

4 medium leeks (white part only), halved, rinsed well, and cut into ¼-inch slices

2 celery stalks, trimmed of leaves, cut into ¼-inch dice

2 sweet red peppers, seeded and deveined, cut into ¼-inch dice

1½ cups chopped cauliflower

4 teaspoons *garam masala** or curry powder, preferably Madras

2 teaspoons minced garlic

⅛ teaspoon cayenne

2 medium tomatoes, peeled, seeded, and chopped or 3 large canned Italian plum tomatoes, drained and chopped

Garam masala is a spice mixture which in India would be prepared to a family's taste. More aromatic than commercial curry powders found on supermarket shelves, tins of already mixed powders are available at Indian markets and some gourmet shops labeled "garam masala." Or mix a teaspoon each of cumin, ground cloves, ground bay leaves, cardamom, cinnamon, and pepper with half a teaspoon of mace and ginger.

1. In a large skillet or sauté pan over moderate heat, heat oil until rippling. Add carrots, leeks, celery, and peppers. Sauté, stirring and shaking the pan occasionally until leeks begin to brown, about 6 to 7 minutes.

2. Add cauliflower, *garam masala* or curry powder, garlic, and cayenne and cook, stirring, 2 minutes. Add tomatoes, stock, salt, and pepper. Turn heat down to simmer and cook, covered, until vegetables are just tender, about 10 minutes. Remove pan from heat and stir in the peanut butter and yogurt. Combine well and transfer to a bowl. Refrigerate, covered, overnight so that the flavors can blend.

A beanery *has meant a cheap eating place since the early 19th century.* Beans were always inexpensive, and beanery *also meant an inexpensive place for blue collar workers to eat.*

Around 1800 the word beanfest *was used by the British for an annual feast and probably derives from the Celtic tradition. The Americans picked up the word soon after and applied it to an employee banquet or picnic.*

½ cup vegetable stock or water
1½ teaspoons salt or to taste
½ teaspoon freshly ground pepper
2 tablespoons peanut butter
2 tablespoons plain yogurt

THE CHICK-PEA PASTRY CRUST

1½ cups all-purpose flour
1 teaspoon salt
½ teaspoon ground coriander
½ cup chick-pea puree, made from cooked or canned chick-peas
½ cup solid vegetable shortening
3 tablespoons water

1. In a bowl mix the flour, salt, and coriander. With fingertips rub the chick-pea puree into the flour until the mixture is flaky.

2. Heat shortening and water in a small saucepan over moderate heat until shortening melts. Slowly pour into flour mixture tossing and mixing with a fork until well blended.

3. Knead briefly on a floured surface and roll out dough ⅛ inch thick. Cut pastry 1 inch larger than a 4-cup casserole. Use scraps for decorating crust, if you wish.

ASSEMBLING PIE

1. Heat vegetable filling in a saucepan over moderately low heat to a gentle simmer. Add water or vegetable stock if mixture is too thick.

2. Preheat oven to 375°.

3. Transfer filling to a 4-cup casserole. Lay pastry over casserole and press overhang against the sides of the casserole to seal.

4. Place casserole in center of oven and bake until crust is light browned, about 25 minutes.

This crust is perfect for other savory pies. It is flaky and flavorful.

THREE-BEAN TERRINE

Although this terrine is only ⅓ Italian, it boasts the colors of the Italian flag. It not only looks pretty (especially set among other foods on a buffet), but the separate layers of pesto-, curry-, and chili-flavored beans melt in your mouth.

SERVES 8 TO 10

THE WHITE BEAN LAYER

- 4 tablespoons unsalted butter
- 1 medium to large onion, chopped fine
- 4 garlic cloves, chopped fine
  Salt to taste
- ½ teaspoon freshly ground pepper
- 1 cup canned cannellini beans, drained and rinsed
- 4 tablespoons pesto, preferably homemade
- 2 eggs

1. Melt butter in a skillet over moderately low heat and add onions. Cover and cook until wilted and lightly golden, about 20 minutes.

2. Add garlic, salt, and pepper and cook uncovered 5 minutes more. Remove from heat.

3. Place beans and pesto in the work bowl of a food processor fitted with the steel blade, add onion mixture, and process to a smooth puree.

4. Add eggs and process to incorporate. Taste and correct seasoning. Scrape into a bowl or plastic container, cover, and refrigerate until chilled and ready to assemble with other layers.

THE GREEN BEAN LAYER

- 4 tablespoons unsalted butter
- 1 medium to large onion, chopped fine
- 4 garlic cloves, chopped fine
- 1½ cups green beans, trimmed and cut into ½-inch pieces
- 1 tablespoon *garam masala* or curry powder
- ½ teaspoon salt, if desired
- ½ teaspoon freshly ground pepper
- ½ tablespoon fresh oregano or ½ teaspoon dried
- ½ teaspoon ground coriander
- 2 eggs

1. Melt butter in a skillet over moderately low heat and add onions. Cover and cook until wilted and lightly golden, about 20 minutes.

2. While onions are cooking, blanch green beans for 5 minutes. Drain.

3. Add green beans, garlic, *garam masala*, salt, pepper, oregano, and coriander to onion mixture. Stir and cook about 10 minutes more or until beans are tender.

4. Scrape into work bowl of food processor fitted with the steel blade and with several on-and-off motions process to a coarse puree.

5. Add eggs and process to just incorporate. Taste and correct seasonings. Scrape into bowl or plastic container, cover, and refrigerate until chilled and ready to assemble with other layers.

THE RED BEAN LAYER

4 tablespoons unsalted butter
1 medium to large onion, chopped fine
4 garlic cloves, chopped fine
1 teaspoon chili powder
½ teaspoon salt, if desired
½ teaspoon freshly ground pepper
2 medium tomatoes, peeled, seeded, and chopped or 4 canned Italian plum tomatoes, drained and chopped
1 cup canned kidney beans, drained and rinsed
2 eggs

1. Melt butter in a skillet over moderately low heat and add onions. Cover and cook until wilted and lightly golden, about 20 minutes.

2. Add garlic, chili powder, salt, and pepper and cook uncovered 5 minutes more.

3. Stir in tomatoes, raise heat to moderate, and cook 10 minutes. Remove from heat.

4. Place beans and cooked mixture in the work bowl of a food processor fitted with the steel blade and puree until almost smooth.

5. Add eggs and process to just incorporate. Taste and correct seasonings. Scrape into bowl or plastic container, cover, and refrigerate until chilled and ready to assemble with other layers.

TO ASSEMBLE AND GARNISH THE TERRINE

2 teaspoons capers, drained
½ sweet red pepper, seeded, deveined, and chopped fine
10 to 12 large cabbage leaves, blanched until pliable

1. Butter a 9-by- 5-by-3 inch loaf pan. Trim any hard ribs from the cabbage leaves. Line the pan with the leaves, overlapping them slightly to cover bottom, sides, and ends of pan. Leave a few leaves to cover top of terrine.

2. Remove three bean mixtures from refrigerator. Start with white bean puree and spoon it into leaf-lined pan. Smooth layer with a spatula and sprinkle capers evenly over top, pressing lightly into surface.

3. Spoon kidney bean puree on top of white bean puree, taking care not to disturb capers. Smooth layer with a spatula. Sprinkle evenly with chopped red pepper; press lightly into surface.

4. Spoon green bean puree over second layer and smooth with spatula. Tap loaf pan several times on counter top to expel any air bubbles.

5. Cover top of terrine with remaining cabbage leaves, folding them in or trimming them to fit.

6. Preheat oven to 350°.

7. Wrap loaf pan completely in aluminum foil, folding edges over to seal. Set the pan in a baking pan in the middle of the oven. Pour boiling water into the pan until it comes halfway up the sides of the loaf pan.

8. Bake for 2 hours or until center of terrine feels firm to the touch. Remove from water and unwrap.

9. Allow to cool for about 15 minutes, then weight with a 2-pound weight (for instance, 2 soup or fruit cans inside another loaf pan). Allow to cool completely. Remove weight, cover, and refrigerate until chilled.

10. To unmold, run a sharp knife around sides of pan then dip pan in hot water briefly. Set a serving platter over top of pan and invert both. The terrine should drop onto the platter. If it doesn't, tap it lightly until it does.

11. To serve, slice and garnish with mayonnaise, flavored, if you like, with Dijon mustard, garlic, or basil.

PREPARATION SHORT-CUT: Because each layer contains both onions and garlic, these ingredients may be combined and cooked all at once to save time. When wilted and golden, divide into thirds and proceed with each layer as directed, using a third of the onion-garlic mixture for each.

SOUPS

COLD GREEN SALAD SOUP WITH TWO PEAS

This soup is our own take-off on a gazpacho. It is very green and even tastes green—as if it had just been picked in a kitchen garden. If a soup can be called thirst-quenching, this is it.

SERVES 4

1 package (10 ounces) frozen tiny peas, thawed

½ pound snow peas, trimmed and chopped coarse

3 cups chicken stock, homemade or canned

½ cup whole unblanched almonds

1 large green (unripe) tomato, cored, seeded, and chopped coarse

½ cup coarse-chopped tender heart of celery

½ cup coarse-chopped sweet green pepper

½ cup coarse-chopped seeded cucumber (peeled only if waxed)

½ cup coarse-chopped romaine lettuce

1 teaspoon minced garlic

½ cup thin-sliced scallions (both white and green parts)

Lime wedges

1. Place thawed peas in a large heatproof bowl. Add chopped snow peas. Reserve.

2. In a saucepan over moderately high heat bring chicken stock to a boil and pour over peas and snow peas.

3. Process almonds in a blender or food processor until they are ground very fine. Add green tomato, celery, pepper, cucumber, romaine lettuce, garlic, and one cup of the broth, including some of the peas. Pulse processor on and off until mixture is consistency of coarse cornmeal. It is important not to overprocess the vegetables. Soup should have texture and a little crunch.

4. Stir vegetable mixture into broth and peas, add scallions, and stir well. Refrigerate, covered, for 4 hours or up to 24. Taste for seasoning and add salt, if necessary. Serve cold accompanied with lime wedges.

CALDO GALLEGO, OR WHITE BEAN SOUP SPANISH STYLE

SERVES 6

1 cup dried Great Northern or navy beans, soaked and drained

½ pound smoked ham, cut into ½-inch dice

8 cups chicken stock, homemade or canned

1 medium onion, sliced

1 pound kale*, tough stems removed, and chopped

3 turnips, cut in half and sliced in ¼-inch half-rounds

3 medium potatoes, cut in eighths

1 teaspoon salt or to taste

1 teaspoon freshly ground pepper

*If kale is unavailable, substitute half a head of cabbage and a few turnip greens, both chopped in fairly large pieces.

1. In a large saucepan or soup pot, cover the beans and ham with the stock, bring to the boil over high heat, turn heat down to gentle simmer, and cook, covered, for 2 hours.

2. Add the onion, kale, turnips, and potatoes. Stir gently into the bean mixture, add the salt and pepper, and simmer, covered, 1 hour more, or until beans are very soft. Serve in large soup bowls.

VARIATIONS: You may add ½ pound boiled ham, ½ stewing chicken, chorizos, and a few links of pork sausage all cut into serving-sized pieces for a hearty 2-course meal, the meats to be served after the soup.

A Catalan peasant version of this soup adds ¼ cup long-grain rice, 1 cup thin egg noodles, and 1 cup cooked chickpeas for the last hour of cooking.

Some find this soup rich enough to be made with water rather than chicken stock. It's flavorful either way.

PINK BEAN
AND SAUSAGE SOUP

●●●

Served with a crusty, coarse-grained bread and fresh sweet butter, then followed with a green salad, this is a wonderfully filling and satisfying winter meal.

SERVES 6

1 can (19 ounces) pink beans, drained and rinsed
4½ cups chicken stock, homemade or canned
1 small onion, chopped fine
¼ sweet green pepper, seeded, deveined, and chopped fine
1 teaspoon minced garlic
1 carrot, pared, sliced thin
2 celery stalks, sliced thin
2 tablespoons unsalted butter or peanut, corn, or safflower oil
3 tablespoons all-purpose flour
1 tablespoon white wine vinegar
1 pound kielbasa (Polish sausage), cut into ¼-inch slices
   Salt to taste
½ teaspoon freshly ground pepper

1. In a large saucepan or sauté pan over moderately high heat combine the beans with 4 cups of the chicken stock, the onion, pepper, garlic, carrot, and celery. Bring to a boil, turn heat down to simmer, and cook, covered for 30 minutes.

2. Meanwhile melt the butter in a small skillet, add the flour, and stir over low heat until lightly browned. Whisk in the remaining ½ cup of stock and keep whisking until a thick, smooth paste is formed. Stir the flour mixture into the hot soup, add the vinegar, and sausage slices. Simmer, covered, for 10 minutes, season with salt and pepper and serve very hot.

This soup can be made with fresh green beans instead of pink beans. Use 1 pound, trimmed and cut into 1-inch pieces. Use ½ pound of sausage.

YELLOW SPLIT PEA SOUP WITH PISTACHIOS

Not all pea soups need a hambone to make them tasty. In this one the split pea is the award-winner but the cumin and the pistachio nuts can be scene-stealers. In this case the supporting cast gives a great performance.

SERVES 6-8

1 tablespoon unsalted butter
1 tablespoon peanut, corn, or safflower oil
1 large onion, chopped coarse
1 celery stalk with some leaves, chopped
6 cups chicken stock, homemade or canned
1 pound yellow split peas
Salt to taste
1 teaspoon freshly ground pepper
1 teaspoon ground cumin
Juice of ½ lemon
2 tablespoons minced parsley
¼ cup chopped pistachio nuts

1. Melt the butter and oil in a soup pot or large saucepan over moderately high heat. Stir in the onion and sauté, stirring frequently, until golden brown. Add the celery and sauté, stirring, until softened.

2. Stir in the chicken stock, bring to a boil, add the split peas, return to the boil, and skim any froth that rises to the surface. Turn down heat to simmer and cook, covered, about 1 to 1½ hours, or until peas are very soft—in about half an hour they will be soft but still firm. Keep cooking.

3. Season to taste with salt; add the pepper, cumin, and lemon juice. Simmer 5 minutes more to allow seasonings to be absorbed.

4. Working in batches, puree the pea mixture in a food processor or blender until smooth and creamy. Return to the pan over moderate heat and simmer a few minutes more. Add more chicken stock or a little water if the soup is too thick. It should be the consistency of sour cream.

5. Garnish with the parsley and sprinkle each bowl of soup with the pistachios.

BLACK BEAN SOUP

This is a recipe we've made for years. It's a standard, a classic. Neither of us remembers where we got it. We do make changes in it once in a while, like adding half a teaspoon of red pepper flakes or a couple of seeded, chopped jalapeño or serrano chilies along with the hambone to satisfy our craving for spices.

SERVES 8

2 cups dried black beans (turtle beans), soaked and drained
¼ cup light Tuscan olive oil
4 medium onions, chopped coarse
1 tablespoon minced garlic
2 carrots, pared and chopped coarse
1 tablespoon ground cumin
4 celery stalks with some leaves, chopped coarse
2 bay leaves
2 tablespoons chopped parsley
1 hambone (preferably from a smoked ham) or smoked butt
1 teaspoon salt or to taste
1 teaspoon freshly ground pepper
⅔ cup dry sherry
2 hard-boiled eggs, sieved
2 lemons, sliced thin

1. In a large soup pot or kettle over high heat bring 8 cups water to the boil. Add the beans, turn heat down to simmer, and skim off any froth that rises to the surface. Cover and cook for 1 hour.

2. Meanwhile, in a skillet over moderate heat, heat oil to rippling and add onions. Sauté, stirring frequently, until just golden, about 4 minutes. Stir in the garlic, carrots, cumin, and celery, and sauté until vegetables soften slightly, about 3 minutes. Ladle about ½ cup of water from the beans and add it to the vegetable mixture. Turn heat down to moderately low and cook for 20 minutes, stirring occasionally, watching to see if vegetables stay moist. If all water evaporates, add a tablespoon or two. Remove from heat and reserve.

3. Add the bay leaves, parsley, hambone, and salt and pepper to the beans. Stir in the cooked vegetables. Cover and cook for 2 hours more, adding a little more hot water from time to time if the beans become too thick.

4. Remove the bone and discard (if using a smoked butt, cut meat in small cubes and reserve). Working in batches, process half the bean mixture in a food processor or blender until pureed smooth. Return to the pot, add the sherry, and cook until hot. Taste and adjust seasonings.

5. Ladle soup into individual warm soup plates and garnish with sieved egg (often just the whites are used), the reserved cubed ham (if butt was used), and slices of lemon.

Other popular garnishes are a dollop of sour cream, a sprinkling of chopped onion, or grated Parmesan.

DAL SOUP

●●●●●●●●●●●●●●●

I n India dried beans are called *dal*. In this recipe we used yellow lentils. You'll notice that one of the ingredients is *garam masala*, an aromatic spice mixture Indian cooks concoct themselves. Good packaged brands may be purchased at Indian food stores or gourmet shops. They are far superior to commercial curry powders found on supermarket shelves. To make your own, *see* directions on p. 68.

SERVES 6

7 ounces yellow lentils (available at Indian, Middle Eastern markets, and some health-food stores)

7 cups chicken stock, homemade or canned

1 medium red-ripe, fresh tomato, peeled, seeded, and chopped coarse

½ small eggplant, peeled and chopped

1 teaspoon turmeric

½ teaspoon salt or to taste

2 tablespoons peanut, corn, or safflower oil

1 medium onion, chopped

1 tablespoon chopped garlic

1 fresh red chili pepper (about 3½ inches long), seeded, deveined, and cut into ⅛-inch dice

1 teaspoon *garam masala* or curry powder, preferably Madras

1 tablespoon minced fresh coriander (cilantro)

1. In a large saucepan over high heat combine the yellow lentils, stock, tomato, eggplant, turmeric, and salt and bring to a boil. Turn heat down to simmer and cook, covered, about 30 minutes or until lentils are just tender.

2. In another large saucepan over moderately low heat, bring the oil to rippling and add onion, garlic, chili, *garam masala* or curry. Cook until onion is limp and transparent, about 10 minutes. Add lentil mixture to onion mixture, sprinkle with coriander, turn heat up to high, and bring to the boil. Turn off heat, ladle into soup bowls, and serve.

*S*everal slang expressions have come into the language because of beans. If we don't list most of them our readers will accuse us of not knowing beans *about beans*. If we get down most of them, though, these same readers might say, "They know how many beans make five," dubbing us shrewd, alert, and knowledgeable.

A VERY COMFORTING LENTIL SOUP

A wonderful, heartwarming soup to make a meal of on a cold, dismal winter evening. It's better than a roaring fire to heat up icy bones.

SERVES 6

1½ cups lentils
 8 cups beef stock, homemade or canned, or water
 1 medium onion, chopped fine
 1 large carrot, cut in ¼-inch dice
 1 celery stalk, cut in ¼-inch dice
 ¼ teaspoon ground cloves
 1 teaspoon freshly ground pepper
 1 tablespoon minced fresh parsley
 1 teaspoon thyme
 1 pound smoked ham hock or piece of smoked ham
 1 tablespoon unsalted butter
 1 tablespoon light Tuscan olive oil
 2 tablespoons minced shallots
 2 tablespoons minced garlic
 1 teaspoon cumin
 1 teaspoon ground coriander
 1 cup heavy cream or milk (optional)
   Salt and freshly ground pepper
   Minced fresh parsley for garnish

1. In a large saucepan or soup pot, combine the lentils with the beef stock, onion, carrot, celery, cloves, pepper, parsley, thyme, and ham hock. Bring to the boil over high heat. Turn heat down to simmer and cook, covered, for about 35 minutes, or until lentils are tender.

2. Remove the ham hock and set aside to cool.

3. In a small skillet melt the butter with the oil over low heat. Add the shallots and garlic and sauté until golden. Add the cumin and coriander and cook 1 or 2 minutes more.

4. Add the garlic mixture to the lentils along with the cream, if desired, and bring the soup back to a simmer, skimming off any foam rising to the surface. Season with salt and more pepper to taste.

5. Remove the meat from the ham hock and cut into tiny dice. Add to the soup. Served ladled into individual soup bowls garnished with a sprinkling of parsley.

The soup may be pureed after step 2, but because it is a country soup, we prefer the heartiness of whole lentils and flecks of other vegetables. This soup becomes even more filling if served with ½-inch thick rounds of French bread fried in garlic butter floating on top.

PUREED SUCCOTASH SOUP

T he Indians (Algonquin, probably) invented succotash but never made it into a soup. Maybe they would have if only they had thought to invent the food processor as well. Pureeing does give the combination an up-to-date elegance.

SERVES 6 TO 8

1 pound onions, sliced thin
1 stick unsalted butter
2 cans Green Giant Corn Niblets, with liquid
1 large baking potato, scrubbed, grated coarse with skin
2 packages (10 ounces each) frozen baby lima beans, thawed
4 cups chicken stock, homemade or canned
  Salt and freshly ground pepper to taste
2 tablespoons fresh lemon juice
  Diced pimento and snipped fresh dill for garnish

1. In a large saucepan or soup pot sauté the onions in the butter, stirring until soft and golden. Add the corn, potato, lima beans, and salt and pepper to taste. Stir until heated through.

2. Add the stock and bring to the boil. Reduce heat and simmer, stirring occasionally, for 20 minutes, or until beans are tender.

3. Transfer the mixture in batches to a food processor or blender and puree until smooth. Return to the pot, add lemon juice, and adjust seasoning. Reheat over low heat until hot. Ladle into warm soup bowls and garnish with pimento and dill.

MOROCCAN TWO-BEAN AND RICE SOUP

Chick-peas and lentils are two prehistoric Middle Eastern and North African beans. Their flavors meld well in this soup and are enriched with two other local favorites, lamb and rice. Each of the main ingredients retains its own texture and shape. As Campbell's might say, "It's the soup you can eat with a fork."

SERVES 8

1½ cups dried chick-peas, soaked and cooked
¼ pound boneless shoulder of lamb cut in ½-inch dice
2 medium onions, chopped fine
1 teaspoon coarse-ground black pepper
½ teaspoon crumbled saffron threads
1 cup lentils
½ cup long-grain rice
1 tablespoon tomato paste
1 cup minced fresh parsley leaves
1 cup minced fresh coriander (cilantro)
1½ cups canned Italian plum tomatoes, drained and chopped fine
Salt and freshly ground pepper to taste

1. Drain the chick-peas and transfer them to a large saucepan or soup pot and combine them with lamb, onions, pepper, saffron, and 2 quarts water. Bring water to the boil, turn down heat, and simmer mixture, covered, for 45 minutes.

2. Stir in the lentils, rice, tomato paste, parsley, coriander, and chopped tomato. Bring soup to the boil, turn down heat, and simmer, covered, for 30 minutes or until the lentils are just tender. Taste for seasoning. Serve hot.

When reheating leftover soup with lentils, bring quickly to the boil and turn off heat. Don't cook or lentils will turn mushy.

CURRIED CREAM OF FAVA AND CAULIFLOWER SOUP

Fava beans are terribly neglected in this country. They've never become popular. Once you taste them, you'll wonder why. They really are a delightful discovery for many cooks.

SERVES 4 TO 6

5 cups chicken or vegetable stock, homemade or canned
1 small cauliflower, washed, trimmed, and cut into small pieces
1 large onion, chopped fine
1 carrot, chopped fine
1 stalk celery, chopped fine
1 sweet green pepper, seeded, deveined, and chopped fine
1 heaping teaspoon minced garlic
1 heaping teaspoon minced fresh gingerroot
3 tablespoons peanut, corn, or safflower oil
1 teaspoon *garam masala** or curry powder, preferably Madras
1 1-pound 3-ounce can fava beans, drained and rinsed
1 cup yogurt
2 tablespoons minced fresh parsley leaves
Salt and cayenne pepper to taste

*See footnote p. 68.

1. In a large saucepan or soup pot bring the broth to a boil and drop in the cauliflower. Cook, covered, for 5 minutes or until just tender. Drain, reserving all the liquid.

2. In the same pot cook the onion, carrot, celery, pepper, garlic, and gingerroot in the oil over moderately low heat, stirring occasionally, about 10 minutes, or until the vegetables are soft. Add the *garam masala* and cook, stirring, 1 minute more.

3. In a blender or food processor puree the mixture with ½ the cauliflower and ½ the fava beans in 1 cup of the broth.

4. Transfer the puree to the pot, add the remaining broth and fava beans, and bring to the boil. Lower heat to simmer and add the remaining cauliflower, yogurt, parsley, salt, and cayenne to taste.

5. Simmer the soup, covered, for 10 minutes. Taste and correct the seasoning. Serve hot.

COLD GREEN SALAD SOUP WITH TWO PEAS

This soup is our own take-off on a gazpacho. It is very green and even tastes green—as if it had just been picked in a kitchen garden. If a soup can be called thirst-quenching, this is it.

SERVES 4

1 package (10 ounces) frozen tiny peas, thawed

½ pound snow peas, trimmed and chopped coarse

3 cups chicken stock, homemade or canned

½ cup whole unblanched almonds

1 large green (unripe) tomato, cored, seeded, and chopped coarse

½ cup coarse-chopped tender heart of celery

½ cup coarse-chopped sweet green pepper

½ cup coarse-chopped seeded cucumber (peeled only if waxed)

½ cup coarse-chopped romaine lettuce

1 teaspoon minced garlic

½ cup thin-sliced scallions (both white and green parts)

Lime wedges

1. Place thawed peas in a large heatproof bowl. Add chopped snow peas. Reserve.

2. In a saucepan over moderately high heat bring chicken stock to a boil and pour over peas and snow peas.

3. Process almonds in a blender or food processor until they are ground very fine. Add green tomato, celery, pepper, cucumber, romaine lettuce, garlic, and one cup of the broth, including some of the peas. Pulse processor on and off until mixture is consistency of coarse cornmeal. It is important not to overprocess the vegetables. Soup should have texture and a little crunch.

4. Stir vegetable mixture into broth and peas, add scallions, and stir well. Refrigerate, covered, for 4 hours or up to 24. Taste for seasoning and add salt, if necessary. Serve cold accompanied with lime wedges.

CREMA DE LIMA (CREAM OF LIMA BEAN SOUP)

This is a South American soup with international overtones. Come to think of it, South America is a continent with international overtones. I guess what we're trying to say is that it's not an indigenous (read Indian) recipe, rather it's a little Spanish, a little French, a little German, and a little Mexican. Anyway, it has a lot of taste.

SERVES 6 TO 8

½ pound lean salt pork without the rind, cut into ¼-inch dice
2 medium onions, chopped
2 celery stalks, chopped
2 carrots, sliced thin
1 tablespoon minced garlic
½ cup minced fresh parsley
1 teaspoon caraway seeds
½ teaspoon red pepper flakes
2 cups dried baby lima beans, soaked, rinsed, and drained
Salt and pepper to taste
2 tablespoons white wine vinegar
1 tablespoon snipped fresh dill
1 cup half-and-half or milk

1. In a soup pot or large sauté pan, cook the salt pork over moderate heat for 10 minutes, stirring often, until golden.

2. Add onions, celery, and carrots and continue cooking, stirring occasionally, for 10 minutes more or until vegetables soften. Add the garlic and cook, stirring, for 1 minute.

3. Add the parsley, caraway, red pepper flakes, the lima beans, 6 cups of water, salt and pepper and bring to the boil. Turn down heat to simmer and cook for 1 hour. Taste for seasoning.

4. Puree the mixture in batches in a food processor or force through a sieve or food mill. Return to the pot and add the vinegar, dill, and half-and-half. Taste again for seasoning and add salt, if necessary.

5. Heat the soup over a moderately low flame until hot but not boiling. Serve as is or garnished with more snipped dill, minced sweet red pepper, or thin-sliced scallions.

MINESTRA DI CECI (CHICK-PEA SOUP)

A stick-to-the-ribs Italian soup, thick, robust, and filling. It can be a meal on its own or part of a multi-course meal if what follows is light and simple.

SERVES 6

3 tablespoons light Tuscan olive oil

2 tablespoons minced garlic

2 leeks (both white and green parts), carefully washed, sliced thin

1 tomato, peeled, seeded, and chopped

2 tablespoons tomato sauce, homemade or canned

1 tablespoon fresh rosemary or 1 teaspoon dried

2 cups cooked or canned chick-peas

2 tablespoons minced fresh basil or 1 tablespoon dried

2 tablespoons minced fresh parsley

6 cups chicken stock, homemade or canned

⅓ pound orzo (or other small pasta such as elbow macaroni)

Salt and freshly ground pepper to taste

1. Heat the olive oil over moderately high heat until rippling in a large saucepan or soup pot. Add the garlic and leeks and sauté until garlic is golden brown. Turn heat down to simmer.

2. Add the tomato, tomato sauce, and rosemary. Simmer for 3 or 4 minutes, stirring constantly.

3. Stir in the chick-peas, basil, parsley, and stock. Turn heat to high and bring to rapid boil. Add the orzo and cook uncovered until the pasta is *al dente*, about 6 to 7 minutes.

4. Remove from heat and adjust seasoning. Serve hot or at room temperature. If you wish, you may pass olive oil at the table to enrich the flavor of the soup.

The texture of this soup can be varied by pureeing two ladlesful of the solids in a food processor or blender and stirring back into the broth to thicken.

PUNGENT CELLOPHANE NOODLE SOUP WITH PORK AND TURNIPS

This soup, followed by a green salad, can be an ample one-dish meal for 2.

SERVES 4

5 scallions (both white and green parts), 3 cut in 2-inch lengths and 2 sliced thin
½ pound trimmed lean pork, cut into 1-inch chunks
2 teaspoons cornstarch
2 teaspoons sake or dry sherry
2 teaspoons soy sauce
¼ teaspoon nutmeg, preferably freshly grated
4-ounce bundle cellophane noodles (available in Asian markets)
4 cups chicken or beef stock, homemade or canned
1 pound turnips, cut in fine julienne strips
1 medium carrot, sliced in paper-thin rounds
¼ teaspoon freshly ground pepper or to taste

1. In a food processor pulse 3 scallions until they are minced, scraping down the sides of the work bowl if necessary. Add the pork and pulse a few times to chop coarsely. Add the cornstarch, sake, soy sauce, and nutmeg and chop to a medium fine texture. Set aside.

2. Place the noodles in a bowl and pour in boiling water to cover. Set aside.

3. Form the chopped meat mixture into balls ¾-inch in diameter. There should be 30 or more.

4. In a large saucepan or sauté pan combine the stock and turnips, cover and bring to a simmer over moderately high heat. Uncover and add the meatballs. Cook for 2 minutes.

5. Turn heat to moderately low. Drain the noodles and cut them with scissors into 4-inch lengths. Add them to the soup along with the carrot and ¼ teaspoon pepper. Simmer gently until carrots are just tender, about 3 or 4 minutes.

6. Taste for seasoning. Sprinkle the remaining scallions over the soup and serve immediately, apportioning the meatballs evenly among the 4 soup bowls.

PASTA E FAGIOLI ALLA VENEZIA

Pasta and bean soup as they prepare it in Venice. This is a classic Italian bean soup often served as a pasta course. It's schizoid. We like it as a soup, albeit a substantial one. Soup or pasta, either way, it's delicious. Served with a salad, cheese, fruit, and a glass of wine, it's perfection.

SERVES 6

¼ cup light Tuscan olive oil
1 cup onion, chopped coarse
1 cup carrot, chopped coarse
1 celery stalk with leaves, chopped coarse
1 tablespoon garlic, chopped fine
3 tablespoons fresh basil, chopped fine or 1 teaspoon dried basil
¼ pound pancetta or prosciutto, chopped fine (optional)
1 cup dried red or white beans soaked, rinsed, and drained
1 cup canned Italian plum tomatoes, chopped
1 sprig fresh rosemary or 1 teaspoon dried rosemary, crushed
¼ teaspoon red pepper flakes or to taste
¼ teaspoon fresh or dried sage
7 cups chicken or vegetable broth, or boiling water
2 cups dried fettuccine, tagliatelle, or egg noodles, broken in pieces

1. Heat the oil in a large, heavy saucepan over moderately high heat. Add onions and sauté until they begin to turn golden. Add carrot, celery, garlic, and basil and cook for a few minutes more, stirring occasionally.

2. Stir in pancetta and sauté for 3 or 4 minutes.

3. Add beans, tomatoes, rosemary, sage, red pepper flakes, and six cups of boiling liquid. Turn heat to high and bring to the boil. Reduce heat to simmer and cook, covered, until beans are tender, about 1 to 1½ hours, stirring occasionally. Add more boiling liquid if needed to cover beans.

4. Transfer about 2 ladlesful of beans and their liquid to food processor, blender, or food mill. Process to a thick puree and stir back into soup.

5. Fifteen minutes before serving, bring soup to a boil and add pasta and any remaining boiling liquid. Stir occasionally until pasta is cooked *al dente* (about 8 to 10 minutes).

6. Remove from heat and stir in salt and pepper to taste.

7. Ladle into soup bowls and sprinkle each serving with Parmesan and a few drops of olive oil, if desired.

Salt and freshly ground pepper
to taste
½ cup freshly grated Parmesan
cheese

ESCAROLE AND WHITE BEAN SOUP

Another inventive Italian soup. Neither light nor delicate, it is filling without being overwhelming. It's the colors and combination of textures that set Italian soups apart. Incidentally, this is called a *minestra*, not a *zuppa*. *Zuppa* has bread as an ingredient, *minestri* do not.

SERVES 4 TO 6

2 cups chicken stock, homemade
  or canned
2 cups water
1 tablespoon thin-sliced garlic
1 head (1 to 1½ pounds)
  escarole, washed, dried, and
  torn into bite-sized pieces
1 can (16 ounces) cannellini
  beans, drained and rinsed
3 tablespoons light Tuscan olive
  oil
½ teaspoon freshly ground pepper
2 eggs, beaten
  Lemon wedges and grated
  Parmesan

1. In a large saucepan bring the stock and water to the boil over high heat, add the garlic and the escarole, stirring to submerge. Cover and cook until tender, about 5 minutes.

2. Add the beans, the oil, and the pepper. Cook, stirring occasionally, for 2 to 3 minutes or until beans are heated through.

3. Stirring gently, slowly pour the beaten eggs in a stream into the saucepan, to form thin strands like those in egg-drop soup. Serve hot, passing lemon wedges and Parmesan at the table.

CREAM OF FRESH PEA SOUP

SERVES 6 TO 8

3 pounds fresh peas, shelled
(about 3 cups)
4 tablespoons unsalted butter
¼ cup all-purpose flour
4 cups hot milk
1 teaspoon salt (or to taste)
¼ teaspoon white pepper
1 quart chicken stock,
homemade or canned
½ cup tofu in ¼-inch dice
(optional)

1. Freeze peas for 1 hour or until hard.

2. Place peas in food processor and pulse on and off until texture resembles coarse meal. Work in batches, if necessary.

3. Make a béchamel sauce: Heat 3 tablespoons of the butter in a saucepan over moderate heat. Whisk in flour until smooth and mixture has no lumps, and cook, whisking, for 3 minutes (do not brown). Gradually add the milk in a slow, steady stream, whisking and blending flour mixture thoroughly with the milk. Turn down heat to simmer, add salt and ¼ teaspoon pepper, and cook 10 minutes. Stir occasionally.

4. Heat stock in a soup pot or large saucepan over high heat until boiling. Stir in peas and reduce heat to simmer. Cook until peas are soft and tender, about 4 minutes.

5. Slowly whisk pea mixture into the béchamel sauce and simmer, stirring occasionally, for 10 minutes. Adjust seasoning.

6. Add diced tofu if desired, and remaining tablespoon butter. Transfer to serving bowls or tureen and dust with remaining pepper.

A SPLIT PEA SOUP LUSH WITH DILL

SERVES 8

2 cups green split peas, soaked, cooked, and rinsed
1 large onion, chopped coarse
2 carrots, chopped
2 celery stalks, sliced thin
3 tablespoons peanut, corn, or safflower oil
2/3 cup snipped fresh dill
4 cups chicken or beef stock, homemade or canned
1 teaspoon crushed peppercorns
1 tablespoon Maggi Seasoning or *tamari* (natural soy sauce)
1 hambone, with some meat attached
Salt to taste
1 cup milk

1. Bring the cooked peas covered with 5 cups of fresh water to the boil in a soup or stockpot. Turn heat to simmer and cook for 10 minutes.

2. In a skillet cook the onion, carrots, and celery in the oil over moderately high heat, stirring, until the onion is soft and golden. Add the vegetable mixture to the simmering split peas along with the dill, stock, pepper, Maggi Seasoning, and hambone.

3. Bring soup to the boil, skimming off any froth that rises to the surface. Turn heat to simmer and cook for 1 hour and 30 minutes.

4. Remove hambone and chop any meat still clinging to it along with any large pieces of meat fallen off into the soup. Reserve.

5. Puree the soup in batches, if you wish, in a food processor or blender. Return to the pot. Add the chopped ham and salt to taste. Thin the soup with the milk, adding a little at a time, until the desired consistency is reached. Serve in hot soup bowls.

We like to garnish soups like this with sliced scallions. But if you prefer a bit of contrasting color, float a thin slice of lemon in each soup bowl, festooned with a small sprig of dill.

MINESTRONE CASALINGA (ITALIAN VEGETABLE BEAN SOUP)

T his is a soup we make from a few basic vegetables plus others we happen to have in the pantry. Onions, carrots, celery, potatoes, white beans, and green beans are essentials. The rest often change with the season. Just be sure there is a variety. Don't put them all in the pot at once. Start with the ones that take the longest to cook, and while one is cooking, prepare and trim the next. Remember, too, that some vegetables give off color—red cabbage, for example, will turn the soup mauve—so be forewarned. And don't worry too much about quantities. A little more or a little less of some of the vegetables really isn't catastrophic.

SERVES 6 TO 10

3 tablespoons light Tuscan olive oil
3 tablespoons unsalted butter
1 cup coarse-chopped onions
1 cup chopped carrots
1 cup chopped celery
1 cup chopped leek (washed well)
2 cloves garlic, minced
2 cups peeled, diced potatoes
2 or 3 peeled, diced turnips
2 cups diced zucchini
1 cup trimmed and sliced green beans
3 cups shredded cabbage (savoy, if available)
2 cups sliced mushrooms
8 cups beef, chicken, or vegetable stock, homemade or canned, or 3 cups canned mixed with 5 cups water
½ cup fresh or frozen peas

1. In a stock or soup pot large enough to hold the ingredients, melt the oil and butter. Over moderately high heat sauté the onions until golden. Lower the heat to simmer and add the carrots. Cook 2 to 3 minutes, stirring occasionally.

2. Repeat this procedure with the celery, then the leek, the garlic, the potatoes, the turnips, the zucchini, the green beans, the cabbage, and the mushrooms, cooking each vegetable for 2 or 3 minutes and stirring occasionally before adding the next.

3. Add the stock, the peas, and the tomatoes with their juice. Turn the heat to high and bring to the boil, stirring once or twice. Lower the heat to simmer and cook, covered, for 3 hours. The cooking may be stopped at any point and resumed later; just be sure to bring the mixture to the boil and then lower the heat to simmer each time.

4. About ½ hour before the soup has completed its cooking time, add the cannellini beans.

5. About 10 minutes before serving stir in the orzo or any small pasta such as *stillette* or *pastene*, if you wish.

1 cup canned Italian plum tomatoes, chopped, with some juice

2 cups canned cannellini beans, rinsed and drained

½ cup orzo (optional)

⅓ cup freshly grated Parmesan cheese

Salt and freshly ground pepper to taste

6. The soup should be quite thick. If it is *too* thick, add a little more hot broth or water (if not served right away, or if there are leftovers, the soup tends to thicken and you may wish to add more liquid when it is reheated).

7. Just before serving, stir in the Parmesan and a good amount of pepper. Transfer to a heated tureen or soup bowls and serve immediately.

Sprinkle soup with chopped parsley, if you like, or stir in a few tablespoonsful of *pesto* to taste. More Parmesan may be passed at the table.

This minestrone, like most cooked soups and stews, tastes even better when refrigerated and reheated up to a week later.

FRENCH GREEN BEAN SOUP WITH SHRIMP

SERVES 4

2 tablespoons unsalted butter

1 medium onion, chopped

½ pound *haricots verts* or small, young string beans, trimmed and chopped coarse

⅓ cup dry white wine

1½ cups fish stock or bottled clam juice

1 tablespoon chopped fresh parsley

⅔ cup heavy cream

Salt and pepper to taste

8 medium shrimp, shelled, deveined, and cut in half

1. In a heavy saucepan melt the butter and sauté the onions until soft and slightly golden. Add the green beans and cook, stirring occasionally, for 5 minutes.

2. Add the wine, 1¼ cups of the stock and the parsley, turn up the heat, and bring to the boil. Lower the heat and simmer partially covered for 5 minutes. Add the cream and continue cooking, covered, for 10 minutes more.

3. Puree the mixture in a food processor or blender and return to the pot. Season with salt and pepper. Heat, stirring, over moderate flame.

4. In a small saucepan combine the shrimp and remaining ¼ cup of stock. Cook over moderate heat until shrimp becomes opaque white.

5. Divide the shrimp evenly among 4 bowls and ladle the soup over them.

COUNTRY KITCHEN VEGETABLE SOUP WITH FAVAS

The vegetables in this soup pretty much keep the shape they were born with or are in generous, bite-sized pieces. So, perhaps, vegetable "stew" would be more apt. The nuts and favas give it an elusive, unfamiliar flavor—and more body. If you could *cook* a walk in the woods on a crisp, fall day, this, we think, is what it would taste like.

SERVES 10

2 9-ounce packages frozen
   artichoke hearts, thawed
   and patted dry
6 tablespoons peanut, corn, or
   safflower oil
6 small white onions, blanched
   and peeled
1 tablespoon minced garlic
1 teaspoon paprika
1 19-ounce can fava (broad)
   beans, rinsed and drained
1 10-ounce package frozen peas,
   thawed
3 carrots, quartered lengthwise,
   cut into 1-inch pieces
1 pound small new potatoes,
   skins on, scrubbed, halved
4 turnips, peeled and quartered
1½ teaspoons salt or to taste
1 bay leaf
½ tablespoon fresh thyme or ½
   teaspoon dried
½ tablespoon fresh basil or ½
   teaspoon dried
¼ cup minced fresh parsley

1. In a soup pot or kettle cook the artichokes in 4 tablespoons of the oil over moderately high heat, stirring, until they are browned. Transfer with a slotted spoon to a paper towel-lined bowl. Set aside.

2. Add remaining 2 tablespoons oil to pot and over moderately high heat cook the onions, stirring, until browned.

3. Reduce heat, add garlic and paprika. Sauté the mixture, stirring, for 2 minutes.

4. Add 4 cups of water, the beans, peas, carrots, potatoes, turnips, and salt. Turn heat to high, bring to the boil, reduce heat to simmer, and cook, covered, for 2 hours, stirring occasionally.

5. Stir in the reserved artichoke hearts, bay leaf, thyme, basil, parsley, cashews, almonds, and enough hot stock to thin the soup somewhat. Simmer, covered, 30 minutes more.

6. Discard the bay leaf and add salt and pepper to taste.

2 tablespoons ground roasted
   cashews (or 2 tablespoons
   cashew butter)
2 tablespoons ground toasted
   slivered almonds
2 to 3 cups hot chicken stock,
   homemade or canned
   Salt and freshly ground pepper
   to taste

LENTIL AND
TWO-PEPPER SOUP

SERVES 4 TO 6

6 tablespoons light Tuscan olive
   oil
3 medium onions, chopped fine
3 medium carrots, cut into small
   dice (about 2 cups)
8 garlic cloves, chopped
7 cups beef stock or canned beef
   broth
¾ cup lentils, picked over and
   rinsed
½ cup sherry
2 sweet red peppers, stemmed,
   cored, and julienned
2 sweet green peppers, stemmed,
   cored, and julienned
   Salt and freshly ground pepper
   to taste

1. Heat the oil in a soup pot over moderately low heat. Add onions, carrots, and garlic. Cook, covered, about 30 minutes or until tender and onions are golden, stirring occasionally.

2. Add beef stock, turn heat to high, and bring to the boil. Reduce heat to simmer, cover, and cook 20 minutes more.

3. Remove from heat and with a slotted spoon transfer solids to a blender or food processor. Add about a cup of liquid to the work bowl and puree. Return puree to pot.

4. Add lentils, sherry, peppers, and salt and pepper to taste. Simmer partially covered for about 25 minutes or until lentils are tender.

5. Correct seasoning and serve garnished with chopped scallions, if you like.

PINTO BEAN SOUP WITH RED PEPPER PUREE

T he way food looks is half its appeal as far as we're concerned—the combination of colors, textures, and shapes, the choice of serving dishes. Swirling red pepper puree into a respectable spiral on the surface of this soup isn't easy at first. It also isn't completely necessary for its enjoyment. But it helps. A little practice is all it takes.

SERVES 6

2 large sweet red peppers
2 tablespoons unsalted butter
2 medium onions, chopped fine
3 cups cooked or canned pinto beans, drained and rinsed
2 cups chicken stock, homemade or canned
1 cup heavy cream or half-and-half
½ teaspoon salt or to taste
½ teaspoon ground white pepper

1. Roast the peppers over an open flame or broil 4 inches from the heat, turning until charred all over, about 5 minutes. Place the peppers in a brown paper bag and twist to seal. Allow to sweat for 10 minutes. Rub off the skins with your fingers, seed and devein, and rinse under cold running water. Chop coarse, puree in blender or food processor, and reserve.

2. In a large saucepan over moderately high heat, melt the butter. Add the onions and sauté, stirring frequently, until just golden, about 3 to 5 minutes.

3. Turn heat to moderate. Add the beans to the onions and continue to cook, stirring gently, for 3 minutes. Add the stock, cover the pan, and cook for 15 minutes.

4. Puree the soup in batches in a food processor or blender and return to the saucepan.

5. Over moderately low heat add the cream and salt and pepper and cook, stirring, until just heated through, about 5 minutes. Ladle the soup into warm soup bowls, spoon a tablespoon or more of the reserved red pepper puree on the surface, and swirl into a spiral.

This soup may be chilled and served cold. Swirl red pepper puree as above.

IMPROVISATIONAL WHITE BEAN, POTATO, AND SAUERKRAUT SOUP

SERVES 4 TO 5

Amounts and proportions in this soup vary with what is left over in the refrigerator. But the three basic ingredients are cooked white beans, diced boiled potatoes, and sauerkraut. Equal amounts of each are nice but not necessary. Heat these ingredients in beef, chicken, or vegetable stock—figure a cup of stock per person, starting with 4 cups. Add leftover cubes of smoked pork or ham, sausage slices (sautéed to render out most of the fat), chicken, smoked turkey, bits of tongue, chopped onion, crumbled bacon, cooked carrots, peas or other cooked vegetables, even leftover coleslaw (in place of the sauerkraut). Use any, all, or none of the above additions. Season to taste with lots of freshly ground pepper, a bay leaf, some caraway seeds, a tablespoon of chopped garlic or a pinch of celery seed and simmer together over moderately low heat for about 30 minutes, stirring occasionally, until the soup is thickened by the disintegration of the potatoes and some of the beans. Serve very hot. If you like, add a dollop of yogurt to each soup bowl or add a tablespoon of Kümmel (caraway liqueur) to the pot while it simmers.

As the name implies, the secret of this soup's success is improvisation. That's how we started—from a vague description of a soup a friend had enjoyed while visiting the Dalmatian coast of Yugoslavia. In neighboring northeastern Italy, around Trieste, this soup is called *la Jota* and is often used as a restorative to brighten "the morning after," especially on New Year's Day. We offer this information with no guarantees.

MEXICAN CHICKEN, GARLIC, AND CHICK-PEA SOUP

Mexican soups are often like soup-and-a-salad all in one. This is representative of the genre.

SERVES 6

6 cups chicken stock, homemade or canned

1 whole chicken breast, with skin and bones

1 whole head of garlic, peeled

1½ tablespoons peanut, corn, or safflower oil

1 medium onion, chopped

1 can (2 ounces) chopped green chilies (mild)

1 canned *chipotle* chili pepper in adobo sauce, drained

1 cup cooked chick-peas, or 1 can (15 ounces) chick-peas, drained and rinsed

1 small ripe avocado, peeled, seeded, and sliced thin

6 radishes, trimmed and sliced thin

2 scallions (both white and green parts), sliced thin

¼ pound Monterey Jack or mild white cheddar cheese cut into ¼-inch dice

1½ limes cut in quarters

1. In a large saucepan heat the stock over moderately high heat to boiling. Add the chicken breast and garlic. Turn heat to simmer, and cook, uncovered, until chicken breast is tender, about 20 minutes. With a slotted spoon transfer garlic cloves to a small bowl. Reserve. Transfer chicken to a plate and reserve stock. When chicken is cool enough to handle, remove skin and bones and discard. Slice meat into thin strips. Reserve.

2. In a small skillet heat the oil over moderate heat until rippling and add onion. Sauté, stirring frequently, until onion is limp and golden, about 4 or 5 minutes. Add green chilies and cook, uncovered, stirring frequently, until mixture is reduced and somewhat dry, about 5 minutes. Remove from heat and reserve.

3. Puree *chipotle* chili in a food processor or blender with ½ cup of the chicken stock and reserved garlic cloves. Add puree and onion-green chili mixture to the reserved chicken stock in the saucepan. Turn heat to moderately high and bring to the boil. Reduce heat to a simmer, add chick-peas, and cook for 15 minutes.

4. Divide reserved chicken strips, avocado slices, radishes, scallions, and cheese among 6 soup bowls. Ladle chicken stock and chick-peas into bowls and serve with lime wedges on the side.

PASTA E CECI
(PASTA AND CHICK-PEA SOUP)

This soup is traditionally made with kale, but Swiss chard may be substituted or tender, young mustard greens, when one or the other isn't available. They're not inter-changeable, but the flavors are related.

SERVES 6

2 teaspoons chopped garlic
2 cups shredded trimmed kale
3 tablespoons light Tuscan olive oil
1 tablespoon tomato paste
½ cup tomato sauce, preferably homemade, or canned Italian plum tomatoes
2 cups canned chick-peas, drained and rinsed
1 carrot, chopped fine
1 onion, chopped fine
1 teaspoon crushed dried rosemary
Salt and pepper to taste
⅓ pound short pasta such as penne or elbow macaroni

1. In a skillet or sauté pan, over moderate heat, sauté the garlic and kale in the oil, stirring occasionally, until the kale is slightly wilted. Add the tomato paste and tomato sauce and cook for 5 minutes more. Set aside.

2. Bring four cups of water to the boil in a soup pot and add the chick-peas, carrot, onion, rosemary, and salt and pepper. Turn heat down to simmer and cook, covered, for ½ hour. Add the garlic-kale mixture to the pot and stir.

3. Simmer the bean and kale mixture very slowly, covered, for 1 hour.

4. Remove half the chick-pea mixture from the pot and puree in batches in a food processor or blender and return to the pot. Stir well. Taste for seasoning and add the pasta. Cook for about 10 minutes or until pasta is *al dente*. Turn off heat and serve.

You may like this soup with a sprinkling of olive oil over each serving. The Italians do not usually add Parmesan to this soup, but if it suits your taste by all means do.

MINTED CREAM OF PEA AND LETTUCE SOUP

A flavorful but delicately elegant soup to serve at a dinner party.

SERVES 4 TO 6

3 tablespoons butter
3 leeks, washed well and sliced into ½-inch rounds
½ head romaine lettuce, washed and shredded
2 cups shelled fresh peas or 1 package (10 ounces) frozen peas, thawed
½ teaspoon sugar
5 cups water or canned chicken broth
½ teaspoon salt or to taste
2 egg yolks
1 tablespoon minced fresh parsley
1 tablespoon chopped fresh mint leaves or 1 teaspoon dried mint
¾ cup heavy cream

1. In a large saucepan, heat the butter and stir in the leeks and lettuce. Cook, covered, over medium heat, stirring occasionally, for 5 to 7 minutes or until well wilted.

2. Stir in the peas and sugar and cook 2 minutes more.

3. Add water (or broth) and salt. Simmer, covered, until peas are just tender, 5 minutes for frozen, 15 for fresh.

4. When peas are cooked, transfer soup in batches to blender or food processor and puree.

5. Return soup to saucepan. When ready to serve, heat through over low heat. Meanwhile, combine the egg yolks, parsley, mint, and cream in a bowl. Pour one cup of hot soup slowly into the egg mixture, stirring to blend well.

6. In a thin stream pour egg-soup mixture into the hot soup, stirring constantly until the egg yolks cook but are incorporated smoothly. Serve hot.

COLD CURRIED
BEAN AND CHICKEN SOUP

Chilled soups can be almost flavorless—not this one, which is piquant and highly aromatic. This soup may be served with warm Indian breads or French bread and butter—or hot vegetable fritters (Pakoras, p. 56) for lunch or a light summer supper.

SERVES 6

4 cups canned chicken broth
1 whole skinless, boneless chicken breast, halved
2 medium onions, chopped
2 small celery stalks with a few leaves, chopped
1 Golden Delicious apple, peeled, cored, and chopped
2 tablespoons peanut, corn, or safflower oil
2 tablespoons *garam masala** or curry powder or more to taste
1 cup cooked or canned Great Northern, navy, or cannellini beans, drained and rinsed
1 cup half-and-half or milk
6 thin lemon slices for garnish

*See footnote p. 68.

1. In a skillet or sauté pan over high heat bring 3 cups of the broth to the boil. Add the chicken and turn heat down to simmer. Cook gently, turning breasts once, for 8 minutes or until just cooked through. Transfer the breasts, reserving the liquid, to a cutting board and chop into ½-inch pieces.

2. In a saucepan over moderate heat, cook the onions, celery, and apple in the oil, covered, for 10 minutes, stirring occasionally, or until the vegetables are soft. Stir in the *garam masala* and continue cooking, stirring, for 2 minutes. Add the remaining 1 cup of broth and stir until heated through. Stir in the beans, cover, and cook 10 minutes more.

3. In a food processor or blender puree the bean mixture and transfer to a bowl. Stir in the reserved 3 cups of broth and the chopped chicken. Allow the mixture to cool and stir in the half-and-half. Chill the soup for at least 3 hours or longer. Ladle into chilled soup bowls and garnish with lemon slices.

You might like to try a garnish of dried apricots, chopped, plumped in warm water for 15 minutes, and drained. Use about 3. The sweet and sour taste of the fruit is a nice counterpoint to the curry flavor. Omit the lemon slices.

RED BEAN SOUP WITH CORNMEAL

This variation on a *minestrone*, garlic bread, and a big green salad make a stalwart, satisfying meal.

SERVES 6

1 cup dried red beans cooked, drained, liquid reserved
¼ cup light Tuscan olive oil
1 medium to large onion, chopped fine
¼ teaspoon crushed dried sage
2 teaspoons minced garlic
1 medium carrot, chopped fine
1 celery stalk, chopped fine
3 tablespoons minced fresh parsley
¼ cup tomato sauce, homemade or canned
1 tablespoon chopped fresh basil leaves or 1 teaspoon dried basil
1 to 2 cups vegetable broth (broth reserved from cooking any vegetable) or canned chicken broth
3 cups shredded cabbage
Salt and freshly ground pepper to taste
¼ cup yellow cornmeal

1. Heat olive oil in a large, heavy saucepan over moderate heat and sauté the onions, sage, garlic, carrot, celery, and parsley for 5 minutes, stirring frequently. Add tomato sauce, stir well, and remove from heat.

2. Puree 1 cup of beans in a food processor or blender and add to the sautéed vegetables. Reserve remaining whole beans.

3. Add reserved cooking liquid to the vegetables and bean puree along with enough vegetable or chicken broth to make 6 cups of liquid.

4. Return saucepan to high heat, bring to the boil, and stir in the cabbage. Lower heat and simmer covered for 30 minutes, stirring occasionally.

5. When cabbage is cooked, add the reserved whole beans. Taste and correct seasoning, adding more salt and pepper if desired.

6. Pour the cornmeal slowly in a thin stream into the soup, stirring all the while to prevent lumping. Cover and simmer for 15 minutes more. Serve, passing grated Parmesan for those who hardly ever have an Italian soup without it—like us.

PASTA
AND RICE

FETTUCCINE WITH RAW SCALLOPS AND TWO PEAS IN SESAME GINGER SAUCE

If you've never tasted raw scallops, you're in for a treat. They're even more delicate and tender than cooked and they almost melt in your mouth. This sauce combines Italian and Chinese ingredients. It has so many different flavors and textures that your tastebuds will be delightfully confused.

SERVES 4 TO 6

2 large egg yolks
2 tablespoons rice vinegar or mild white wine vinegar
1 tablespoon fresh lemon juice
1 tablespoon minced fresh gingerroot
Salt and pepper to taste
½ cup peanut, corn, or safflower oil
2 tablespoons sesame oil
¼ cup heavy cream
1 pound fettuccine cooked *al dente*, drained, and refreshed under cold water
2 scallions (both white and green parts), sliced thin
1 pound scallops (cut into bite-sized pieces if large ocean scallops)
1 cup cooked peas, cooled
½ pound snow peas trimmed, cut diagonally into 4 pieces
1 tablespoon toasted sesame seeds

1. In a food processor or blender combine the egg yolks, vinegar, lemon juice, gingerroot, and salt and pepper. With the motor running add the two oils, heavy cream, and 2 tablespoons hot water in a stream. Blend well.

2. In a large serving bowl toss the fettuccine with the scallions, scallops, both peas, and the dressing, coating all the ingredients well. Serve at room temperature sprinkled with the sesame seeds.

OVEN-BAKED RICE WITH PEAS, CELERY, AND SAUTÉED PECANS

SERVES 6

1 medium onion, chopped fine
2 tablespoons peanut, corn, or safflower oil
2 celery stalks, sliced thin
Salt and freshly ground pepper to taste
1 cup long-grain rice
2 cups hot chicken stock, homemade or canned
1 tablespoon unsalted butter
⅓ cup pecan pieces
1 10-ounce package frozen tiny peas, thawed

1. Preheat oven to 375°. In a heatproof casserole over moderate heat, sauté the onion in the oil until golden, about 5 minutes, stirring occasionally. Add the celery and salt and pepper and cook 2 minutes more, stirring.

2. Add the rice and stir until it is well coated with the oil. Stir in the stock and bring to the boil.

3. Cover the casserole, transfer to the oven, and bake for 17 minutes.

4. While the rice is baking, melt the butter in a small frying pan and sauté the pecans for 2 or 3 minutes.

5. Uncover the rice and stir in the pecans and peas and taste for seasoning. Return casserole to oven, covered, for 5 minutes more or until all the liquid has been absorbed. Fluff with 2 forks before serving or transfer to a serving dish.

PILAF OF RICE AND GREEN SPLIT PEAS

SERVES 6

¼ cup peanut, corn, or safflower oil
1 medium onion, chopped fine
1 teaspoon minced garlic
2 cups long-grain or basmati rice, rinsed
2½ cups chicken stock, homemade or canned
3 tablespoons fresh lemon juice
½ cup dried green split peas, soaked and drained
1 teaspoon cinnamon
1 teaspoon ground cumin
Salt and freshly ground pepper to taste

1. In a saucepan over moderate heat, bring the oil to rippling and sauté the onion until golden. Add the garlic and rice and stir until the rice is coated with the oil.

2. Stir in the stock, lemon juice, split peas, cinnamon, cumin, and salt and pepper to taste. Bring the liquid to the boil, then turn heat to simmer. Cover and cook for 25 minutes or until all the liquid is absorbed and the rice is tender. Let stand, covered, 5 minutes more, fluff with two forks, and serve.

One-half stick of unsalted butter, cut in tiny bits, may be added before fluffing the pilaf.

FASHIONS, FADS, AND FANCIES

*B*eans have had their ups and downs in food fashion. Yes, even hundreds of years ago there were food fads. The potato found favor at one point in the 16th century—it was a new taste sensation from the New World—so the fava, the lentil, and the chick-pea became old hat to be eaten out of necessity rather than choice. But, fortunately, the new world also had produced French Beans (the shapely kidney bean renamed, no doubt, by Public Relations people of the day who knew even then the panache of anything French) and limas (dubbed "butter beans"), both of which were grown at first for their delicate flowers and attractive foliage, but soon their delicious seeds and pods graced the tables of Charles II of England and Louis XIV of France. These were fashionable tables indeed, and soon everyone was clamoring for pulses (what beans are called in England) and haricots (their name in France) and fagioli (what they called "the poor man's meat" in Italy).

FETTUCCINE WITH SMOKED SALMON AND GREEN BEANS

We usually don't like to cook smoked salmon—it can become overly salty and fishy tasting. However, here it is merely warmed by tossing in the pan with the fettuccine and retains its delicacy.

SERVES 4 TO 6

3 tablespoons unsalted butter
1 onion, chopped fine
½ pound string beans, trimmed, cut into 1-inch pieces
1½ cups heavy cream or half-and-half
2 tablespoons grated Parmesan cheese
1 pound egg or spinach fettuccine cooked *al dente* and drained
¼ pound smoked salmon (Nova Scotia), cut into ¼-inch strips
2 tablespoons snipped fresh dill
1 teaspoon freshly ground black pepper

1. Melt the butter in a sauté pan and cook the onion over moderate heat until just transparent. Add the string beans and sauté until softened, about 5 minutes.

2. Add the heavy cream or half-and-half and the cheese and cook, stirring occasionally, for 5 minutes more.

3. Add the fettuccine, the smoked salmon, the dill, and the pepper. Toss over the heat until well-combined and heated through. Serve immediately.

TORTELLINI IN CREAMY BEAN SAUCE

E ven if you have to puree the beans from scratch, this dish takes only 15 minutes, start to finish. If you like, use green tortellini, or a combination of green and white for eye-appeal.

SERVES 4

1½ quarts chicken stock, homemade or canned
1 pound cheese- or chicken-stuffed fresh tortellini
1 cup cannellini bean puree
½ cup milk
¼ teaspoon nutmeg, preferably freshly grated
Salt and white pepper to taste
½ cup grated Parmesan cheese

1. In a saucepan bring the stock to a boil over high heat. Stir in the tortellini. Return to the boil, stir once, reduce heat to moderately high, and cook until tortellini are almost tender, about 5 minutes. Drain, reserving the stock for another use.

2. Meanwhile, over moderate heat, combine the puree with the milk, nutmeg, and salt and pepper. Cook, stirring, about 5 minutes, until heated through and slightly thickened.

3. Stir the cooked tortellini into the hot bean sauce and cook, stirring occasionally, until pasta is tender, about 3 to 5 minutes. Remove from heat, sprinkle with Parmesan and stir gently to blend. Transfer to warmed platter and serve, passing additional Parmesan at the table.

CANNELLINI CARBONARA

We often experiment, substituting beans for pasta. This carbonara was especially successful. It works as the centerpiece of a meal or can be served as a side dish.

SERVES 4

3 ounces pancetta (bacon, not smoked but salted, available at Italian markets and specialty food stores), cut into ½-inch dice

½ stick unsalted butter, at room temperature

¼ cup heavy cream or half-and-half

1 teaspoon minced garlic

2 1-pound cans cannellini beans, drained and rinsed under very hot water

1 large egg yolk at room temperature

3 tablespoons grated Parmesan cheese plus additional cheese for passing
Freshly ground black pepper to taste

1. In a skillet or sauté pan cook the pancetta in 1 tablespoon of the butter over moderate heat, stirring occasionally, for 7 or 8 minutes or until browned.

2. In a small saucepan simmer the cream and the garlic, swirling the pan occasionally, for 5 minutes. Keep warm.

3. Melt 2 tablespoons of the remaining butter in the skillet containing the pancetta, add the cannellini, and warm, covered, over low heat, for 5 minutes.

4. In the small saucepan whisk together the garlic-cream mixture and the egg yolk and pour the mixture over the beans. Add the remaining 1 tablespoon of butter cut into bits and the 3 tablespoons Parmesan and remove pan from heat. Sprinkle generously with pepper and toss carbonara gently until it is combined. Serve immediately, passing additional Parmesan.

FUSILLI, CANNELLINI, AND BROCCOLI IN GORGONZOLA SAUCE

SERVES 6

½ pound fusilli (corkscrew-shaped pasta)

1 bunch broccoli, cut into small florets, stems reserved for another use

1 15-ounce can cannellini beans, drained and rinsed

1 cup heavy cream or milk

1 teaspoon minced garlic

1 teaspoon freshly ground black pepper

½ pound Gorgonzola, rind discarded, at room temperature

1 stick unsalted butter, at room temperature

¼ cup grated Parmesan cheese, plus more for passing

¼ cup minced fresh parsley leaves

1. In a large pot of boiling salted water cook the fusilli for 8 minutes or until *al dente*.

2. While the fusilli are cooking, cook the broccoli for 2 minutes in a saucepan of boiling water. Add the beans and bring to the boil. Remove from heat and drain.

3. In a small saucepan bring the cream or milk to the boil, turn heat down to a simmer, add the garlic and pepper, and cook for 5 minutes. Stir in the Gorgonzola and ½ the stick of butter. Cook, stirring, until the sauce is smooth.

4. Drain the fusilli and return them to the kettle. Add the broccoli, the beans, the remaining butter, the Parmesan, and the parsley. Toss gently.

5. Add the Gorgonzola Sauce and toss the mixture to combine well. Serve immediately, passing more Parmesan at the table.

HOPPIN' JOHN OR BLACK-EYED PEAS AND RICE

This is a conglomeration of the many versions of Hoppin' John cooked all over the South. It's somewhat basic—but you can add meat (in the case of soul food cooks it's usually hog jowl, hog maw, pig tails, snouts, etc.) and more generous quantities of flavorings, such as red pepper, molasses, garlic, thyme, and onion. White cooks often embellish this simple fare with milk, cream, bread crumbs, chopped pecans, bacon bits, or other extras for textural interest.

SERVES 4

1 cup black-eyed peas, rinsed and drained
½ pound lean bacon, sliced thick and cut into two-inch pieces
1 cup unconverted long-grain rice
1 medium onion, chopped fine
1 teaspoon minced garlic
½ teaspoon Tabasco sauce or ½ teaspoon red pepper flakes
1 small sweet red or green pepper, seeded and deveined, in ½-inch dice
1 bay leaf
½ teaspoon thyme
Salt and freshly ground pepper to taste

1. In a large saucepan over high heat bring 5 cups of water to the boil, add the beans, turn heat to simmer, and cook beans gently, covered, for about 45 minutes or until tender but not mushy.

2. In a skillet fry the bacon until crisp. Drain on paper towels. Reserve. In the bacon fat, over moderate heat, sauté the onions and garlic, stirring frequently, until just golden. Reserve.

3. When the beans are done tip the pot and gauge the amount of liquid left. There should be about 2½ cups. If not, add more liquid. Add the rice, Tabasco or red pepper flakes, pepper, bay leaf, thyme, salt and pepper, and reserved bacon and onion mixture (including fat from pan). Stir well to combine.

4. Cook, covered, over moderately low heat for 20 minutes or until rice is tender. Turn off heat and allow to rest for about 15 minutes on top of stove or in a very low (250°) oven. Remove the bay leaf before serving.

This recipe serves 4 generously as a main dish with the addition of sliced ham, perhaps some cooked mustard or collard greens, and a salad. Cornbread is the traditional accompaniment.

MOROS Y CHRISTIANOS I (CUBAN BLACK BEANS AND RICE)

SERVES 4

¼ cup light Tuscan olive oil
1 medium onion, chopped fine
1 sweet green pepper, seeded, deveined, and chopped fine
2 teaspoons minced garlic
2 red, ripe tomatoes, chopped coarse or 4 canned Italian plum tomatoes, drained and chopped coarse
Salt and freshly ground pepper to taste
2 cups cooked black beans, drained or 1 can (15 ounces), drained and rinsed
1 cup unconverted long-grain rice

1. In a medium saucepan over moderately high heat, heat the oil until rippling. Add the onion, garlic, and pepper and sauté, stirring frequently, until onion is translucent. Add the tomatoes and cook, stirring, until well blended and thickened, about 3 or 4 minutes. Season with salt and pepper to taste. Turn heat down to simmer.

2. Stir in the beans, cover, and simmer gently while the rice is prepared.

3. In a saucepan over high heat bring 2 cups of salted water to the boil, add the rice, turn heat down to simmer, and cook, covered, for 18 minutes or until rice has absorbed all the liquid.

4. Mound rice on a warm serving plate and create a well in the center. Pour beans into the well and serve.

MOROS Y CHRISTIANOS II (CUBAN BLACK BEANS AND RICE)

SERVES 8

2 cups black beans, soaked
2 pounds ham butt, in ½-inch cubes
2 tablespoons chopped garlic
1 bay leaf
½ teaspoon thyme
¼ cup chopped fresh parsley, preferably flat-leaf
4 tablespoons light Tuscan olive oil
2 medium onions, chopped fine
1 sweet green pepper, seeded, deveined, and chopped fine
2 red, ripe tomatoes, chopped coarse or 4 canned Italian plum tomatoes, drained and chopped coarse
1½ tablespoons distilled white vinegar
1 teaspoon red pepper flakes or Tabasco sauce to taste
2 cups unconverted long-grain rice

GARNISHES

2 hard-boiled eggs, chopped
1 medium onion, chopped fine
1 lemon, cut into eighths
1 lime, cut into eighths
4 radishes, sliced thin

1. Place beans in a large saucepan with 2 quarts of water, the ham, garlic, bay leaf, thyme, and parsley. Bring to the boil over high heat, then immediatly turn heat to simmer and cook, covered, 1½ hours or until beans are almost tender.

2. In a large skillet or sauté pan, over moderate flame, heat the oil until rippling and add onions and pepper. Sauté, stirring frequently, until onion is translucent. Add tomatoes, vinegar, red pepper flakes or Tabasco. Turn heat to moderately low and simmer, uncovered, stirring frequently, until sauce is well blended and thickened, about 10 minutes.

3. Drain any liquid from beans. Return beans to pot and stir in the sauce. Turn heat to very low, cover the pot, and allow beans to absorb sauce flavorings while preparing the rice.

4. In a medium saucepan over high heat bring 4½ cups of salted water to the boil, add the rice, turn heat down to simmer, and cook, covered, for 18 minutes or until rice has absorbed all the liquid.

5. Transfer rice to a warm serving platter and top with the beans. Pass garnishes separately.

This is a more elaborate, extended version of the traditional Cuban recipe. Each cook has his own variations on the basic theme—this is just another.

RISI E BISI (RICE AND PEAS)

This springtime dish is a Venetian specialty. Renowned for the quality of their seafood, Venetians are also famous for their local peas. Rice and peas is another of the infinite varieties of northern Italy's risotto—but a very special version. It's been around for centuries, and its appeal continues.

SERVES 4 TO 6

2 tablespoons light Tuscan olive oil

2 tablespoons unsalted butter
Salt to taste and about 5 grindings of pepper

½ cup celery or fennel, chopped fine

1 medium onion, chopped fine

1 tablespoon chopped fresh parsley

1 cup Arborio rice (Italian short-grain rice, available at Italian markets, specialty food stores, and many supermarkets) or other short-grain Italian rice

4 cups hot chicken stock, homemade or canned

2 cups shelled fresh peas or 1 package (10 ounces) frozen tiny peas

⅓ cup freshly grated Parmesan plus additional cheese for passing

1. Melt the olive oil and 1 tablespoon of the butter in a saucepan over moderate heat. When the foam subsides add the salt and pepper, the celery or fennel, and the onion. Sauté, stirring frequently, for about 7 or 8 minutes or until the vegetables soften and begin to brown around the edges. Add the rice and cook, stirring, until the grains are thoroughly coated with the oil and butter, about 2 or 3 minutes.

2. Ladle in the hot stock 1 ladleful at a time and continue cooking over moderate heat, stirring constantly, until liquid is absorbed. Repeat with another ladleful, stirring constantly. Repeat procedure until rice is creamy and tender but still chewy and all the stock has been transferred, about 20 to 25 minutes in all.

3. At this point the rice is almost cooked. Add the peas and combine well. Cook another 5 minutes.

4. Remove the pan from the heat. Add remaining tablespoon butter and the Parmesan. Stir to combine well, cover the pan, and allow it to stand 4 or 5 minutes. Taste for seasoning. Serve immediately accompanied by additional grated cheese.

SUPPLÌ AL TELEFONO (TELEPHONE WIRES) OR RISOTTO CROQUETTES

SERVES 4 TO 6

2 cups leftover Risi e Bisi
(p. 115)

3 ounces prosciutto or other
dry-cured ham, cut in
¼-inch dice (about ½ cup; or
use same quantity cooked
diced shrimp, flaked cooked
fish, etc.)

3 tablespoons freshly grated
Parmesan cheese

2 tablespoons minced fresh
parsley

½ teaspoon freshly ground pepper

1 egg, beaten

3 tablespoons milk

½ cup fine dried bread crumbs

½ cup fine-ground blanched
almonds

1 teaspoon grated lemon zest

½ teaspoon salt

½ cup all-purpose flour

3 ounces mozzarella, cut into 12
2½-inch cubes
Peanut, corn, or safflower oil
for deep frying

1. Combine in a bowl the 2 cups of leftover Risi e Bisi, prosciutto, Parmesan, parsley, pepper, and 1 tablespoon of the beaten egg, using your hands to blend thoroughly. Spread mixture in an even layer in a rectangular pan. Refrigerate, covered with plastic wrap, until firm enough to work with, about 1 hour. In a bowl, whisk together the remaining egg and the milk and refrigerate, covered.

2. To start preparing croquettes, remove egg-milk mixture from refrigerator. Combine bread crumbs, almonds, lemon zest, and salt in a dish. Set aside. Mound flour on a sheet of waxed paper.

3. With a sharp knife divide rice mixture into 12 equal portions. Picking up one portion at a time, press a cube of mozzarella in the center, and using your hands, form rice into a 2-inch ball enclosing the cube. (If the rice mixture is sticky, flour hands lightly.) Roll each ball in flour, shaking off excess, then dip into egg mixture, allowing excess to drip back into bowl, and roll in bread crumb mixture to coat evenly. Repeat with each ball and set in a waxed-paper-lined baking dish or large plate. Let stand at room temperature until coating is set, about 30 minutes.

4. Pour oil into a wide saucepan to a depth of 2 inches. Turn heat to high and bring oil to temperature of 365° on a deep fat thermometer or until a bread cube sinks and returns immediately to the surface, turning golden.

5. Lower croquettes into hot oil with a slotted spoon 2 or 3 at a time. Do not overcrowd. Fry, turning once, until golden brown, about 3 minutes. Transfer to paper towels to drain. Repeat with remaining croquettes. Serve immediately.

This recipe works equally well with any leftover risotto. The croquettes are a nice accompaniment to a main dish that has a gravy or 2 or 3 may be served as a first course, on a plate ladled with a pool of light tomato sauce.

BEAN THREAD NOODLES WITH GARLIC PEANUT SAUCE

SERVES 4

2 packages (5 ounces each) bean thread noodles (Japanese *saifun* or Chinese cellophane noodles, available at Asian markets)
2 tablespoons minced fresh coriander (cilantro)
1 teaspoon minced garlic
1 cup creamy peanut butter
1 cup chicken stock, homemade or canned
3 tablespoons rice vinegar
2 tablespoons Chinese or Japanese dark sesame oil
½ teaspoon sugar
½ teaspoon dry mustard
2 tablespoons soy sauce
2 tablespoons toasted sesame seeds
4 scallions (both white and green parts), cut into ½-inch pieces

1. With scissors cut the noodles into 5-inch or 6-inch lengths. Place them in a metal or other heatproof bowl and cover with boiling water. Allow them to soften, stirring occasionally, for 5 minutes. Drain in a colander and refresh under cold running water. Dry by patting with paper towels. Set aside.

2. In a food processor or blender process the coriander, garlic, peanut butter, and ½ cup of the stock until well combined. Stir the remaining stock, vinegar, sesame oil, sugar, dry mustard, and soy sauce together in a small pitcher and with the motor running add this mixture to the peanut butter in a slow stream. Process until very smooth.

3. Transfer noodles to a serving bowl and pour peanut sauce over them. Toss to coat well. Add the sesame seeds and scallions and toss again. Serve at room temperature.

RISOTTO CON FAGIOLI (ITALIAN RICE WITH CHAMPAGNE AND BEANS)

This is a first course in Italy, and it can be here, too. However, it is filling enough to serve as a luncheon or supper main dish accompanied by a salad.

SERVES 6 TO 8

6 tablespoons unsalted butter
1 medium onion, chopped fine
2 cups Arborio rice or other short-grain rice
½ cup dry Champagne or dry white wine
pinch of saffron threads (optional)
½ teaspoon freshly ground pepper
6 cups hot chicken stock, homemade or canned, or vegetable broth
2 cups cooked or canned cannellini beans, drained and rinsed
1 cup grated Parmesan cheese
Salt to taste

1. Melt 3 tablespoons of the butter in a saucepan and sauté the onion over moderate heat, stirring, until the onion is just golden, about 4 or 5 minutes. Turn heat up to moderately high and add the rice, stirring for 2 to 3 minutes, so that it is well coated with the butter and very hot.

2. Add the Champagne and pepper and cook quickly, stirring, until the Champagne is absorbed, about 3 to 5 minutes.

3. Turn heat down to moderate and add the hot stock 1 cup at a time. Simmer the mixture, stirring constantly, until the stock is absorbed, about 2 or 3 minutes. Continue to add stock 1 cup at a time, simmering and stirring the mixture until the rice is just *al dente*—soft on the outside, still crunchy but tender at the center. Stir in the beans, combine well, and cook about 2 minutes more or until beans are heated through.

4. Remove saucepan from heat, stir in remaining butter, Parmesan, and salt. Combine until Parmesan is completely melted. Serve immediately.

A generous pinch of saffron may be added with the Champagne to impart a beautiful golden color and an elusive taste to the risotto. Incidentally, the Champagne need not be bubbly; flat is fine. It's the flavor, not the bubbles, that count. Think of this dish when you have leftover Champagne, if you ever do.

RED BEANS AND RICE, HAITIAN STYLE

Every Caribbean island has its own version of beans and rice (so does New Orleans). This one is from Haiti.

SERVES 8

2 tablespoons peanut, corn, or safflower oil

¼ pound salt pork, cut into ½-inch dice, parboiled for 15 minutes

1 medium onion, chopped fine

2 cups cooked red kidney beans or 1 1-pound can, drained and rinsed

4 scallions (both white and green parts), sliced thin

¼ cup chopped fresh parsley

2 teaspoons kosher salt

½ teaspoon Tabasco sauce or more to taste

2 cups unconverted long-grain rice

4½ cups water or canned chicken broth

1. In a large skillet or sauté pan over moderate heat, heat the oil until rippling. Add the salt pork and sauté for 3 minutes, stirring. Add the onions and sauté, stirring, until onions are translucent, about 4 or 5 minutes. Stir in the beans and ¼ cup of water and cook until water has evaporated.

2. Stir in the scallions, parsley, salt, Tabasco, and rice. Mix well. Slowly add the water or chicken broth. Turn heat to high and bring to the boil. Immediately turn heat down to simmer and cook the mixture, covered, for about 20 to 30 minutes or until all the liquid has been absorbed.

EGYPTIAN LENTILS IN TOMATO SAUCE WITH RICE AND MACARONI

SERVES 6 TO 8

1 cup dried lentils, rinsed
1½ cups unconverted long-grain rice
1 cup elbow macaroni
3 tablespoons peanut, corn, or safflower oil
2 fresh red chili peppers, seeded, deveined, and chopped fine
1½ cups homemade Tomato Sauce (recipe follows)
2 tablespoons vinegar
1 large onion, chopped coarse

1. Place lentils in a saucepan with enough water to cover by 1 inch. Turn heat to high, bring to the boil, turn heat down to simmer, and cook, covered, 35 minutes or until tender. Drain and transfer to a large bowl. Set aside.

2. Bring 3 cups of salted water to the boil over high heat. Pour in rice and turn down heat to simmer. Cover and cook for 18 minutes or until all the water is absorbed and rice is tender. Fluff with a fork and add to lentils.

3. Bring 2 quarts of salted water to the boil over high heat. Pour in macaroni, turn heat down to moderate, and boil macaroni, uncovered, stirring occasionally, about 10 minutes. Test for tenderness. Drain and add to lentils and rice.

4. In a small skillet over moderate heat bring 1 tablespoon of the oil to rippling and add chilies. Sauté, stirring, for 2 minutes. Add the Tomato Sauce, ½ cup of water, and the vinegar. Turn heat down to low and simmer gently, stirring frequently, for 5 minutes. Remove from heat and reserve.

5. In a large skillet over moderately high heat bring the remaining 2 tablespoons of oil to rippling and add the onion. Sauté, stirring frequently, until limp and brown at the edges, about 10 minutes.

6. Toss lentils, rice, and macaroni together and transfer to a large serving platter. Garnish top with sautéed onions and pour the reserved Tomato Sauce over all. Serve immediately.

TOMATO SAUCE

MAKES ABOUT 4 CUPS

¼ cup olive oil
1 medium onion, chopped fine
½ sweet green pepper, seeded, deveined, chopped
1½ teaspoons minced garlic
1 can (28 ounces) Italian plum tomatoes, undrained, chopped
1 tablespoon chopped fresh parsley
½ teaspoon oregano
½ teaspoon thyme
1 bay leaf
1 teaspoon salt or to taste
½ teaspoon freshly ground pepper or more to taste

1. In a saucepan over moderate heat bring the oil to rippling. Add the onion, pepper, and garlic. Sauté, stirring frequently, until the vegetables are soft, about 5 minutes. Turn heat down to moderately low.

2. Stir in the tomatoes, parsley, oregano, thyme, and bay leaf and cook, covered, until sauce is thickened. Season with salt and pepper.

The sauce can be stored, tightly covered, in the refrigerator for several days. It freezes successfully, for long storage.

SOYBEAN: THE GREAT IMPERSONATOR

*A*mericans are not so bad at inventing soybean products themselves. There is a process which turns soy protein isolate into filaments and then colorless, tasteless fibers. These fibers are then spun like textile fibers into foods that look and taste like anything you want them to—nuts, fish, beef, pork, chicken, you name it. One of the first of these soy products was BacO's— fake bacon bits that look and taste a lot like fried and crumbled bacon. It's cheaper than bacon (but not by much), has more protein and absolutely no bacon fat (no cholesterol). It's even kosher!

Soybean isolates are used to extend meat. They cost only small change per pound and when rehydrated triple in bulk and can be used by food producers to "beef up" inexpensive chopped meat, sausages, or inexpensive cuts in combination dishes. They are also used in analogues or the vegetarian meats that imitate beef, pork, poultry, fish, and seafood. As we said, these soy products can be made by skilled food technicians to look and taste like the real thing—but they must be labeled as such. Of course, this means artificial flavors and colors must be used—so if you have allergies, beware. No one is really trying to deceive you but technological food can offer you problems.

RUM-LACED BLACK BEANS AND RICE, VIRGIN ISLAND STYLE

The Virgin Islands are noted for their rum. It seems natural that it would find its way into the Islands' favorite dish.

SERVES 8

1 pound dried black beans, soaked, drained, and rinsed
2 large onions, chopped coarse
1 tablespoon minced garlic
2 stalks celery, including leaves, chopped fine
2 medium carrots, pared and chopped coarse
1 bay leaf
½ teaspoon freshly ground pepper
½ teaspoon oregano
½ teaspoon thyme
¼ cup minced fresh parsley
1 tablespoon kosher salt
4 tablespoons unsalted butter
¼ cup dark rum
2 cups unconverted long-grain rice, simmered 18 to 20 minutes in 4½ cups water
1 cup sour cream
8 lime wedges

1. In a large saucepan over high heat bring 8 cups water to the boil and add beans, onion, garlic, celery, carrots, bay leaf, pepper, oregano, thyme, and parsley. Turn heat down to simmer. Cover and cook beans 1½ hours or more until beans are almost done, checking liquid occasionally and adding more water if necessary.

2. Preheat oven to 350°.

3. Remove bay leaf. Add salt, half the rum, and the butter, stirring, to blend well. Transfer bean mixture to a large casserole, cover, and bake in oven until beans are completely tender, about 30 minutes.

4. Remove casserole from oven, stir in the remaining rum, and serve over the rice, passing sour cream and lime wedges at the table.

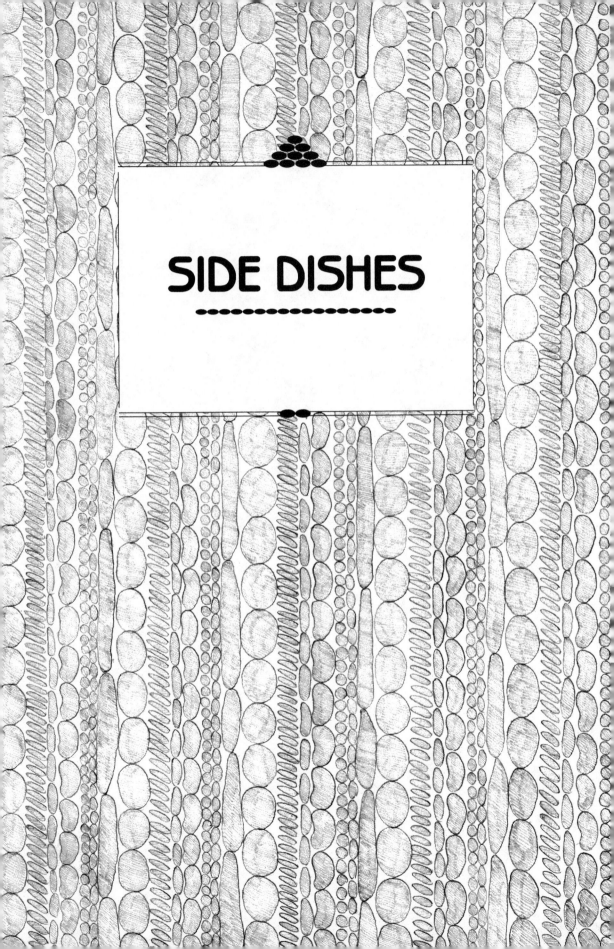

SIDE DISHES

SOFT AND SAVORY CORN AND LIMA BEAN CUSTARD

SERVES 4

2 tablespoons unsalted butter
1 medium onion, chopped fine
½ sweet green pepper, seeded,
   deveined, and cut into
   ¼-inch dice
½ sweet red pepper, seeded,
   deveined, and cut into
   ¼-inch dice
1 package (10 ounces) frozen
   baby lima beans, thawed
1 cup (12 ounces) Green Giant
   Corn Niblets, drained or 1½
   cups fresh corn kernels (from
   3 to 5 ears)
½ teaspoon freshly ground pepper
   or more to taste
   Salt to taste
3 eggs, beaten
1 cup heavy cream
1 teaspoon dry mustard

1. In a medium saucepan or skillet over moderately high heat melt the butter. When the foam subsides add the onion and peppers; sauté, stirring frequently, until vegetables are soft but not browned, about 2 or 3 minutes. Stir in lima beans, corn, pepper, and salt to taste. Sauté, continuing to stir frequently until vegetables are heated through, about 2 minutes.

2. With a rubber spatula transfer mixture to top of double boiler set over simmering, not boiling, water. Whisk eggs, cream, and mustard in a bowl and add to vegetables. Cook, stirring constantly, until custard thickens enough to heavily coat the back of a metal spoon, about 20 minutes. Mixture should be creamy smooth, not set, but very thick. Remove from heat, transfer to a warm serving bowl, and serve immediately.

GOLDEN GARLIC LENTIL FLAN

A versatile dish, this flan may be served hot, at room temperature, or cooled—so it spans the seasons.

SERVES 4 TO 6

½ pound garlic cloves, unpeeled
1 cup chicken stock, homemade or canned
1 teaspoon unsalted butter
½ teaspoon sugar
½ teaspoon white wine vinegar or lemon juice
½ teaspoon salt or to taste
½ teaspoon freshly ground white pepper or to taste
½ teaspoon ground coriander (cilantro)
2 whole eggs
1 egg yolk
1½ cups heavy cream, warmed (or a combination of cream and milk or skimmed milk)
1 cup cooked and drained yellow lentils

1. In a medium saucepan, cover the garlic cloves with water and bring to the boil. Cook for 5 minutes. Drain, refresh garlic under cold running water, and peel.

2. Return garlic to saucepan and add stock, butter, sugar, vinegar or lemon juice, salt, pepper, and coriander. Bring to the boil and reduce heat to simmer. Cook, uncovered, for about 30 minutes or until the liquid is reduced to almost a glaze and the garlic is very soft.

3. Preheat the oven to 300°.

4. Scrape the garlic and glaze into the work bowl of a processor fitted with the steel blade. Add the whole eggs, yolk, cream, and cooked lentils (these may be cooked while you prepare the recipe to this point) and process to a smooth puree.

5. Pour the custard into a greased 2-quart soufflé mold. Place the mold on a roasting pan in the middle of the oven and pour enough boiling water into the pan to reach halfway up the sides of the mold.

6. Bake for 30 to 35 minutes or more until the flan puffs slightly, feels springy, and a toothpick inserted in the center comes out clean. Remove from oven and allow to stand in its hot water bath for 10 minutes.

7. Run a sharp knife around the edge of the flan and unmold onto a warm serving dish. Cut in wedges. Serves 6 as a side dish or 4 for lunch or light supper.

It makes a nice accompaniment to medallions of lamb, grilled fish, or a selection of steamed vegetables.

CUMIN-SPICED COUSCOUS WITH PEAS

SERVES 6

2 cups chicken stock, homemade or canned
1 stick unsalted butter, cut in small pieces
1 teaspoon ground cumin
¼ teaspoon cayenne pepper
1½ cups cooked fresh peas or 1 10-ounce package frozen tiny peas, thawed
2 cups instant couscous (available at specialty food shops and some supermarkets)
2 tablespoons minced fresh coriander (cilantro) leaves or 3 tablespoons fresh parsley leaves
Salt and freshly ground pepper to taste

1. In a saucepan bring the broth, butter, cumin, and cayenne to the boil.

2. Stir in the peas and couscous, cover, and turn off heat. Allow to stand for 4 minutes.

3. Add coriander or parsley and, using two forks, fluff the mixture. Transfer to a warm covered dish and serve.

Full of energy was the first meaning of full of beans. A little after the turn of the century this changed to mean "you don't know what you're talking about." Just beans! means nonsense! To spill the beans started with gypsy reading and means to tell all, to give away a secret and to confess. Old bean is an affectionate way to address a friend in Britain. And if you don't have a penny to your name, you don't have a bean in your jeans. A beany is a little hat that sits on the back of the head (bean).

PINTO BEANS WITH LIME JUICE AND GREEN CHILIES

SERVES 4

2 tablespoons unsalted butter
1 tablespoon fresh lime juice
1 small hot green chili (jalapeño or serrano) seeded, deveined, and minced
½ teaspoon salt or to taste
2 cups cooked or canned pinto beans, rinsed and drained
Freshly ground pepper

1. In a medium saucepan melt the butter over low heat and stir in the lime juice, minced pepper, and salt.

2. Raise heat to simmer and add the beans and pepper. Toss gently to coat and glaze beans. Cook, stirring occasionally, for 2 or 3 minutes or until beans are heated through.

THE AMERICAN PANTRY

*B*eans from the Americas along with tomatoes, corn, and other exotics took a while—some took centuries—to be accepted and integrated into the world's cuisines. They were late-comers, but some, like the bean, the potato (Pizzaro discovered it along with Peru), and the tomato eventually dominated some regional and national cuisines and became such staples in many that most of the world thinks of them as indigenous to those countries. The tomato dominates the food of southern Italy, chocolate monopolizes French and Swiss dessert trays, the potato is synonymous with Irish cookery. The bean? It's the star of many national dishes of peasant origin in France, Italy, the Middle East, Russia, Brazil, Mexico, India, China and Japan. Of course, not all the beans in these dishes are of Mexican origin—but most of them excepting India's, China's, and Japan's can call South Of The Border their original homeland.

LEBANESE SPINACH WITH LENTILS AND LEMON

SERVES 6

½ pound lentils
¼ cup light Tuscan olive oil
1 medium onion, sliced thin
1 tablespoon minced garlic
2 tablespoons chopped fresh coriander (cilantro)
1 package (10 ounces) frozen chopped spinach, thawed
2 medium boiling potatoes, peeled and sliced into ⅛-inch rounds
Salt to taste
½ teaspoon freshly ground pepper
¼ cup fresh lemon juice or more to taste

1. Place the lentils in a saucepan over high heat and cover with water. Bring to the boil, turn down heat to simmer, and cook, covered, 20 minutes. Set aside.

2. In a sauté pan over moderately high heat bring the oil to rippling and sauté the onions until browned, about 12 minutes. Stir in the garlic and coriander, add the spinach, and sauté 5 minutes more, stirring frequently.

3. Add the potatoes and the lentils with their liquid, season with salt and pepper, and bring to the boil. Turn heat down to simmer and cook, covered, for 1 hour or until thick.

4. Stir in the lemon juice and serve.

You may also serve this dish at room temperature or chilled.

ITALIAN HERBED GREEN BEANS AND CARROTS WITH ANCHOVIES

SERVES 6

4 tablespoons unsalted buttter
1 teaspoon chopped garlic
¾ pound green beans, trimmed, and cut into 2-inch pieces
6 medium carrots, cut into 2-by-¼-inch julienne strips
Salt and freshly ground pepper
3 tablespoons chopped fresh parsley
2 teaspoons fresh marjoram or ½ teaspoon dried
1 teaspoon chopped fresh rosemary or ¼ teaspoon dried, crushed
4 flat anchovies, drained and mashed
Grated zest of 1 lemon
2 teaspoons fresh lemon juice

1. In a large skillet or sauté pan melt the butter over moderate heat and sauté the garlic until golden.

2. Add the beans, carrots, salt and pepper to taste, parsley, marjoram, and rosemary and toss to combine. Cover and cook, stirring occasionally until just tender, about 10 or 12 minutes. If vegetables stick, add a tablespoon or two of water.

3. Uncover and add the anchovies, lemon zest, and lemon juice. Cook, stirring and tossing for 2 minutes. Serve with roasted, grilled, or broiled fish or chicken.

LIMA BEANS WITH GARLIC BUTTER

SERVES 4 TO 6

1 pound dried lima beans, soaked, drained, and rinsed

2 slices bacon

½ teaspoon freshly ground pepper

1 teaspoon salt or to taste

6 large garlic cloves

2 tablespoons unsalted butter, softened

1 tablespoon minced fresh parsley

1 tablespoon minced chives or 1 scallion (both white and green parts), sliced very thin

1. Preheat oven to 325°.

2. Place the beans in an ovenproof casserole. Arrange the bacon slices on top, sprinkle with pepper, and add boiling water to cover by 1 inch. Cook, covered, in the oven for 2½ hours or until the beans are very tender. Stir in the salt.

3. In a small saucepan, over high heat bring 2 cups of salted water to the boil. Add the garlic, turn down heat to moderate, and boil 15 minutes, or until garlic is soft. Drain and, in a small bowl, mash into the softened butter with the parsley.

4. With a perforated spoon remove the beans from the casserole and transfer to a warm serving bowl. Cut the bacon into small dice and mix along with the garlic-butter mixture into the beans. Sprinkle with chives and serve.

MINTED GREEN BEANS WITH TOMATO

SERVES 4 TO 6

1 medium onion, chopped fine
2 tablespoons peanut, corn, or
  safflower oil
1 tablespoon minced garlic
4 tablespoons minced fresh mint
  or 2 tablespoons dried
5 canned whole Italian plum
  tomatoes, drained and
  chopped coarse
  Salt and freshly ground pepper
  to taste
1 pound green beans, trimmed
2 tablespoons unsalted butter, cut
  in small pieces, or softened

1. In a skillet or sauté pan cook the onion in the oil over moderate heat, stirring until soft and golden. Add the garlic and the mint and cook, stirring, for 1 to 2 minutes. Add the tomatoes and simmer, stirring occasionally, for about 15 minutes or until sauce is thickened. Add salt and pepper to taste.

2. Plunge the beans into a saucepan of boiling water and cook for 4 to 6 minutes or until just tender but not at all soft. Drain well and transfer to a serving bowl. Toss with the butter and sauce. Serve immediately.

GREEN PEAS
WITH SHREDDED LETTUCE

SERVES 6

1 small or medium onion, chopped fine
½ stick unsalted butter
1 head Boston lettuce, rinsed and shredded
1 tablespoon minced fresh thyme or 1 teaspoon dried
¼ cup minced fresh mint or 1 teaspoon dried
1 bay leaf
2 packages (10 ounces each) frozen tiny peas, partially thawed
½ teaspoon sugar
Salt and freshly ground pepper to taste

1. In a saucepan sauté the onion in the butter, stirring, until translucent and soft. Add the lettuce, thyme, mint, and bay leaf and cook the mixture over moderate heat, stirring, for 3 or 4 minutes.

2. Add the peas, sugar, and salt and pepper to taste and cook, covered, for 5 minutes.

3. Discard the bay leaf and taste for seasoning. Transfer to a heated serving bowl and serve. Or spoon the peas into 6 large Bibb lettuce leaves and arrange on a serving platter.

GREEN BEANS WITH WHITE TURNIPS

SERVES 4 TO 6

1 pound green beans, trimmed and cut in half
2 tablespoons unsalted butter
½ cup diced (¼ inch) boiled or smoked ham
½ cup diced (¼ inch) white turnips
½ cup thin-sliced scallions (both white and green parts)
¼ teaspoon salt or to taste
¼ teaspoon freshly ground pepper

1. Cook the beans in a saucepan of boiling salted water until barely tender, about 4 to 6 minutes, drain in a colander and refresh under cold running water. Drain again and set aside.

2. Melt the butter in the same saucepan. Add the ham and sauté over moderate heat for 2 minutes. Add the turnips, stir well, and cover. Cook until turnips are just tender, about 2 minutes. Add the scallions, beans, and salt and pepper. Toss together and cook, over high heat, stirring occasionally, until beans are heated through and any liquid has been evaporated, about 1 or 2 minutes.

BY ANY OTHER NAME

*S*ometimes beans are misnamed. The black-eyed pea is an example. It's not really a pea but a relative of the mung bean which made its way to our southern states over the silk route from China into the Near East and thence to Arabia, East Africa across to West Africa and through the slave trade to the Caribbean Islands and then to our Dixie mainland. This almost around the world tour didn't take 80 days but rather a couple of thousand years, most likely. During their grand tour their origins became a little fuzzy so that most people believe that Africa is the homeland of black-eyed peas. Today, fresh black-eyes are grown in our southern states and are available only in summer; dried black-eyes are grown in California and shipped to all parts of the world, even to Africa and the Far East. It's magical in a way how transplanted foods can find their way home.

SUCCOTASH

Succotash is a North American Indian dish, a simple mixture of corn and beans. There are many variations. This is a basic recipe using corn and lima beans, the limas being the beans of record for a century now, at least. Because corn stalks were the natural bean poles of the Indians (this clever device was appropriated by the first colonists), it was also natural for the two to be cooked together.

SERVES 4

1 cup cooked fresh lima beans
1 cup cooked fresh corn kernels
  or 1 can (12 ounces) Green
  Giant Corn Niblets, drained
2 to 3 tablespoons unsalted
  butter
  Salt and pepper to taste

1. Combine beans and corn in a steamer over boiling water and steam for 3 minutes.

2. Transfer to a serving dish, stir in butter, and season with salt and pepper to taste.

This is the basic recipe, but, as they say, there are as many variations of it as there are cooks. Some add cream, some diced sweet red peppers. A New England version combines corn and limas with shredded corned or dried beef and potatoes. Diced turnips find their way into some recipes. Navy beans, green beans, black-eyed peas, various seasonings, and other vegetables, chicken, you name it, all have found their way into succotash—but if it isn't based on corn and beans, it should be renamed.

DUTCH BAKED BEANS WITH BEER

SERVES 6 TO 8

1 pound dried kidney beans
(your choice), soaked, drained,
and rinsed
2 small ham hocks
1 teaspoon minced garlic
1 bay leaf
2 tablespoons peanut, corn, or
safflower oil
2 red, ripe tomatoes, chopped or
3 canned Italian plum
tomatoes, drained and chopped
1 sweet green pepper, seeded,
deveined, and chopped
1 large onion, chopped
2 celery stalks, with some leaves,
chopped
Salt to taste
1 teaspoon freshly ground pepper
1 can beer, light or dark

1. Combine beans, ham hocks, garlic, and bay leaf in a large saucepan, cover with 1 inch of water, and bring to the boil. Turn heat down to simmer and cook covered loosely about 2 hours or until beans are tender. (Check once in a while to be sure beans are not dry. Keep covered with 1 inch of water throughout cooking process.) Drain, reserving the cooking liquid. Remove and discard bay leaf. Strip off meat from hocks, dice, and return to beans.

2. In a large skillet or sauté pan over moderate heat bring oil to rippling and sauté, stirring frequently, tomatoes, pepper, onion, and celery until all vegetables are just soft. Add beans, salt and pepper, and beer. Bring to simmer and cook, uncovered, for 20 minutes, adding some of the reserved cooking liquid if beans become too dry. Transfer to serving bowl and serve with corn bread and a fresh green salad.

PARTY CREAMED PEAS AND POTATOES

This recipe can easily be cut in half for a family dinner.

SERVES 12

2 teaspoons sliced garlic

2 medium onions, chopped coarse

2 pounds new potatoes, peeled and cut in quarters

1½ tablespoons unsalted butter

1 cup milk
Salt to taste

¼ teaspoon white pepper (or more to taste) or ⅛ teaspoon cayenne

2 packages (10 ounces each) frozen tiny peas, thawed

1. Cook garlic, onions, and potatoes in a large saucepan of boiling, salted water about 20 minutes or until potatoes are fork tender. Drain and mash with potato masher or put through ricer and return to saucepan.

2. Over very low heat add butter, milk, and pepper, stirring to combine thoroughly. Add peas and stir gently to distribute through potato mixture until peas are just heated through, about 1 minute.

The head is known by some as the bean. Baseball has given us the bean ball, a pitched ball aimed at the batter's head. To bean someone means to hit them on the head. Bean bags were first used by children in 1887 and they were blowing peas at each other through a pea-blower in 1821, a pea-shooter by the 1860's, then bean-shooters by 1889.

GREEN BEANS SAUTÉED WITH GARLIC BREAD CRUMBS AND WALNUTS

SERVES 4

1 pound green beans, trimmed
2 tablespoons peanut, corn, or safflower oil
3 tablespoons unsalted butter
1 tablespoon minced garlic
8 anchovy fillets, chopped fine
½ cup fresh bread crumbs
¼ cup walnuts, chopped coarse
Freshly ground pepper to taste

1. In a sauté pan or skillet cook the green beans in the oil over moderately high heat, stirring constantly, for 4 or 5 minutes or until they are crisp-tender.

2. Turn down the heat to moderate and stir in the butter, coating the beans well. Add the garlic and anchovies and stir until most of the anchovies have dissolved.

3. Add the bread crumbs and sauté, stirring, until the crumbs are golden. Stir in the walnuts and plenty of freshly ground pepper and serve.

GREEN BEANS VINAIGRETTE WITH RED ONION AND FRESH CORIANDER (CILANTRO)

This recipe travels well, and because it should be served warm or at room temperature, it's great for picnics or for backyard barbeques.

SERVES 4

1 medium red onion, chopped fine

1 pound green beans, trimmed and cut in half

2 tablespoons red wine vinegar
Salt and pepper to taste

½ teaspoon powdered mustard

3 dashes Maggi Seasoning

¼ cup light Tuscan olive oil

2 tablespoons chopped coriander leaves (cilantro)

1. Place the onion in a large bowl.

2. In a steamer set over boiling water steam the green beans, covered, for 5 to 6 minutes or until just tender. Add to onions.

3. In a small bowl whisk the vinegar together with the salt and pepper, mustard, and Maggi Seasoning. Add the oil in a slow stream, whisking, until the dressing is combined and emulsified.

4. Pour dressing over beans and onions, sprinkle with coriander, and toss well. Serve warm or at room temperature.

GREEK TAVERNA-STYLE BLACK-EYED PEAS IN OIL AND LEMON

SERVES 8 TO 12

1 pound dried black-eyed peas, soaked and drained

2 medium onions, chopped coarse

1 teaspoon freshly ground pepper plus ½ teaspoon or to taste

1 bay leaf

1 teaspoon salt

¼ cup fresh lemon juice

½ cup light Tuscan olive oil

1 tablespoon minced garlic

½ teaspoon oregano
Grated zest of 1 lemon

1. In a large saucepan place the black-eyed peas, onions, 1 teaspoon of the pepper, and bay leaf; add 6 cups of water and bring to the boil over high heat. Immediately turn heat to simmer; cook, uncovered, until the peas are tender but still firm, about 25 minutes. Add the salt and cook 2 minutes more. Drain the peas and place in a serving bowl.

2. Whisk the lemon juice, olive oil, garlic, and oregano together in a small bowl and pour over the peas. Toss gently to coat evenly. Season with the remaining ½ teaspoon of the pepper (or more to taste), salt if needed, and lemon zest. Serve at room temperature or chill, covered, in the refrigerator until 20 minutes before serving.

GREEN BEANS IN DILLED TOFU SAUCE

SERVES 4 TO 6

1 pound green beans, trimmed and sliced diagonally into 1-inch pieces

THE SAUCE
4 garlic cloves, unpeeled
4 ounces tofu, drained on paper towels and cut into pieces
¼ cup fresh lemon juice
2 teaspoons Dijon mustard
¼ cup snipped fresh dill
Salt to taste
½ cup corn or safflower oil

1. In a steamer set over boiling water steam the beans, covered, for 5 to 6 minutes or until just tender. Keep warm.

2. In a small saucepan cook the garlic cloves in boiling water to cover for 5 minutes (or they may be steamed with the beans). Drain and slip off the skins.

3. In a food processor or blender process the garlic, tofu, lemon juice, mustard, dill, and salt to taste until the mixture is smooth. With the motor running add the oil in a slow stream until the sauce is combined and emulsified. Pour some of the sauce over the beans and toss. Store any remaining sauce in a covered jar in the refrigerator. Keeps for 1 to 2 weeks. Use to dress other cooked vegetables or beans such as black-eyed peas or pink beans.

A garnish of chopped scallions, chopped parsley, or chopped coriander (cilantro) adds color, texture, and fresh flavor interest.

QUICK COUSCOUS AND CHICK-PEAS WITH GARLICKY RED PEPPER SAUCE

SERVES 4 TO 6

THE COUSCOUS

- 2 tablespoons unsalted butter
- 1 medium onion, chopped fine
- 2 cups chicken stock, homemade or canned
- 1 cup medium-grain instant couscous
- 1 cup chick-peas, cooked or canned, drained and rinsed
- 1½ cups leftover chicken, pork, or lamb, cut into ½-inch dice (optional)
- 3 tablespoons chopped fresh coriander (cilantro) for garnish

1. In a medium saucepan over moderately high heat melt the butter and sauté the onion until translucent, about 3 or 4 minutes. Add the chicken stock and bring to the boil.

2. Pour the couscous in a stream into the boiling liquid, stirring constantly. Boil for 2 minutes, remove from heat, and stir in the chick-peas and leftover meat, if desired.

3. Cover and allow to stand until the couscous is tender, about 10 to 20 minutes. Fluff the mixture with two forks. Garnish with the fresh coriander (cilantro) and serve with the sauce.

THE SAUCE

- ⅓ cup light Tuscan olive oil
- 1 tablespoon plus 1 teaspoon paprika
- 2 teaspoons minced garlic
- ½ teaspoon salt
- ⅛ teaspoon cayenne pepper or more to taste

1. Mix all the ingredients in a small bowl until thoroughly blended. Pass sauce at the table.

PERSIAN PUMPKIN AND LENTIL CASSEROLE

Pumpkin is not particularly popular in this country as a vegetable, but it has its advocates, especially among Middle Eastern peoples. It has a natural affinity for lentils and the combination works well with the seasonings. Try it. You'll discover there are other uses for it besides pumpkin pie.

SERVES 6 TO 8

2 tablespoons unsalted butter	
1 medium onion, chopped fine	
1 cup lentils	
3 cups 1-inch cubes of pared pumpkin	
1 tablespoon fresh lemon juice	
2 teaspoons minced fresh parsley	
1 teaspoon salt or to taste	
½ teaspoon ground ginger or 1 teaspoon fresh grated gingerroot	
¼ teaspoon freshly ground pepper	
¼ teaspoon ground cumin	
2 scallions (both white and green parts), sliced thin	

1. Melt butter in a large saucepan over moderate heat. When the foam subsides add the onion; cook, stirring occasionally, until just golden.

2. Add the lentils and toss to combine and coat lentils with butter. Pour in enough cold water to cover, turn heat to moderately high and bring to the boil. Turn down heat to simmer and cook, covered, stirring occasionally, until lentils are barely tender, about 20 minutes.

3. Add pumpkin, lemon juice, parsley, salt, ginger, pepper, and cumin. Stir well to mix, cover and cook until pumpkin is tender, about 20 minutes.

4. Stir scallions into lentil-pumpkin mixture and serve hot in a covered vegetable dish.

PEAS AND CUCUMBER IN DILL

SERVES 4

4 tablespoons unsalted butter
2 large cucumbers, pared, cut in half lengthwise, seeded, cut in half again lengthwise, then cut in ½-inch pieces
Salt to taste
1 package (10 ounces) frozen tiny peas, thawed
1 tablespoon snipped fresh dill
Freshly ground pepper to taste

1. Melt butter in a sauté pan or large skillet over moderately high heat. When foam subsides add cucumbers and sauté, stirring and tossing, until just crisp-tender, not soft, about 2 minutes. Turn heat to simmer, sprinkle with salt, add peas, and cook, stirring, until heated through, about 1 minute.

2. Add dill and a generous amount of pepper and toss to combine thoroughly. Transfer to warm serving dish.

SAUTÉED DILLED FAVA BEANS

SERVES 4 TO 6

2 tablespoons unsalted butter
2 pounds fresh young fava beans, shelled
¼ cup fresh lemon juice
¼ cup snipped fresh dill
Salt and freshly ground pepper to taste

1. Melt the butter in a large skillet or sauté pan over moderately high heat. When foam begins to subside, add the beans and sauté, stirring for 3 minutes.

2. Add the lemon juice and stir to combine. Sprinkle with dill and salt and pepper. Serve immediately.

If young fava beans are unavailable, boil mature beans in water to cover for 8 to 10 minutes, or until tender. Drain, pat dry, and peel off outer seed coat. Proceed as above.

TEN-MINUTE BLACK BEANS WITH TOMATOES AND CORIANDER

SERVES 4

1½ tablespoons peanut, corn, or safflower oil

1 medium onion, chopped

1 teaspoon chopped garlic

6 fresh plum tomatoes peeled, seeded, and chopped or 1 can (14 ounces) Italian plum tomatoes, drained and chopped

1 can (16 ounces) black beans, drained and rinsed

½ teaspoon Tabasco sauce

½ teaspoon salt or to taste

2 tablespoons chopped fresh coriander (cilantro)

1. Heat the oil in a small skillet or saucepan over moderately high heat and add the onions and garlic. Sauté, stirring, until onion is almost translucent but still firm, about 2 minutes. Add tomatoes and cook, stirring frequently, for 2 minutes more.

2. Add the black beans, Tabasco, and salt and stir to combine. Cover skillet and cook until beans are heated through, about 2 minutes.

3. Remove from heat and stir in 1 tablespoon of the coriander. Transfer to serving dish and sprinkle with remaining coriander. Serve immediately.

GREEN BEANS WITH BASIL-WALNUT VINAIGRETTE

SERVES 6

1 teaspoon coarse-chopped garlic
12 to 15 basil leaves (a little more, not less, can't hurt)
½ teaspoon salt or to taste
½ teaspoon freshly ground pepper
1 teaspoon Maggi Seasoning
4 tablespoons white wine vinegar
¼ cup light Tuscan olive oil
¼ cup walnut oil
1½ pounds young green beans, trimmed, left whole if small, cut in half if large
2 scallions (both white and green parts), sliced thin
Chopped walnuts for garnish (optional)

1. In a food processor or blender, pulse on and off the garlic, basil, salt, pepper, and Maggi Seasoning with the vinegar until smooth. With the motor running add the oils in a slow stream until combined and emulsified.

2. In a steamer filled with water to just below steamer basket, steam the beans over moderately high heat for 8 to 10 minutes or until tender. Refresh beans under cold running water. Drain well.

3. Place the beans in a serving bowl and pour the vinaigrette over them. Toss to coat thoroughly. Toss a few times more as they cool. Serve at room temperature or chilled, garnished with a few chopped walnuts, if desired.

PEARS, GREEN BEANS AND BACON, BAVARIAN STYLE

SERVES 6 TO 8

6 firm pears, peeled, cored, halved, and cut into ¼-inch slices
¼ cup fresh lemon juice
1 teaspoon grated lemon zest or a 3-inch strip of lemon zest, julienned
1 pound young green beans, trimmed, cut in 2-inch lengths
6 slices bacon
¼ cup sugar
2 tablespoons red wine vinegar
Salt and freshly ground pepper to taste

1. In a large saucepan over moderate heat combine the pears, 2 tablespoons of the lemon juice, the lemon zest, and about ⅓ cup of water. Cook, stirring occasionally, for 5 minutes, or until the pears are crisp-tender.

2. In a saucepan of boiling salted water cook the green beans for 5 minutes or until just tender. Refresh them under cold running water and drain.

3. In a skillet cook the bacon over moderate heat until crisp, transfer to paper towels to drain, and crumble. Reserve.

4. Pour off the fat in the skillet leaving enough to coat it. Add the sugar, the vinegar, and the remaining lemon juice. Cook over moderately high heat, scraping the brown bits from the bottom and sides of the pan, until the mixture is syrupy.

5. Drain the pears and add them to the skillet along with the green beans. Turn the heat to moderately low and cook, stirring and tossing gently, until heated through, about 2 minutes. Transfer to warm serving dish and sprinkle with salt and pepper and the reserved bacon.

FRIJOLES REFRITOS
(MEXICAN REFRIED BEANS)

SERVES 6

THE BASIC BEANS

2 cups dried black, pinto, kidney, or pink beans, soaked, drained, and rinsed
2 medium onions, chopped fine
2 teaspoons chopped garlic
1 bay leaf or ½ teaspoon dried *epazote* (a distinctive Mexican herb available in Mexican and Hispanic food stores)
2 tablespoons peanut, corn, or safflower oil
1 tablespoon salt or to taste
Freshly ground pepper to taste

1. In a saucepan over high heat cover the beans with an inch of cold water and bring to the boil. Add the onions, garlic, and bay leaf and lower the heat to simmer. Cook gently, loosely covered, for 1½ to 2 hours, adding more boiling water as it evaporates.

2. When the beans are soft, wrinkled, and breaking open, add the oil, salt, and a generous amount of pepper. Continue cooking, uncovered, for 30 minutes more, adding no more water. The beans should be thoroughly soft, almost mushy, and there should be a good deal of bean gravy.

THE REFRIED BEANS

1 recipe for Basic Beans (above)
6 tablespoons peanut, corn, or safflower oil
1 medium onion, chopped fine
2 teaspoons minced garlic
1 fresh, ripe tomato, peeled, seeded, and chopped

1. Working in batches, puree beans and their liquid *roughly* in a food processor. Do not use a blender; there is not enough liquid for a blender to do this step properly. If you do not own a processor it is best to mash the beans a few tablespoons at a time, right in the skillet, using a sturdy fork or potato masher.

2. Heat 2 tablespoons of the oil over moderate heat in a skillet. Add the onion and garlic and sauté until the onion is translucent. Add the tomato and cook 2 or 3 minutes. Add a little of the remaining oil and several tablespoons of the pureed beans, mashing them with a fork into the vegetables until they are incorporated. Repeat with more oil and more beans, mashing and stirring with each addition until all the beans are incorporated and you have a thick, creamy, somewhat dry paste. Use for tacos, for enchiladas, for stuffing green chilies (p. 202), or for other Mexican dishes. May also be used as a side dish.

TROPICAL FRUITED LENTILS

SERVES 6

1 cup dried lentils
2 tablespoons raisins or currants
1 teaspoon minced garlic
1 small onion, chopped
1 large fresh, ripe tomato, peeled, seeded, and chopped or 3 canned Italian plum tomatoes, drained and chopped
1½ tablespoons peanut, corn, or safflower oil
1 thick slice fresh pineapple, cut into chunks, or ⅔ cup canned pineapple chunks, drained
½ medium-firm banana, peeled and sliced
1 small Golden Delicious apple, pared, cored, and diced
Salt and freshly ground pepper to taste

1. Rinse lentils and place in a saucepan with raisins and water to cover. Bring to the boil over high heat. Reduce heat to simmer and cook, covered, for 25 minutes. Drain and set aside.

2. In the work bowl of a food processor puree the garlic, onion, and tomato until smooth. In a skillet over high heat, heat the oil until rippling and cook the puree, stirring and scraping, for 3 minutes. Turn heat down to a simmer and add pineapple, banana, apple, salt, and pepper. Cook 5 minutes more.

3. Add lentils to the puree and fruit and simmer uncovered, for 10 minutes, stirring occasionally or until the lentils are fairly dry and creamy textured. Serve.

Lentils made in this manner go especially well with smoked meats, ham steaks, fried chicken, spareribs, and roast pork.

GREEN BEANS IN BASIL-ANCHOVY SAUCE

SERVES 4 TO 6

1½ pounds fresh green beans
6 tablespoons light Tuscan olive
   oil
2 medium onions, sliced thin
4 ripe tomatoes peeled, seeded,
   and chopped or 6 canned
   Italian plum tomatoes, drained
   and chopped
   Salt, if desired
   Freshly ground pepper
2 tablespoons chopped fresh
   parsley
   Bay leaf
3 garlic cloves, halved
4 flat anchovy fillets

1. Trim beans and drop them into saucepan of boiling salted water. Cook for 7 to 10 minutes or until just tender. Drain and refresh under cold running water.

2. In a large skillet or sauté pan heat 4 tablespoons of the oil, add the onions and cook them, covered, for 10 minutes over moderately low heat until soft and turning golden.

3. Add tomatoes, salt, pepper, parsley, bay leaf, and thyme. Raise heat to moderately high and cook, stirring occasionally, for 10 to 15 minutes or until well thickened. Remove bay leaf and discard.

4. Add green beans, reduce heat to simmer, and cook, covered, for 5 minutes.

5. Meanwhile, puree the basil, garlic, anchovies, and remaining oil in a blender or food processor fitted with the steel blade. Add puree to bean mixture, stir through until heated, and serve.

For a one-dish meal, steam 2 pounds mussels. Remove from shells, combine with green beans, and add basil-anchovy puree.

BLACK FOREST LENTILS WITH FRUITS AND VEGETABLES

SERVES 4 TO 6

½ cup lentils, rinsed
2 tablespoons raisins
3 slices bacon or 1½ tablespoons peanut, corn, or safflower oil
2 cloves garlic, chopped
1 small onion, chopped
½ cup diced carrots, blanched
1 cup fresh green beans, trimmed, cut into 2-inch lengths, and blanched
1 Granny Smith or other tart apple, peeled, cored, and diced
1 Bosc or other firm-fleshed pear, peeled, cored, and diced
Salt, if desired
Freshly ground pepper

1. Place lentils in a saucepan with the raisins and water to cover. Bring to the boil over high heat, reduce to simmer and cook, covered, for 25 minutes or until lentils are tender. Drain and set aside.

2. While lentils are cooking, fry the bacon in a skillet until crisp. Drain on paper towels and crumble. Pour off all but 1½ tablespoons of the fat. (If omitting bacon, add oil to the pan.)

3. In the same skillet sauté garlic and onion until wilted and golden. Add carrots and sauté 5 minutes, stirring frequently. Add green beans, apple, and pear and sauté a few minutes more.

4. Add the lentils and simmer over low heat, uncovered, stirring occasionally, for 10 minutes. The lentils should be somewhat dry, but creamy-textured.

5. Turn into a serving dish and sprinkle with crumbled bacon.

TWICE-COOKED GREEN BEANS WITH GARLIC AND VODKA

SERVES 6

2 tablespoons soy sauce
1 tablespoon vodka
1 teaspoon sugar
4 cups peanut, corn, or safflower oil for deep frying
1½ pounds green beans, trimmed
1 tablespoon minced garlic
1 teaspoon red pepper flakes

1. In a bowl combine the soy sauce, vodka, and sugar.

2. In a sauté pan or wok heat the oil to 375° and fry the beans, a small handful at a time, for 20 seconds. Transfer each batch of fried beans with a slotted spoon to paper towels to drain. Allow the oil to return to 375° before adding next handful.

3. When all the beans are fried, pour off all but 2 tablespoons of oil; turn heat to high and stir-fry the garlic and red pepper flakes for 10 to 15 seconds.

4. Add the fried beans and stir for 15 seconds more or until all the beans are coated with garlic.

5. Add the vodka–soy sauce mixture to pan and stir for another 30 seconds or until the beans are heated through and combined well with the sauce.

6. Transfer beans to serving dish and pour remaining sauce in pan over them. Serve immediately.

The beans may be deep-fried several hours beforehand and set aside. Just before serving, continue with steps 3 to 6.

PINK BEANS IN THE PORTUGUESE MANNER

SERVES 8

5 strips bacon, cut in 1-inch pieces
1 large onion, chopped
1 tablespoon minced garlic
1 pound pink kidney beans, soaked and drained
1 teaspoon cinnamon
½ teaspoon ground cloves
½ teaspoon allspice
1 teaspoon ground cumin
1 can (28 ounces) Italian plum tomatoes, chopped, juice reserved
2 tablespoons dark molasses
1 tablespoon salt or to taste
1 teaspoon freshly ground pepper

1. In a soup pot over moderate heat fry the bacon until brown. Add the onion and sauté, stirring frequently, until transparent. Stir in garlic and turn down heat to moderately low. Cook until onion turns golden.

2. Add the beans, cinnamon, cloves, allspice, cumin, tomatoes and their reserved juice and enough water to cover. Turn heat to high and bring to the boil. Turn heat down to simmer and cook, covered, 1½ hours. Uncover and cook 30 minutes more or until beans are just tender and sauce is thickened.

3. Add molasses, salt, and pepper and continue cooking 15 minutes more until sauce is very thick.

A CURIOUS BEAN BONANZA

*T*he soybean is the largest cash crop in the United States today. But only yesterday, about 1900 to be exact, it was practically unknown here, a legume curiosity. Even in Europe it was unknown until the 17th century. It is now our prime source of edible oil and protein. Amazing!

Thanks go partly to Commodore Matthew Perry who brought the soybean here from the Far East in 1854. Nobody ate it, however. We washed with it (its oil was used in soaps), painted our houses with it, and varnished our dining tables with it. In other words it was used industrially, not gustatorially—and just for its oil. Nobody thought of eating it whole, fresh or dried. Its oil couldn't be used for cooking or salads then because it is very unstable, oxidates easily, which means it consequently goes bad quickly and tastes awful. Then someone invented the hydrogenation process and the food industry discovered a new darling, using the oil first to make margarine and then other soy products as additives, supplements, extenders, and cattle feed.

BAKED BEANS WITH MAPLE SYRUP AND BOURBON

SERVES 4 TO 6

1 pound dried pea beans or Great Northern beans, cooked, liquid reserved

1 tablespoon dry mustard

½ teaspoon freshly ground pepper

1 tablespoon minced fresh gingerroot (or ½ teaspoon ground ginger)

1½ cups cider vinegar

1½ cups strong brewed coffee (preferably espresso)

½ cup U.S. Grade B maple syrup, or ½ cup U.S. Grade A plus 1 teaspoon unsulphured molasses

2 medium onions, chopped fine

¼ pound lean salt pork with rind

½ cup bourbon

1. Preheat oven to 275°.

2. Transfer beans to a two-quart bean pot or earthenware casserole (or enameled cast-iron Dutch oven or a saucepan with a heavy, tight-fitting lid).

3. Combine mustard, pepper, ginger, and vinegar in a bowl with coffee, maple syrup, and 1½ cups of bean cooking liquid. Stir well and pour mixture over beans in pot. If the mixture doesn't cover beans, add more cooking liquid.

4. Add onion to beans and stir to combine.

5. Score *fat side* of pork in ½-inch diamond pattern. Do not cut through rind. Place scored side up on beans.

6. Cover pot and bake in the center of the oven for 6½ to 7 hours. Remove beans from oven and stir in bourbon. Add ½ to 1 cup of the reserved cooking liquid, if beans appear dry. Recover pot and return to oven for 1 hour more.

7. Remove cover from beans (they should be moist, but most of the liquid should have been absorbed) and bake 30 minutes more or until top of beans appears crusty. Interior will be almost dry and syrupy.

Do *not* use high-grade maple syrup straight in this dish. The flavor is much too subtle and needs the boost of molasses to assert itself. If you'd rather use all molasses instead of maple syrup, substitute 6 tablespoons of dark unsulphured molasses plus ¼ teaspoon ground cloves and ¼ teaspoon ground cinnamon.

SERVING SUGGESTION: Baked beans are classically served with frankfurters or ham but we prefer the color and crunch of cauliflower, broccoli, and tomatoes at room temperature tossed with a creamy mustard-mayonnaise dressing. The cauliflower and broccoli should be little more than blanched.

CREAMED CORN AND BABY LIMAS

SERVES 6 TO 8

2 cups fresh baby lima beans or 1 package (10 ounces) frozen baby limas, thawed
1 medium onion, chopped fine
¼ cup (½ stick) unsalted butter
1 cup milk
2 12-ounce cans Green Giant Corn Niblets, drained
½ cup heavy cream
Salt to taste
½ teaspoon freshly ground pepper or more to taste

1. If using fresh limas, plunge them into a saucepan containing 1½ cups of boiling water and cook over moderate heat for 15 minutes. Drain and set aside. If using frozen limas, cook in same manner for only 3 minutes, drain, and set aside.

2. In a saucepan over moderate heat sauté the onions in butter, stirring frequently, until they are just beginning to turn golden, about 4 minutes. Add the limas and ½ cup of the milk and cook the mixture, stirring, until the milk is absorbed, about 5 minutes. Add the corn and remaining ½ cup milk and cook another 5 minutes or until milk is absorbed.

3. Add the cream, salt, and pepper and cook the mixture until it thickens a little. Transfer to a serving bowl and serve with additional fresh pepper.

GREEN BEANS WITH POTATOES AND ZUCCHINI

SERVES 6

1 pound green beans, trimmed and cut in half
1 large potato, peeled and sliced into ⅛-inch rounds
½ cup light Tuscan olive oil
1 medium zucchini, cut into ¼-inch slices
1 tablespoon chopped parsley, preferably flat-leaf Italian
½ cup chopped fresh tomato or canned Italian plum tomatoes, drained and chopped
1 medium onion, sliced thin
1 tablespoon dried basil or 12 fresh basil leaves, chopped
Salt to taste
½ teaspoon freshly ground pepper

1. In a large saucepan over high heat bring 3 cups of water to the boil and blanch the beans and potatoes until water returns to the boil. Drain.

2. In a large skillet or sauté pan over moderately high heat, bring the oil to rippling and stir in the green beans and potatoes. Add the rest of the ingredients, turn heat down to moderately low and cook, covered, until green beans and potatoes are just tender, about 15 to 20 minutes. Transfer to a warm serving bowl.

The seasonings in this dish can be varied by substituting 1 teaspoon rosemary for the basil, 1 teaspoon minced garlic for the onion, and 1 cup of chicken stock for the tomatoes. Sauté the garlic and rosemary for a few minutes before adding the rest of the ingredients.

NEW MEXICAN SPINACH AND PINTO BEANS

SERVES 4

2 tablespoons bacon drippings or peanut, corn, or safflower oil
1 tablespoon crushed dried red chili or 1 teaspoon red pepper flakes
1 medium onion, chopped fine
1 teaspoon minced garlic
1 package (10 ounces) frozen chopped spinach, thawed
1 can (16 ounces) pinto beans, drained and rinsed
1 teaspoon vinegar
Salt to taste

1. In a large skillet over moderately high heat bring the fat or oil to rippling. Add the dried chili, stir for 30 seconds. Add the onion. Sauté until translucent and add the garlic. Stir for 30 seconds and add the spinach, pinto beans, and vinegar.

2. Sauté 10 minutes, stirring frequently, and serve.

*L*entils have given us the word lens for a convex-concave polished optical glass the very shape of the bean.

The English have given us many of our slang expressions using and based on the word bean. But oddly enough, perversely enough, they call beans pulses.

The French gave us the word we use for the whole bean family: legume. But in French the word légume means vegetable and includes all of them, beans, too—but not just beans, which are called légumes secs when they're the dry kind.

FAVA BEANS FLAVORED WITH LEMON, GARLIC, AND SMOKED SALMON

SERVES 4 TO 6

2 pounds fresh young fava beans
Juice of 1 lemon
¼ cup peanut, corn, or safflower oil
¼ cup water or more
1 teaspoon salt or to taste
½ teaspoon white pepper
4 large garlic cloves, crushed
1 tablespooon unsalted butter
2 slices smoked salmon (about ⅛ pound)

1. Shell the fava beans and place in a saucepan with a tight-fitting lid.

2. Add lemon juice, oil, water, salt, pepper, and garlic. The beans should just barely be covered with liquid. Add more water, if necessary.

3. Mix and bring to the boil over high heat. Cover, turn heat down to simmer, and cook for 45 minutes or until beans are very tender and most of the water has evaporated. If there is too much liquid, remove cover and boil rapidly to reduce.

4. Meanwhile, melt the butter in a small frying pan over low heat and add the salmon slices. As they begin to lose their satiny gloss and turn light pink, break up the slices into shreds. Continue to sauté for 2 minutes.

5. Add smoked salmon to beans, mix through, and serve.

SUGGESTION: A teaspoon of yogurt or sour cream on each serving is a refreshing and pretty touch.

MAIN DISHES

CHOCOLATE CHILI WITH PINTO BEANS

Mexicans use chocolate a lot in cooking—mole sauces are most familiar in this country. Here we use cocoa powder to add a dark, rich color and flavor very much in keeping with chili's origins. In other words, it's not just a gimmick.

SERVES 6 TO 8

1½ pounds lean pork, diced fine or ground coarse
1½ pounds lean beef, diced fine or ground coarse
¼ cup olive or vegetable oil
5 medium onions, chopped coarse
2 cups tomato juice
3 cups water
5 tablespoons chili powder, or to taste
3 tablespoons ground cumin
3 tablespoons oregano
3 tablespoons unsweetened cocoa powder
3 tablespoons cinnamon
1 tablespoon salt or to taste
2 tablespoons garlic, chopped fine
3 tablespoons masa harina* or stone-ground white cornmeal
2 cans (1 pound each) pinto beans, drained and rinsed
Chopped onion, shredded lettuce, grilled flour tortillas

*See footnote, p. 162

1. In a large sauté pan or flameproof casserole, cook the pork and beef over moderate heat, stirring frequently, until both meats lose their pink color but are not browned, about 20 minutes. Transfer to a bowl and set aside.

2. Heat the oil in the same pan until rippling and add the onions. Sauté, stirring occasionally, until soft and translucent, 10 to 20 minutes.

3. Stir the reserved meat into the onions. Add the tomato juice, 3 cups of water, the chili powder, cumin, oregano, cocoa, cinnamon, and salt. Blend. Turn the heat to high and bring to the boil; reduce heat and simmer, uncovered, for 1 hour. Stir occasionally.

4. Taste for seasoning. Add more chili powder if you like your chili really searing. Cook 30 minutes longer.

5. Stir in the garlic, masa harina or cornmeal, and beans. Simmer for 10 minutes more until the beans are heated through.

6. Serve with suggested chili garnishes (see recipe p. 162).

Chunks of peeled and cored apples (2 medium), a handful of raisins, and some sliced stuffed olives can be added along with the beans for flavor and textural interest that combines the Middle East with our Southwest—to the advantage of both. Ice-cold dark beer is the beverage we suggest as a foil for this pungent stew.

PINTO BEAN CHILI CON CARNE

SERVES 8

2 tablespoons peanut, corn, or safflower oil

2 large onions (or 4 medium), chopped

2 tablespoons garlic, chopped

2½ pounds coarse-ground lean bottom round beef

¼ cup masa harina* or all-purpose flour

1 can (35 ounces) Italian plum tomatoes, chopped, juice reserved

4 cups beef or chicken stock, homemade or canned

6 tablespoons chili powder

1 tablespoon ground cumin or more to taste

1 teaspoon oregano

1 teaspoon cinnamon

1 teaspoon freshly ground black pepper

1 tablespoon salt or to taste

2 tablespoons cider vinegar

2 fresh jalapeño peppers, seeded, deveined, and chopped or 2 canned *chipotle* chilies

4 cups cooked pinto beans or 2 cans (16 ounces each), drained and rinsed

*Masa harina is finely milled cornflour used in Mexican cooking. Quaker makes it in this country and it's widely available. Look in the Hispanic section of your supermarket—or substitute all-purpose flour.

1. In a large sauté pan or Dutch oven over moderate heat, heat the oil until rippling. Add the onions and sauté, stirring frequently, until golden brown, about 10 minutes. Add the garlic and continue sautéing, stirring, for 2 minutes more.

2. Add the ground beef and cook, stirring until meat loses its red color. Sprinkle the mixture with the masa harina and continue stirring until it is incorporated and cooked through, about 2 minutes.

3. Stir in all the remaining ingredients (including reserved tomato juice) except the pinto beans, turn heat to high, and bring to a simmer. Immediately turn heat to moderate and simmer gently, covered, for 1½ hours, stirring occasionally to keep it from sticking. Add a little hot water if the mixture seems too thick.

4. At end of cooking time spoon off excess fat on the surface of the chili, if necessary. Add the beans, stir through, and continue cooking 5 to 10 minutes more. It may be served at this point or held, after cooling to room temperature, in the refrigerator for several days. Bring back to room temperature and reheat over moderately low heat. (If a film of orange-colored fat congeals on the surface of the chili, remove as much as possible before bringing to room temperature.)

5. Serve with corn tortillas, sourdough bread, biscuits, corn bread, or saltines.

GARNISHES: We like to spoon on chopped onions, grated Parmesan, shredded lettuce, and, perhaps, a dollop of sour cream or crème fraîche at the table. These garnishes can be varied with chopped fresh coriander (cilantro), chopped scallions, chopped cucumber, rings of pickled jalapeño, and/or chopped sweet peppers. Any one or a combination of these garnishes may be used, or you may serve the chili without any—it's flavorful and hearty enough on its own.

VEGETABLE CHILI VARIATION: Omit the beef and substitute a cup of bulgur wheat. Add chopped carrots, sweet peppers, celery, drained Green Giant Corn Niblets or hominy, zucchini, sliced green beans, cabbage, or other vegetables. Cook for only an hour and add quick-cooking vegetables with the beans toward the end of the cooking time. Kidney beans, pink beans, or black beans may be used in place of the pinto beans.

PIQUANT KIDNEY BEAN AND SAUSAGE STEW

Like all stews, this one improves in flavor if allowed to cool (uncovered) and chill (covered) in the refrigerator overnight.

SERVES 4 TO 6

2 cups dried kidney beans, soaked and drained

2 celery stalks with leaves, chopped coarse

1 small sweet green pepper, chopped coarse

2 onions, chopped coarse

1 tablespoon garlic, chopped fine

1 pound smoked sausage or kielbasa, cut in ½-inch slices, sautéed and drained of fat

½ teaspoon red pepper flakes or more to taste

2 teaspoons Worcestershire sauce

4 scallions (both green and white parts), sliced thin

½ cup chopped fresh parsley

¼ cup wine vinegar (optional)

1. In a large saucepan or sauté pan cover the kidney beans with 6 cups of water and bring to the boil.

2. Stir in celery, pepper, onions, garlic, sausage, red pepper flakes, and Worcestershire sauce. Turn heat to simmer and cook, covered, for 50 minutes to 1 hour, or until the beans test tender. (May be made to this point and set aside until serving time.)

3. Before serving stir in the scallions, reserving a tablespoon for garnish. Sprinkle with vinegar.

DFINA—EGYPTIAN HIDDEN TREASURE BEEF STEW

This is a rich beef stew with two secrets—the sour flavor of sorrel and the surprise of finding a creamy-textured hard-boiled egg *in its shell* hidden in each serving. The original recipe we got from a young friend, Annie Pitt, calls for a blanched calf's foot added with the meat. If your butcher can accommodate you, by all means add it.

SERVES 6

2 pounds lean beef chuck, cut into 1-inch cubes

6 small new potatoes, scrubbed

2 large onions, chopped (sautéed in oil until golden, if you prefer)

1 pound Great Northern beans or chick-peas, soaked and drained

1 heaping tablespoon minced garlic

6 eggs in their shells

1 teaspoon allspice

1 teaspoon freshly ground pepper
Salt to taste

1 pound fresh sorrel (sour grass), stems removed, blanched, drained, and chopped

1 tablespoon light Tuscan olive oil

1. Place all the ingredients—with the exception of the salt, sorrel, and oil—in a large saucepan over moderately high heat. Add water to cover and bring to the boil. Turn heat down to low simmer and cook, covered, for 4 hours. Or preheat oven to its lowest setting and after simmering gently on top of the stove for ½ hour complete the cooking time in the oven.

2. An hour before serving sauté the sorrel in the oil in a skillet over moderate heat for 3 minutes, stir into the stew, and continue cooking until serving time. The meat will be falling-apart tender and the eggs will be hard-boiled but creamy-textured. Serve with buttered rice.

TAGINE MALSOUKA, OR TUNISIAN MEAT PIE IN FILO DOUGH

SERVES 6

1 pound lean boneless lamb, cut into 1-inch cubes
2 tablespoons peanut, corn, or safflower oil
¼ pound dried Great Northern beans, soaked and drained
½ teaspoon freshly ground pepper or more to taste
¼ teaspoon crumbled saffron threads
½ teaspoon cinnamon
½ teaspoon allspice
6 eggs
Salt to taste
¼ pound unsalted butter
12 sheets of filo dough
1 egg yolk, beaten, for glazing crust

1. In a large saucepan or sauté pan over moderately high heat brown the lamb in the oil. Add the beans and cover with water. Stir in the pepper, saffron, cinnamon, and allspice and bring to a boil.

2. Turn down heat to simmer and cook gently, covered, for about 2 hours or until the beans and meat are tender and the liquid is reduced to a thick gravy. (Check periodically during cooking time and add a little more water if too much evaporates.)

3. Turn heat down to low and break the eggs one at a time into the mixture, stirring well after each addition. Add salt to taste and keep stirring until eggs have set a little and are creamy. Remove from heat and set aside.

4. Preheat the oven to 375°.

5. Butter a large baking dish. Brush 4 of the filo sheets with butter and fit them into the dish so that the edges come up and fold over the sides (keep the stack of filo sheets covered with a damp tea towel so they don't dry out while you're working). Transfer half of the lamb mixture into the pastry-lined dish and cover with another 4 sheets of filo each brushed with butter. Spoon in the rest of the lamb mixture and cover the top with the last 4 sheets of filo, each brushed with butter. Tuck in the folded edges and brush the top with the beaten egg yolk. Bake for 40 minutes.

6. Turn oven heat to 450° and bake 15 minutes more or until pastry is crisp and a deep golden color. Serve from the baking dish accompanied by a cool green salad, and buttered couscous or rice.

COLD JULIENNED CHICKEN WITH SPICED PINTO BEAN SAUCE

I n smaller portions this can be served as an appetizer. It's also useful at a buffet dinner where people are eating from dishes resting in their laps, and cutting food on a plate is a problem.

SERVES 6

Lettuce leaves for lining a serving plate
2 cups julienned cooked white meat chicken
1 tablespoon minced scallion
1 small cucumber, peeled, seeded, and julienned
1 heaping teaspoon minced garlic
2 teaspoons peeled and minced fresh gingerroot
1 cup pureed pinto beans
1 tablespoon rice vinegar
1½ tablespoons soy sauce or tamari
1 teaspoon sugar
1 tablespoon chili paste with garlic (at Asian and specialty food stores)
1 tablespoon dark sesame oil (at Asian and specialty food stores)

1. Line the serving plate with lettuce leaves and heap the julienned chicken in the center.

2. In a bowl combine the rest of the ingredients and stir well.

3. Pour the sauce over the chicken and serve.

THE SOYBEAN UNMASKED

T he soybean has a 40% protein content, and high quality protein at that, almost the same as meat in its amino acid balance. Still it is only significant as a human food in China and Japan—although it does sneak into our stomachs in disguised form and in huge quantities. The most familiar is still margarine. American margarine producers use close to 2 billion pounds of soybean oil a year (twice the amount of any other vegetable oil, animal fat, or non-fat dry milk).

BEAN AND PUMPKIN STEW WITH TWO MEATS

SERVES 8 TO 10

1 pound trimmed lean bottom round, cut into 1-inch cubes

1 pound trimmed lean boneless pork shoulder, cut into 1-inch cubes

½ cup all-purpose flour

3 tablespoons peanut, corn, or safflower oil

2 tablespoons unsalted butter

3 large onions, chopped coarse

2 tablespoons chopped garlic

1 sweet red pepper, chopped coarse

1 sweet green pepper, chopped coarse

½ teaspoon oregano

½ teaspoon crushed rosemary

½ teaspoon thyme

1 can (28 ounces) Italian plum tomatoes with juice

2 cups chicken stock, homemade or canned
Grated zest of 1 orange

2 pounds pumpkin, peeled, seeded, and cut into 1-inch chunks (or any winter squash such as butternut or Hubbard)

1 cup dried navy beans, cooked and drained

2 teaspoons salt or to taste

1 teaspoon freshly ground pepper

1. Dredge the beef and pork cubes in the flour until well coated. In a large sauté pan or Dutch oven heat 2 tablespoons of the oil until rippling and brown the meat on all sides in batches. Add a little more oil if meat sticks. As it is browned transfer with a slotted spoon to a large bowl.

2. Add the butter to the pan, and the onions, garlic, peppers, oregano, rosemary, and thyme. Stir and reduce heat to simmer and cook, stirring occasionally, until the onions are lightly browned, about 10 minutes.

3. Add the meat and any of its juices to the pan. Add the tomatoes with their juice, the broth, and the orange zest. Turn heat to high and bring to the boil. Reduce to a slow simmer and cook loosely covered for about 2 hours, or until the beef and pork are almost tender.

4. Add the pumpkin and beans to the stew and continue to simmer gently about 45 minutes or until the pumpkin and the meats are tender when pierced with a fork. Season with salt and plenty of pepper. Serve hot or make a day in advance and reheat over moderately low heat. Like most stews and soups this one will taste even better after standing.

BLACK-EYED PEAS WITH SWEET AND HOT SAUSAGES

SERVES 6

½ teaspoon minced garlic
¼ pound sweet Italian sausages,
   cut into ½-inch rounds
¼ pound hot Italian sausages, cut
   into ½-inch rounds
2 cans (16 ounces each)
   black-eyed peas, drained
   and rinsed
¼ cup fresh lemon juice
⅔ cup sun dried tomatoes in oil,
   drained and chopped fine
   or 5 tablespoons tomato paste
¼ cup minced celery
¼ cup minced fresh parsley
1 small onion, minced
   Salt and freshly ground pepper
   to taste

1. In a skillet cook the garlic, sweet sausage, and hot sausage over moderate heat, stirring and pressing on the sausage to remove fat. Cook until well browned, about 10 minutes. Drain on paper towels.

2. In a large saucepan combine the black-eyed peas, lemon juice, and sun dried tomatoes with 1¼ cups of water. Bring to the boil over moderately high heat. Add the sausages, turn heat down to simmer, and cook 2 or 3 minutes to meld flavors.

3. Just before serving, add the celery, parsley, and onions. Remove from heat and add salt and pepper to taste. Serve hot alone or over cooked rice.

APPLE AND BLACK BEAN PICADILLO

SERVES 6 TO 8

- 4 tablespoons peanut, corn, or safflower oil
- 4 medium onions, chopped coarse
- 2 tablespoons chopped garlic
  Salt to taste
- 1 teaspoon freshly ground pepper
- 2 pounds chopped very lean beef or 1 pound chopped beef plus 1 pound chopped lean pork (shoulder or butt)
- 1 can (35 ounces) Italian plum tomatoes, drained and chopped
- 3 canned jalapeño peppers, seeded and sliced into rings
- 1 can (4 ounces) chopped green chilies
- 2 pieces (4-inches by 1-inch) orange zest, julienned into slivers
- ½ cup raisins or currants
- ½ teaspoon cinnamon
- ½ teaspoon ground cloves
- ½ teaspoon allspice
- ½ teaspoon nutmeg, preferably freshly grated
- 2 large tart apples, peeled, cored, and cubed
- 1 can (16 ounces) black beans, drained and rinsed
- ¼ cup capers, drained

1. In a large sauté pan over moderately high heat, heat the oil until rippling, add the onions, garlic, salt, and pepper and sauté, stirring frequently, until onions are just golden.

2. Add the meat and cook, stirring, until it loses its red color.

3. Stir in the tomatoes, jalapeños, orange zest, raisins, and the spices. Simmer, uncovered, 20 to 30 minutes.

4. Ten minutes before serving, mix in the apples, beans, and capers; stir and simmer over low heat so that apples do not become mushy.

5. Transfer to deep serving bowl or covered dish and serve with rice.

CASSOULET

Cassoulet is French country (Southwest) baked beans. It takes time and effort. It can be prepared all at once, of course, but it can also be done piecemeal over two or three days, then assembled and baked later. This recipe serves a lot of diners and serves them well. But there's no reason why batches of it can't be frozen for baking at another time for another meal—with the oven doing all the work.

SERVES 10 TO 12

FOR THE BEANS

2 pounds dried Great Northern beans, soaked and drained

½ pound fresh pork rind, boiled for 20 minutes, refreshed under cold water, and cut into pieces 1″ square

1 pound lean salt pork or slab bacon, blanched for 10 minutes in 2 quarts of water, drained, refreshed under cold water, and patted dry

1 large onion, chopped coarse

4 medium carrots, sliced
Bouquet garni of ½ teaspoon thyme, 5 large cloves of garlic, peeled, small bunch of parsley, 2 bay leaves, and 3 cloves, all tied in cheese cloth
Salt to taste

1. In a large stockpot or kettle over high heat, bring 6 quarts of water to a rolling boil. Pour in the soaked beans, pork rind, salt pork, onion, carrots, and bouquet garni. Bring to the boil again, reduce heat to simmer and cook gently, uncovered, for 1½ hours. Skim off scum that rises to the surface during cooking time. Add more boiling water, if necessary, to keep beans just covered. Salt to taste at end of cooking time, cover, and allow beans to rest in cooking liquid until ready to use. Skim off fat when cooled.

FOR THE PORK

2½ to 3 pounds boned pork loin, all fat removed

2 garlic cloves, crushed in a press
Salt and freshly ground pepper to taste

1. Preheat oven to 500°. Rub the roast with garlic, salt, and pepper and place in a roasting pan with a cup of water. Roast at high heat for 15 minutes. Reduce oven to 350° and continue roasting for 1¼ hours more or until a meat thermometer registers an internal heat of 175°. Set aside. Reserve pan juices.

FOR THE LAMB

3 tablespoons peanut, corn, or safflower oil

2½ to 3 pounds boned lamb shoulder, cut in 2-inch chunks

2 medium onions, chopped fine

1 tablespoon minced garlic

6 tablespoons tomato paste

½ teaspoon thyme

½ teaspoon oregano

3 cups dry white wine or vermouth

3 cups beef or chicken stock, homemade or canned

Salt and freshly ground pepper to taste

1. In a large skillet or sauté pan over moderately high heat, heat the oil until rippling and brown the lamb chunks a few pieces at a time. Transfer browned pieces to a dish and repeat until all the lamb is browned.

2. Turn heat to moderate, add the onions to the pan and sauté, stirring frequently, until golden brown. Stir in the garlic and cook for 1 minute. Return the meat to the pan, stir a few times, and add the tomato paste, thyme, oregano, wine, and stock. Bring the liquid to a simmer. Season with salt and pepper, cover, and cook slowly for 1½ hours. Remove from heat and skim off fat when cooled.

FOR THE SAUSAGE

2 pounds hot Italian sausage or chorizos, cut into ½-inch rounds

1. Brown sausage pieces in a skillet over moderate heat. Drain on paper towels.

ASSEMBLING THE CASSOULET

Freshly ground pepper

2 cups fresh, coarse bread crumbs

½ cup minced fresh parsley

3 teaspoons minced garlic

3 tablespoons unsalted butter, melted

1. Drain the beans, reserving the liquid. Discard the bouquet garni. Cut the salt pork into ¼-inch slices. Set aside.

2. Cut the pork loin into 1 to 1½-inch chunks.

3. In a large (8 quart) casserole or baking dish spread a thick layer of beans. Cover with a layer each of pork, lamb, salt pork, and sausage. Repeat layers of beans and meats, ending with a last layer of beans. Add the pan juices from the lamb and pork loin and enough bean liquid to just barely cover the solids.

4. Mix the bread crumbs, parsley, and garlic together and spread evenly over the top of the casserole. Drizzle the melted butter over the bread crumbs. Set aside until ready to bake, or refrigerate. If freezing in 2 or 3 batches, do not spread with bread crumbs until transferred to baking dish and thawed.

5. Preheat oven to 400°.

6. On top of stove bring the casserole to a simmer over moderate heat. Remove from heat and set in upper half of oven. Bake for 20 minutes or until a crust has formed on top. With a wooden spoon, break the crust pushing it down into the cassoulet. Turn the oven down to 350° and bake another 20 minutes. Repeat crust procedure and baste surface with some of the juices. Repeat again in 15 minutes. Bake for 10 minutes more and serve from casserole. After a light first course or none at all, the only accompaniment cassoulet needs is a lively green salad made with a few pungent greens such as arugula, endive, and watercress. Keep the dessert simple—a refreshing fruit is right.

Instead of lamb you might want to substitute 2 ducks (about 5 pounds each), cut into at least 8 serving pieces each. Brown the duck pieces in batches evenly on both sides, set aside, and continue recipe for the lamb, using the duck instead. Be sure to skim off as much fat as possible after duck has cooled. This is best accomplished by chilling in the refrigerator until fat has congealed on top.

SORCERER'S APPRENTICE

*B*eans have always been associated with magic—and ghosts and witches. The story of Jack and the Beanstalk *relies on their magical qualities—growing a stalk so high it reached the sky, and overnight, too! Fortune tellers "toss" the beans to read the future—or "spill the beans" which has come to mean to tell all. The ancient Greeks believed Apollo, the sun god, was responsible for ripening the offerings of the earth, so they celebrated his name by holding "bean feasts," sacrificing to him the first of the year's bean crop. The Celts also held bean feasts or "Beanos" (not to be confused with the variation on Bingo, called Beano because it uses lima beans as markers) and on Twelfth Night a bean was hidden in a festive cake, the finder of the bean being crowned King of the evening's revels. These cakes are still being baked in some European countries—one example is France's Galette de Rois.*

BRAISED CHICKEN MIDDLE EASTERN STYLE WITH EGGPLANT AND CHICK-PEAS

SERVES 4 TO 6

2 medium eggplants, pared, cut into ½-inch thick pieces about 1½ inches long and 1 inch wide

1 tablespoon plus ¼ teaspoon salt

⅔ cup peanut, corn, or safflower oil

1 3-pound broiler-fryer chicken, cut into 8 pieces

3 medium onions, sliced thin

1 tablespoon plus 1 teaspoon sesame seeds, toasted for 1 minute in a dry skillet

2 teaspoons minced garlic

½ teaspoon cumin

½ teaspoon allspice

¼ teaspoon mace

¼ teaspoon ground cloves

1 can (1 pound) Italian plum tomatoes, drained and chopped

1 can (15 ounces) chick-peas, drained and rinsed

3 tablespoons plus 2 teaspoons fresh lemon juice

¼ teaspoon freshly ground pepper

2 tablespoons minced fresh flat-leafed parsley

1. In a bowl sprinkle the eggplant with 1 tablespoon of the salt, toss to mix well and transfer to a colander to drain for 30 minutes. Rinse under cold running water, drain, and dry with paper towels. Reserve.

2. In a large skillet or sauté pan heat the oil over moderately high heat until rippling. Gently add half the eggplant and fry, turning frequently, until eggplant begins to brown. Remove pieces with a slotted spoon or tongs to drain on paper towels. Repeat with remaining eggplant.

3. Pour off all but about 3 tablespoons of the oil and over moderate heat sauté as many pieces of chicken as will fit into the pan without touching, skin side down, until deep golden brown, about 10 minutes. Turn pieces with tongs and brown second side, about 6 to 8 minutes. Remove to drain on paper towels and repeat procedure with remaining pieces of chicken.

4. To the skillet add the onions. Turn heat to moderately high and sauté, stirring frequently until lightly browned, about 6 to 8 minutes. Stir in 1 tablespoon of the sesame seeds, the garlic, cumin, allspice, mace, and cloves and sauté, stirring, for 1 minute. Add tomatoes, chick-peas, 3 tablespoons of the lemon juice, and the salt and pepper.

5. Add chicken pieces. Bring to the boil, reduce heat to simmer, and cook until meat is so tender it separates easily from the bones, about 50 minutes.

6. Stir in reserved eggplant and parsley and simmer 10 minutes more. Taste and adjust seasoning. Transfer to serving platter and sprinkle with remaining lemon juice and sesame seeds.

This dish needs nothing more than a simple green salad and some rice or pita bread to complete the menu.

GARBURE—A MEAL-IN-ITSELF FRENCH COUNTRY SOUP

SERVES 10

2 pounds fresh ham such as hock, picnic shoulder, or pork butt

1 pound pork belly (unsmoked) or very lean salt pork, blanched 5 minutes and drained

3½ quarts water

1 pound dried Great Northern beans, soaked and rinsed

1 medium whole onion stuck with 2 or 3 whole cloves

3 tablespoons peanut, corn, or safflower oil

3 medium onions, sliced

2 leeks, trimmed, split lengthwise, carefully rinsed, and cut into 2-inch pieces

2 medium turnips, pared and quartered

1 tablespoon minced garlic plus 2 whole cloves garlic
Bouquet garni (3 sprigs of parsley, ½ teaspoon dried thyme, 1 bay leaf, and ½ teaspoon dried marjoram, all tied in a double layer of cheesecloth)

1 teaspoon freshly ground pepper

¼ teaspoon cayenne
Salt to taste

1. Place the ham hock and pork belly in a large soup pot or Dutch oven. Pour in 3½ quarts of water, turn heat to high, and bring to the boil. Turn down to simmer and cook, partially covered, 1 hour, skimming froth frequently.

2. Add to the pot the beans and the whole onion stuck with cloves. Continue simmering 1 hour longer, skimming froth as necessary.

3. In a skillet bring the oil to rippling over medium heat and add the sliced onions and leeks. Cover tightly and "sweat" the vegetables until they are soft, about 3 or 4 minutes. Add these to the pot along with the turnips. Turn the heat to moderate and bring to the low boil, uncovered.

4. Add the minced garlic and the bouquet garni. Add pepper and cayenne; cook, uncovered, 45 minutes. Add salt to taste.

5. In a blender or food processor, puree the garlic cloves, parsley, and bacon to a smooth paste and add to the pot. Add the cabbage, potatoes, and sausage. Turn up heat to high, bring to a boil, and then turn down heat to simmer. Cook, uncovered, 30 minutes.

6. When ready to serve remove meats to a platter, moisten with a few tablespoons of soup, cover loosely with foil, and keep warm. The soup should be very thick, almost porridgelike. If it is not, boil down to thicken. Taste and adjust seasoning.

7. Serve the soup as a first course, ladling it over slices of French bread in warm soup bowls. As a second course, slice the meats and serve them with the cornichons and hot peppers. Of course, the meat can be cut in small chunks and served in the soup.

1 medium head cabbage (green
  or savoy), trimmed and
  chopped coarse
2 or 3 sprigs parsley
2 slices bacon
3 medium boiling potatoes
  (about 1 pound) pared, cut
  in eighths
1 pound French garlic sausage, if
  available, or Italian cotechino,
  simmered for ½ hour in water,
  drained
10 thin slices of French bread run
  under the broiler for a few
  seconds, cornichons, pickled
  jalapeño or other hot
  peppers for garnish

A really authentic garbure would be served with a confit of duck and enriched with the fat from the confit. However, the soup is rich enough without it and the confit could cause a real imbalance in anyone (everyone!) watching his or her cholesterol.

ANCIENT PEAS AND CLUES

For the Greeks and the Romans legumes were important. They not only ate chick-peas and lentils, but peas—fresh and dried. They had learned of peas from the Aryans, that Eastern group of invaders, who probably found out about them from the Chinese—who were the first to eat them green. The pea spread throughout the Mediterranean as fast as the Romans did. The Aryans had already brought them into India. In the Middle Ages peas were an important source of protein in Europe. In a little reverse trade, the colonists brought them to the New World. In the middle 19th century the pea figured in the study of family traits and heredity. It was, if you remember your high school science courses, the Silesian priest and botanist, Gregor Johann Mendel (of Mendelian Law fame) who grew many generations of garden peas, crossing and hybridizing them to discover what characteristics are passed on to offspring under varying conditions and with various matings. His was the basis of all modern research into genetics and it was the pea that gave him the clue.

RAGOUT OF LAMB AND WHITE BEANS PROVENÇALE

SERVES 6 TO 8

5 tablespoons unsalted butter
5 tablespoons light Tuscan olive oil
½ cup minced shallots
2 tablespoons minced garlic
1 can (35 ounces) Italian plum tomatoes, drained and chopped coarse
1½ teaspoons thyme
1 teaspoon salt or to taste
1 teaspoon freshly ground pepper
1 tablespoon minced fresh parsley plus ½ cup
1 bay leaf
4 pounds boneless lamb shoulder, cut into 1-inch chunks
½ teaspoon sugar
1 tablespoon all-purpose flour
1 cup dry white wine
2 cups beef stock, homemade or canned
1 large sweet red pepper, cored, seeded, and cut in ½-inch dice
3 cups cooked Great Northern beans
1 can (2 ounces) flat anchovy fillets, drained and rinsed

1. In a medium saucepan melt 2 tablespoons of the butter and 2 tablespoons of the oil over moderate heat. Add the shallots and 1 tablespoon of the garlic and sauté for 1 minute or until golden. Add the tomatoes and cook, stirring frequently, for 5 minutes. Add thyme, salt and pepper, 1 tablespoon of the parsley, and bay leaf. Turn heat to low, partially cover, and simmer, stirring occasionally, until the juices evaporate and the mixture thickens, about 20 to 30 minutes. Set aside.

2. Preheat oven to 350°.

3. Dry the lamb on paper towels. In a large skillet or sauté pan, melt 1 tablespoon of the remaining butter and 2 tablespoons of the remaining oil over high heat. Add the lamb chunks in batches without crowding and sauté, turning them until they are browned on all sides, about 15 minutes altogether. Remove them as they are done with a slotted spoon and reserve in a bowl. If the meat begins to stick during browning, add more oil.

4. Pour off fat from the pan and add remaining butter and melt over moderate heat. Return lamb and its accumulated juices to the pan, sprinkle with sugar and flour, and cook for 2 minutes, stirring and tossing, until meat is glazed and well browned. Transfer lamb with a slotted spoon to a large heat-proof casserole.

5. Add the wine to the skillet. Turn the heat to high and bring to the boil, scraping up any brown bits clinging to the bottom and sides of the pan, until the wine is reduced to 3 or 4 tablespoons, about 3 to 5 minutes.

6. Add the reserved tomato mixture and the beef stock, bring to the boil, and pour over the lamb in the casserole. Cover tightly and bake in the center of the oven for 1½ hours or

until the lamb is tender when pierced with a fork. Remove from the oven, let cool, and refrigerate overnight.

7. Scrape away and discard any congealed fat from the top of the ragout. Remove and discard the bay leaf. Place the casserole, covered, over moderately low heat on top of the stove.

8. In a small skillet heat 1 tablespoon of the oil over moderate heat, add the pepper and cook, stirring frequently, until just tender, about 6 to 8 minutes.

9. Add the pepper and white beans to the casserole and stir in gently. Cook, covered, for 15 minutes. Add the remaining garlic, the remaining ½ cup of parsley, and the anchovies. Stir to combine. Cover the casserole and cook 5 minutes more. Taste for seasoning and serve.

MEXICAN-STYLE GREEN BEANS WITH CARROTS AND CHORIZO

SERVES 4

1 tablespoon unsalted butter
1 chorizo sausage, casing removed, crumbled
3 medium carrots, scraped, cut into ¼-inch sticks then into 2-inch lengths
½ pound green beans, cut into 2-inch lengths
1 teaspoon fresh lemon juice
1 tablespoon Dijon mustard
Salt and freshly ground pepper to taste

1. In a skillet over moderate heat melt the butter and add the chorizo. Sauté, stirring frequently, until most of the fat has been rendered out.

2. Add the carrots and cook, covered, for 5 minutes.

3. Stir in the green beans and cook, covered, 5 minutes more or until vegetables are crisp tender.

4. Turn heat to low and stir in lemon juice, mustard, salt, and pepper. When well combined, transfer to warm platter and serve.

NEW ORLEANS BABY LIMAS WITH SAUSAGE AND RICE

SERVES 8

1 pound dried baby lima beans
   (butterbeans or white
   limas), soaked and drained
1 medium onion, chopped
1 large carrot, chopped fine
2 teaspoons chopped garlic
1 pound smoked sausage such as
   kielbasa or andouille, cut
   into 1-inch slices
1 teaspoon Tabasco sauce or to
   taste
1 large bay leaf or 2 small, left
   whole
½ teaspoon thyme
½ teaspoon freshly ground pepper
   Salt to taste
2 cups unconverted long-grain rice
½ cup minced parsley

1. In a large saucepan or soup pot over moderately high heat place all the ingredients, except the salt, rice, and parsley, with enough water to cover by 1 inch (about 2 quarts) and bring to the boil. Reduce heat to simmer and cook, covered, for 1½ to 2 hours or until beans are tender but not falling apart. Add salt to taste. There should be some liquid in the pot, enough to form a rich gravy. Remove cover and allow to cool slightly for 15 minutes. Cover pot and allow ingredients to steep in the gravy for 2 hours or more before reheating.

2. In a saucepan over high heat bring 4½ cups of water to the boil, pour in the rice, reduce heat to simmer, and cook rice, covered, for 18 to 20 minutes or until all the liquid is absorbed.

3. While rice is cooking, gently reheat beans, covered, over moderately low heat. Serve over rice. Sprinkle each serving with parsley.

SAVORY OXTAIL AND WHITE BEAN STEW FRAGRANT WITH FENNEL

SERVES 6

3 pounds trimmed oxtails, cut by butcher into 2-inch pieces

¼ cup peanut, corn, or safflower oil

2 medium onions, chopped

1 tablespoon minced garlic

3 cups canned beef broth

1 pound fennel, sliced thin

½ teaspoon oregano

½ teaspoon marjoram

1 pound dried Great Northern or white kidney beans, soaked and drained

2 scallions (both white and green parts), sliced thin

2 tablespoons minced fresh parsley

1. In a large saucepan or sauté pan over moderate heat, brown the oxtails in batches in 2 tablespoons of the oil. Transfer them to a bowl.

2. In the same pan over moderate heat sauté the onions, stirring frequently, in the remaining 2 tablespoons of oil until soft. Add the garlic and cook until golden.

3. Return the oxtails and any accumulated liquid to the pan with the onion-garlic mixture. Add enough broth to just cover them. Add the fennel, oregano, and marjoram and bring to the boil. Turn down heat to simmer and cook, covered, adding more broth when necessary to keep the oxtails just covered, for 1½ hours.

4. Stir in the beans and enough water, if needed, to just cover the solids. Turn heat to high, bring to the boil, and skim off any froth. Turn down heat to simmer and cook, loosely covered, for another 1½ hours, or until the beans are tender.

5. Remove 1 cup of the beans and puree in a food processor or blender. Stir puree into the stew, transfer to a deep covered dish or tureen, sprinkle with scallions and parsley and serve.

BRAZILIAN FEIJOADA— NATIONAL DISH OF BLACK BEANS AND RICE WITH WHAT-HAVE-YOU OF PIG

A *Feijoada Completa* is not a dish to serve to the faint-of-heart. We mean that literally. Feijoada, like cassoulet, is a guaranteed artery-clogger. If the consumers of this dish are near and dear to you, you should post the equivalent of a "Surgeon General's Warning" on your dining table: *This Dish Could Be Dangerous To Your Health.*

It is delicious, however, and probably you wouldn't want to make it more than once a year anyway. It is not cheap to prepare, by any means. It requires time and determination—in the cooking, it goes without saying, and in the shopping as well. The combination of flavors, textures, and colors is unique and exciting and should be experienced in the country of origin. Barring that possibility we offer a recipe that, although not authentic in ingredients, makes a pass at authenticity of flavor and texture. Only true aficionados can tell if it's a completed pass or not.

SERVES 8 TO 10

THE MEATS

- 1 3-pound smoked beef tongue, soaked in cold water overnight, drained, simmered in water to cover for 2½ hours, skinned, and trimmed of fat and gristle
- 1½ pound piece of jerked beef (beef jerky), soaked in cold water overnight, drained, and simmered in water to cover for 30 minutes
- 2 pigs' feet, well scrubbed, each cut into quarters

1. In a very large soup pot or stockpot bring 12 cups (3 quarts) of water to the boil and add the beans, bay leaf, beef jerky, pigs' feet, and slab bacon. Bring to a boil again and skim off any froth that rises to the surface. Turn heat down to simmer, cover, and cook for 1 hour.

2. Uncover and add the tongue and pork butt. Cover and continue cooking 1 hour more. Check water occasionally to be sure beans are moist and soupy.

3. Heat bacon drippings in a large skillet or sauté pan over moderate heat and add the onions and garlic. Sauté, stirring frequently, for about 5 minutes, or until soft and just golden. Stir in the tomatoes, peppers, orange zest, and salt and pepper. Add 2 cups of the beans and their liquid to the sauce. Mash them into the sauce, stir, and simmer 15

½-pound piece lean smoked
slab bacon

3 pounds fully cooked smoked
pork butt (optional)

1 pound chorizo sausage or
kielbasa sausage, cut into
2-inch pieces

1 pound hot Italian sausage, cut
into 2-inch pieces

THE BEANS

2 pounds dried black beans,
soaked, rinsed, and drained

1 bay leaf

3 tablespoons bacon drippings or
lard

4 medium onions, chopped

2 tablespoons chopped garlic

1 cup chopped, drained Italian
plum tomatoes

2 small hot red peppers, seeded,
deveined, and chopped fine

2 4-inch strips of orange zest

1 teaspoon salt or to taste

1 teaspoon freshly ground pepper

THE ACCOMPANIMENTS

(recipes follow)

    Brazilian Rice

    Farofa

    Pepper and Lime Sauce

    Shredded Greens

4 or 5 large navel oranges,
peeled, sliced thin, or
chunked

FAROFA

½ pound unsalted butter

2 medium onions, chopped
coarse or sliced thin

1 pound uncooked Cream of
Wheat

    Salt to taste

2 tablespoons minced parsley

---

minutes more to combine and thicken. Remove from heat
and set aside.

4. Preheat oven to 250°.

5. After beans have cooked for the second hour, remove
tongue to a heatproof platter, cover with foil, and place in a
low oven to keep warm.

6. Add the sausages and stir in the reserved sauce. Check for
moistness and simmer, covered, for 1 hour more.

7. Lift out all the meats and transfer to the platter along with
the tongue. Skim fat from surface of beans. Remove beans
from heat.

8. Slice all the meats. Leave the sausages in 2-inch pieces.
Transfer the beans—which should have a somewhat soupy
consistency—to a large bowl or tureen. Arrange the meats
on a serving platter. Place the accompaniments—the rice,
farofa, pepper and lime sauce, greens, and sliced oranges—in
separate bowls.

9. Each diner ladles a generous portion of beans over the rice,
selects some of the meats, and adds the accompaniments.

Cachaca, a potent Brazilian rum, is traditionally downed with
feijoada to aid digestion. But your favorite rum will do nicely—or
beer to cool the palate.

ACCOMPANIMENTS

Authentic farofa is made from manioc or cassava meal. Cream
of Wheat, which this recipe calls for, is available everywhere
and serves as a more than satisfying substitute.

1. In a large skillet or sauté pan over moderate heat, melt 4
tablespoons (½ stick) of the butter. When the foam subsides add the onions and, stirring frequently, sauté until
they turn golden brown, about 7 to 9 minutes.

2. Stir in the remaining butter and when it has melted, stir in
Cream of Wheat and salt. Turn heat down to low and
cook, stirring constantly, until cereal grains are separate and
lightly browned. Add the parsley and stir to combine.
Transfer to a serving bowl and pass at the table to be
sprinkled over the feijoada.

SHREDDED GREENS

4 pounds collard greens, kale,
 or mustard greens, trimmed of
 tough stems and shredded
 into ¼-inch strips
½ pound lean salt pork or bacon,
 in small dice
 Salt to taste
½ teaspoon freshly ground pepper

1. Blanch greens in 4 quarts of boiling water for 3 minutes. Drain in colander, pressing down on greens to extract as much liquid as possible.

2. In a large skillet or sauté pan over moderately high heat, fry salt pork, stirring frequently, until crisp. Transfer with slotted spoon to paper towels to drain and reserve pork fat.

3. In the same skillet, heat pork fat until smoking. Add greens and cook, stirring frequently, until tender, about 5 to 10 minutes. Add salt to taste and pepper. Transfer to serving bowl and top with crisp pork bits.

MOLHO DE PIMENTA E LIMAO (PEPPER AND LIME SAUCE)

2 red, ripe tomatoes, chopped or
 1 cup chopped and drained
 canned Italian plum tomatoes
2 small hot red peppers, seeded,
 deveined, and chopped fine
 or 4 bottled Tabasco peppers,
 drained and chopped fine
½ cup fresh lime juice
½ cup light Tuscan olive oil
1 large red onion, chopped fine
1 tablespoon minced parsley
1 tablespoon minced garlic

1. In a small bowl mix all the ingredients. Allow to steep for at least an hour before serving—or refrigerate covered until ready to use.

Authentic Pepper and Lime Sauce recipes often call for some of the bean liquid, scooped from the pot while the feijoada is simmering, to be added to the sauce. If you would like to be more authentic add about ¼ cup bean liquid, retrieved during second hour of cooking and reserved for this purpose.

BRAZILIAN RICE

3 tablespoons bacon fat or light
 Tuscan olive oil
1 large onion, chopped
2 teaspoons chopped garlic
 Salt to taste
½ teaspoon freshly ground pepper
2 cups unconverted long-grain
 rice
4½ cups water or canned chicken
 broth
1 cup chopped and drained
 canned Italian plum tomatoes

1. In a saucepan over moderate heat, heat the fat until it ripples, add the onion and sauté, stirring constantly, until soft and just golden, about 5 minutes. Add the garlic, salt and pepper, and stir for 1 minute more.

2. Add the rice, stir for 3 to 4 minutes or until all the grains are coated with oil and are beginning to brown. Add the water and tomatoes and bring to the boil. Turn heat down to simmer, cover, and cook for 18 to 20 minutes or until all the liquid has been absorbed. Transfer to heated serving bowl and serve just as a bed for the beans.

CASSEROLE OF BEANS WITH CHICKEN BREASTS AND VEGETABLES

SERVES 6

1 pound dried navy beans, soaked, rinsed and drained

2 large carrots, pared

2 medium onions, halved

1 bay leaf

½ teaspoon dried thyme or 1 tablespoon fresh thyme

½ teaspoon crushed rosemary or 1 tablespoon fresh rosemary

1 teaspoon freshly ground pepper

2 tomatoes, peeled, seeded, and chopped or 3 canned Italian plum tomatoes, drained and chopped

3 whole chicken breasts with bones and skin (about 4 to 4½ pounds)

1 tablespoon salt

1 tablespoon minced garlic

¼ cup minced fresh parsley

1. In a large stock pot or sauté pan over high heat, bring 2 quarts of water to the boil. Add beans, carrots, onions, bay leaf, thyme, rosemary, and pepper. Turn heat down to simmer and cook, partially covered, skimming any foam occasionally, for 45 minutes. Add tomatoes.

2. Add the chicken breasts and cook, partially covered, 45 minutes more.

3. Remove the chicken breasts, skin and debone them, discarding both, and cut into ½-inch slices. Return to beans. With a slotted spoon remove the carrots and onions and chop coarsely. Return to beans.

4. Add the salt, garlic, and parsley and turn heat to high. Bring to the boil, turn heat down to simmer, and cook, uncovered, 5 minutes. Taste and adjust seasoning. Discard bay leaf and serve.

If there is too much liquid left after chicken breasts are removed, turn up heat and boil down while skinning, boning, and slicing chicken. Turn down heat before returning chicken to beans.

ITALIAN COUNTRY DISH OF LENTILS WITH COTECHINO SAUSAGE

SERVES 6

1 cotechino sausage (about 3 inches in diameter by 8 inches long)
2 tablespoons peanut, corn, or safflower oil
1 small onion, chopped fine
1 celery stalk, chopped fine
1 bay leaf
¼ cup chopped parsley
¼ teaspoon crushed rosemary
1 cup lentils, rinsed and drained
½ teaspoon freshly ground pepper
Salt to taste
1 teaspoon fresh lemon juice

1. Soak cotechino well covered with water for about 4 hours or overnight. Drain and place in a large pot with 3 quarts of water, cover, and over high heat, bring to the boil. Turn heat to low and cook for 2½ hours. *Do not* puncture the skin during cooking. When cooking time is completed, turn off heat and allow to rest in the cooking liquid for ½ hour.

2. About an hour before cotechino is through resting, heat the oil in a saucepan over moderate heat and when rippling add the onion and sauté, stirring frequently, until golden. Stir in the celery and cook, for a minute more. Add the bay leaf, parsley, rosemary, and lentils and stir until they are well coated with oil.

3. Add 2 cups or ladlesful of the cotechino cooking liquid to the lentils and pour in enough simmering water to cover. Turn heat down to moderately low and simmer gently, covered, for 35 minutes or until lentils are tender. Add more cotechino cooking liquid, if necessary, to keep lentils just covered.

4. About 5 minutes before lentils are done, stop adding water. If there is still water in the pot, uncover, turn up heat to moderate and evaporate it while stirring the lentils. Add pepper and salt to taste and stir in lemon juice.

5. Remove the cotechino from its liquid and cut into ½-inch slices. Discard any skin. Transfer lentils to a heated oval platter and arrange the slices of cotechino, overlapping, down the center.

COTECHINO SAUSAGE WITH WHITE BEANS AND TOMATO SAUCE

This recipe is as different from the previous cotechino recipe as an Irish Beef Stew is from goulash. Only the cotechino remains the same.

SERVES 6

1 cotechino sausage (about 3 inches in diameter by 8 inches long)
¼ cup light Tuscan olive oil
1 medium onion, chopped
1 tablespoon chopped garlic
½ teaspoon dried basil
½ teaspoon oregano
½ teaspoon red pepper flakes
1 large carrot, chopped
1 celery stalk, chopped
1 can (35 ounces) Italian plum tomatoes, chopped coarse, with juice
3 cups cooked or canned white kidney beans or cannellini, drained and rinsed
Salt and freshly ground pepper to taste

1. Soak cotechino well covered with water for about 4 hours or overnight. Drain and place in a large pot with 3 quarts of water. Cover, and over high heat, bring to the boil. Turn heat to low and cook for 2½ hours. *Do not* puncture the skin during cooking. When cooking time is completed, turn off heat and allow to rest in the cooking liquid for ½ hour.

2. While the cotechino is resting, heat the oil in a flameproof casserole or large saucepan over moderate heat. When rippling add the onion and sauté, stirring frequently, until golden. Stir in the garlic and sauté until it begins to color. Add the basil, oregano, red pepper, carrot, and celery and cook, stirring occasionally for 5 minutes. Add the chopped tomatoes and their juice, turn heat down to moderately low, and cook at a slow simmer for 20 minutes. Add the beans and cook 5 minutes more.

3. Preheat oven to 350°.

4. Remove the cotechino from its liquid and cut into ½-inch slices. Discard any skin and transfer slices to casserole. Cover and place casserole in the middle third of the oven and cook for 20 minutes. If the sauce seems too watery, return to the top of the stove, uncover, turn heat to high, and reduce liquid. Add salt and pepper if necessary. Stir and serve.

GREEN BEAN
AND PROSCIUTTO FRITTATA
(OPEN-FACED OMELET)

SERVES 4

6 eggs
½ teaspoon salt or to taste
½ teaspoon freshly ground pepper
1½ cups chopped boiled or
    steamed green beans
½ cup julienned prosciutto
    (available at Italian markets)
1 cup grated Parmesan cheese
3 tablespoons butter

1. Beat eggs until well blended.

2. Add salt, pepper, green beans, prosciutto, and Parmesan and mix thoroughly.

3. Heat butter in a large skillet (12 inches) over moderate heat. Allow foam to subside and pour in egg mixture. Move the green beans and prosciutto slivers around with a wooden spoon or rubber spatula to distribute them evenly. Turn heat to low and cook frittata, shaking the pan occasionally, until it is set except for a thin layer of uncooked egg on the surface, about 12 to 15 minutes of very slow cooking.

4. While frittata is cooking, preheat broiler. When frittata reaches the stage described above, remove from heat and broil 2 inches from heat until top is set but not browned, about 30 seconds to 2 minutes. Cut into wedges and serve from skillet or transfer to warm platter and serve immediately.

THREE-BEAN PUMPKIN AND CHORIZO STEW

SERVES 6

1 tablespoon chopped garlic

2 large onions, sliced

¾ cup light Tuscan olive oil

½ cup dried red kidney beans, soaked and drained

½ cup dried lima beans, soaked and drained

½ cup dried chick-peas, soaked and drained

½ pound chorizo sausage, sliced

1 cup homemade or canned tomato sauce

2 cups beef stock, homemade or canned

1 teaspoon cayenne

3 cups peeled pumpkin, cut into ½-inch dice

½ cup minced fresh parsley
Salt and freshly ground pepper to taste

1. In a large saucepan over moderately high heat sauté the garlic and onions in the oil, stirring frequently, until golden, about 7 to 10 minutes. Add the beans, the chorizo, tomato sauce, beef stock, and cayenne. Bring to the boil, turn down heat to simmer, and cook the mixture, covered, stirring occasionally, for 2 hours or until the beans are tender.

2. Add the pumpkin and cook 20 minutes longer, covered, or until pumpkin is tender.

3. Stir in parsley and salt and pepper to taste. Transfer to heated, covered, serving dish.

*A*gain, because beans are cheap and plentiful and always have been, the expressions *not worth beans* or similarly, *worth beans* have been around since the 13th century. Americans, always more expansive than others, changed these expressions in 1860 to *not worth a hill of beans.*

GINGERED WHITE BEAN SALAD WITH CHICKEN AND CHUTNEY

SERVES 4 TO 6

1 cup dried Great Northern beans, cooked and cooled
3 slices bacon, cooked till crisp, drained and crumbled
3 tablespoons vegetable oil
2 tablespoons white wine vinegar
1 small onion, minced
¾ cup diced cooked chicken
½ teaspoon salt
½ teaspoon freshly ground pepper
½ cup minced fresh parsley
½ cup shredded romaine lettuce
3 tablespoons minced crystallized ginger
2 tablespoons chopped walnuts
1 tablespoon chopped fresh coriander (cilantro)
3 tablespoons mango chutney or bottled chutney

1. Place the beans in salad bowl and add the rest of the ingredients.

2. Toss gently to combine. Chill, covered, for 1 hour. Toss again and serve.

WHERE THERE'S A CURD THERE'S A WAY

Soybeans were first cultivated in China around 3000 B.C. But it took thousands of years for even the ingenious Chinese to invent bean curd. It happened about 200 A.D. Like in our West, there were range wars in China. Chinese farmers fought off Tartar and Mongol herdsmen, their mortal enemies and perhaps, because of this enmity, never developed a taste for milk and dairy products. Instead they make their own kind of milk from the soybean and soybean cheese.

CHICKEN DINNER IN A POT WITH GREEN BEANS AND BLACK-EYED PEAS

SERVES 4 TO 8

1 3½- to 4-pound chicken, cut
   into 8 serving pieces
2 carrots, grated coarse
1 sweet green pepper, seeded,
   deveined, and cut into
   ½-inch dice
1 sweet red pepper, seeded,
   deveined, and cut into
   ½-inch dice
8 scallions (both white and green
   parts), sliced thin
2 medium red, ripe tomatoes,
   chopped or 4 canned Italian plum
   tomatoes, drained and chopped
2 cups chicken stock, homemade
   or canned
   Salt to taste
1 teaspoon freshly ground pepper
½ pound green beans, cut into
   2-inch lengths
¼ small head of cabbage, shredded
2 cups cooked or canned
   black-eyed peas, drained
   and rinsed
½ cup snipped fresh dill
½ cup chopped parsley
4 ounces dry thin egg noodles
2 egg yolks
⅔ cup sour cream, crème fraîche,
   or yogurt
¼ cup fresh lemon juice

1. In a large saucepan or soup pot, combine chicken, carrots, peppers, scallions, and tomatoes. Add stock, 3 cups water, salt to taste, and pepper. Bring to the boil over moderately high heat, turn heat down to simmer and cook, loosely covered, for 45 minutes, skimming froth occasionally. Turn off heat and allow to rest for 5 minutes. Skim off any fat from surface.

2. Turn on heat and return chicken to simmer. Add the green beans, cabbage, and black-eyed peas. Cook for 15 minutes.

3. Add the dill, parsley, and egg noodles and cook until noodles are tender, about 5 minutes.

4. In a small bowl whisk the egg yolks and sour cream until well blended. Gradually whisk in ¼ cup of the hot cooking liquid and stir the mixture into the pot. Stir in the lemon juice. Taste and adjust seasoning. Serve in large soup bowls.

With an adjustment in cooking time this can be turned into a fish stew rather than chicken. Substitute 8 small fillets of firm-fleshed fish (tile or monkfish work well) for the chicken, combine *all* the ingredients up to and including the black-eyed peas, and simmer for 15 to 20 minutes or until the fish flakes when tested with a fork. Continue with steps 3 and 4. Fish stock or bottled clam juice may be substituted for the chicken stock, if desired.

TWO-TEXTURED WHITE BEANS WITH SAUSAGE AU GRATIN

SERVES 6

2 cups chopped canned Italian plum tomatoes with their juice

1 recipe Piquant White Bean Puree (p. 239)

½ teaspoon crumbled sage

3 cups cooked Great Northern or white kidney beans or canned cannellini beans, drained and rinsed

12 small sweet Italian sausages, pricked well with a fork

½ cup fine, fresh bread crumbs

½ cup freshly grated Parmesan cheese

4 tablespoons (½ stick) unsalted butter, melted

1. In a saucepan over moderate heat bring the tomatoes to the boil. Turn heat down to simmer and add the bean puree and the sage. Stir until well combined. Stir in the whole beans and cook until heated through.

2. In a skillet cook the sausages in ½ cup water, covered, over high heat until the water is nearly evaporated. Remove cover, turn heat down to moderate, and brown sausages, turning them frequently.

3. Preheat oven to 375°.

4. Transfer the bean mixture to a 3- to 4-quart shallow baking dish and arrange the sausages in one layer over the beans, pressing them into the mixture.

5. In a bowl combine the bread crumbs and the Parmesan. Sprinkle the mixture over the beans and sausages. Drizzle the melted butter over the dish and bake in the oven for 30 to 40 minutes or until the top is golden brown and the bean-sausage mixture is bubbling.

FRAGRANT BAKED SHORT RIBS WITH BEANS, BARLEY AND POTATOES (CHOLENT)

A Jewish dish of Palestinian origin usually served at the end of the Sabbath services. Often this dish was cooked in the neighborhood baker's oven—left from Friday before sundown until Saturday afternoon. Originally made with chick-peas rather than beans, olive oil instead of chicken fat and lamb rather than short ribs. The Diaspora changed its name as well as its ingredients, from *hamim* (Hebrew for hot) to *cholent* (a variation, it is thought, of the Yiddish word *shul-ent*, meaning conclusion of the synagogue service).

SERVES 6 TO 8

1 cup dried white beans, lima beans, or chick-peas prepared by Quick Soaking Method
3 tablespoons rendered chicken fat
3 medium onions, chopped
3 garlic cloves, crushed
4 small baking potatoes, peeled, cut into ¾-inch pieces
½ cup barley
3 pounds short ribs of beef, trimmed of fat
1 teaspoon salt or to taste
1 teaspoon freshly ground pepper
1½ teaspoons paprika
1 tablespoon flour

1. Drain beans. Set aside.

2. In a heavy saucepan or casserole over moderate heat, heat the chicken fat. Add the onions and garlic and sauté for 10 minutes or until golden, stirring frequently.

3. Add the drained beans, potatoes, and barley to the onions and stir until combined.

4. Place the meat in the center of the pot. Combine salt, pepper, paprika, and flour and sprinkle mixture over meat.

5. Add boiling water to cover ½ inch above ingredients.

6. Cover and cook over very low heat for 4½ hours, checking the pot every so often to see that the ingredients do not burn and adding a little water only if necessary (the finished dish should be very thick with almost no liquid remaining).

7. Set oven to 500°. Fifteen minutes to ½ hour before serving, remove cover and place pot in oven. When top starts to brown and become crusty, crush the crust into the rest of the beans and allow a second crust to form.

8. Serve from the saucepan, spooning bean mixture and meat into each plate.

SMOKY RED BEANS AND RICE WITH HAM HOCKS AND SAUSAGE

SERVES 6

3½ to 4 pounds ham hocks (about 6)
10 cups water
3 cups chopped celery
3 medium onions, finely chopped
3 sweet green peppers, finely chopped
6 bay leaves
2 teaspoons white pepper
2 teaspoons thyme
2 tablespoons minced garlic
1½ teaspoons oregano
1 teaspoon freshly ground black pepper
1 teaspoon Tabasco sauce or more to taste
1½ pounds smoked sausage (preferably andouille, kielbasa, or other well-smoked pork sausage) cut into bite-sized pieces
1 pound dried red kidney beans, soaked, drained, 6 cups of liquid reserved
4 cups Special Rice (recipe follows)

1. In a large saucepan or Dutch oven place the ham hocks, water, and the rest of the ingredients, excepting the sausage, beans, and rice. Stir, cover, and bring to the boil over high heat. Reduce heat and simmer for 30 minutes, stirring occasionally, until meat is tender.

2. Remove ham hock from pot and set aside.

3. Add the drained beans and 4 cups of soaking liquid to remaining liquid in the pot. Bring to the boil over high heat. Turn heat down to simmer and cook for 30 minutes, stirring occasionally.

4. Add sausage and 2 cups boiling water and continue to simmer, stirring and scraping bottom of pan often for 30 minutes or more until beans are very tender and almost falling apart. Beans should not be dry. They should be slightly soupy.

5. Add the ham hocks to the beans and cook over low heat, stirring, for 10 minutes more, to heat through.

6. To serve, place a generous amount of rice in the center of a dinner plate, add a ham hock to one side and a few pieces of sausage to the other. Spoon a goodly amount of red beans around the rice. Pick out and discard bay leaves.

SPECIAL RICE

SERVES 6

2 tablespoons butter
2 medium onions, chopped fine
2 teaspoons minced garlic
1 teaspoon salt
½ to 1 teaspoon freshly ground pepper
2 cups unconverted long-grain rice
4½ cups chicken stock, homemade or canned, or water

1. In a medium saucepan with a cover, melt butter over moderate heat and sauté onions and garlic until wilted and lightly golden.

2. Add salt, pepper, and rice. Stir until rice is hot and thoroughly coated with butter. Fry a moment longer.

3. Add liquid to the pot. Do not stir. Bring to the boil, then lower heat to simmer and cook, covered, for 20 minutes or until all liquid is absorbed and rice is tender.

FISH STEAKS GRILLED IN MISO MARINADE

SERVES 4 TO 6

½ cup miso (light, dark, or in-between)
6 tablespoons water
¼ cup mirin (rice wine) or sweet sherry
4 to 6 fish steaks, ½-inch to ¾-inch thick, patted dry with paper towels
1 tablespoon toasted sesame seeds
1 teaspoon freshly ground pepper

1. In a small saucepan over moderately low heat cook the miso, water, and mirin, stirring occasionally, until it forms a thick paste, about 4 minutes.

2. Pour mixture into a baking pan or flat dish and arrange fish steaks on top in a single layer. Allow to marinate for 15 minutes and turn steaks over. Cover and refrigerate at least 6 hours or overnight, turning once or twice.

3. Drain fish, reserving the marinade for another use, if desired, and grill fish in preheated broiler or on a prepared charcoal grill about 2 inches from heat source until just opaque, about 3 minutes on each side. Arrange on a serving platter, sprinkle with sesame seeds and pepper, and serve.

CRANBERRY BEAN AND SHRIMP FRITTATA (OPEN-FACED OMELET)

Cranberry beans are very popular in Italy. You'll find them fresh, at the greengrocer's in a pod streaked with red and tan. Pinto beans can stand in for them when they're not available. But you should find them canned at the supermarket.

SERVES 4 TO 6

1 pound medium shrimp, boiled 1 minute, shelled, and cut in half lengthwise

1½ cups cooked or canned cranberry (borlotti, Roman) beans, rinsed and drained

8 eggs

2 tablespoons minced fresh parsley

½ teaspoon salt or to taste

1 can (4 ounces) whole green chilies, drained and cut into ¼-inch dice

⅛ teaspoon cayenne or more to taste

½ teaspoon freshly ground pepper

1 tablespoon peanut, corn, or safflower oil

2 tablespoons unsalted butter

3 tablespoons grated Parmesan cheese

1. Place shrimp and beans in a medium bowl.

2. Beat eggs, parsley, salt, green chilies, cayenne, and pepper until well blended. Stir into shrimp and beans.

3. Heat butter and oil in a large skillet (12 inches) over moderate heat. Allow foam to subside and pour in egg mixture. Turn heat to low and cook frittata, shaking the pan occasionally, until it is set except for a thin uncooked layer of eggs on the surface, about 12 to 15 minutes of very slow cooking.

4. While frittata is cooking, preheat broiler. When frittata reaches stage described above, remove from heat and sprinkle with Parmesan. Broil 2 inches from heat until top is lightly browned, about 30 seconds to 2 minutes. Cut into wedges and serve from skillet or transfer to warm platter and serve immediately.

This is a quick supper dish, especially nice on a summer evening served with crusty French bread and a fresh salad or at brunch accompanied by popovers with juicy crisp melon to start.

Unlike a French omelet, a frittata is firm and set, yet not dry.

CATALAN-STYLE BAKED SALT COD WITH BEANS

SERVES 4

1¾ pounds pure white salt cod, as thick as possible (available at Italian and Hispanic markets)
½ pound dried Great Northern beans, soaked and drained
1 hambone
1 leek, trimmed and well rinsed
1 teaspoon salt or to taste
½ teaspoon freshly ground pepper
2 tablespoons minced garlic
1 tablespoon plus 1 teaspoon paprika
¾ cup dry sherry
¼ cup minced fresh parsley

1. In a large bowl soak salt cod in plenty of water and place in the refrigerator for 36 hours or more or until most of the salt has leached out and the fish is pliable. Change the water often, whenever you think of it, during soaking.

2. Place the beans in a saucepan with enough water to cover along with the hambone and leek. Bring to the boil over moderately high heat, turn down heat to simmer, and skim off any foam rising to surface. Cook, covered, 1 hour, then add 1 teaspoon salt and pepper. Continue cooking until beans are tender, about 1 hour, adding more water, if necessary.

3. Preheat oven to 350°.

4. Drain cod and pat dry with paper towels. Cut into 4 serving pieces. Heat oil in a large skillet or sauté pan over moderate heat until rippling and add cod. Sauté, turning, until lightly golden brown on both sides, about 2 minutes per side. Transfer to a baking dish in which the fish fits snugly.

5. In the same skillet over moderately high heat, stir 1 tablespoon of the garlic, paprika, and sherry and boil for 1 minute. Pour over fish. Sprinkle remaining garlic, paprika and parsley over cod and bake until fish is opaque in the center, about 15 to 20 minutes. Serve immediately on a warm platter surrounded by the beans.

SHRIMP WITH BEANS ANNA CAPRI

SERVES 4

2 tablespoons light Tuscan olive oil

1 tablespoon chopped garlic

½ teaspoon red pepper flakes

1 pound medium shrimp, shelled and deveined (for appearance only)

1 tablespoon capers, drained

12 black brine-cured olives, halved and pitted

12 cherry tomatoes, halved

1 can (16 ounces) cannellini beans, drained and rinsed

½ cup dry white wine

1 tablespoon fresh lemon juice

1 tablespoon chopped fresh parsley

½ teaspoon salt or to taste

¼ teaspoon freshly ground pepper

2 tablespoons unsalted butter

1. In a large skillet or sauté pan, heat the oil over moderately high heat. Add the garlic and red pepper flakes and sauté until garlic is golden.

2. Add the shrimp and sauté for 1 minute, stirring. Add the capers, olives, and tomatoes and cook, stirring, 1 minute or until tomatoes are softened but still hold their shape.

3. Add the beans, the wine, the lemon juice, the parsley, and the salt and pepper. Cook for 1 minute. Add butter, 1 tablespoon at a time, stirring till blended. Serve.

*I*f the Pilgrims followed the Indians' lead in planting beans with corn, later farmers substituted beanwood to stake their vines. By 1821 this name was changed to beanpole, a long, thin stick which soon came to mean a tall, skinny person like Abe Lincoln—in France, the excessively thin are called haricot vert (string bean, just as here).

CURRIED WHITE BEAN AND MUSSEL SALAD WITH TWO PEPPERS

SERVES 4 TO 6

3 pounds mussels, steamed in 1 cup white wine for 5 minutes, shelled and cooled

1 10-ounce package frozen tiny peas, thawed

4 scallions (both white and green parts), sliced thin

4 tablespoons minced coriander leaves (cilantro)

1 roasted (over open flame or in oven) sweet red pepper, skinned, seeded, and deveined, and cut into ¼-inch dice

1 large jalapeño pepper, seeded and deveined, chopped fine

1 tablespoon fresh lemon juice

THE DRESSING

1 teaspoon minced garlic

¾ cup peanut, corn, or safflower oil

2 teaspoons curry powder or *garam masala*

1 teaspoon cumin

½ teaspoon allspice

¼ cup white wine vinegar

2 tablespoons Dijon mustard
Salt and freshly ground pepper to taste

1. Combine all the salad ingredients in a large serving bowl, cover, and refrigerate.

2. Make the dressing by cooking the garlic in 1 tablespoon of the oil over moderate heat in a small skillet, stirring, until it just starts to turn golden. Add the curry powder, cumin, and allspice and cook, stirring, for 1 minute. Stir in remaining oil and remove from heat.

3. In a food processor or blender combine the vinegar, mustard, salt, and pepper. With the motor running add the oil mixture in a slow stream until the dressing is combined and emulsified.

4. Pour the dressing over the cooled salad and toss gently to combine. Return salad, covered, to refrigerator to chill for at least 2 hours or overnight to allow flavors to meld. Remove from refrigerator 1 hour before serving. Toss again, gently, and serve at room temperature.

MOCK CRAB WITH PEAS, BEANS, POTATOES, AND CHILIES

This dish was completely improvised at the stove one night when both our kids unexpectedly decided to stay home for dinner—even though they were tired of sampling bean recipes. We had only used mock crab (a Japanese synthesis of antique origin that processes pollack fish and snow crab together and is sold under several brand names in this country, one of which is Sea Legs Supreme) in salad and a deviled crab appetizer but never before in a main dish. This one now has become a standard one-dish meal at our house.

SERVES 4 TO 6

1 large onion, quartered, each quarter cut into ⅜-inch slices

1 tablespoon chopped garlic

2 tablespoons peanut, corn, or safflower oil

Salt to taste

½ teaspoon freshly ground pepper or more to taste

4 medium potatoes, peeled, cut into ¾-inch dice, boiled for 10 minutes, and drained

1 can (4 ounces) whole green chilies, cut into ¼-inch dice, juice reserved

2 or 3 pickled jalapeño peppers, halved, sliced thin

1 package (10 ounces) frozen tiny peas

1. In a large skillet or sauté pan, over moderately high heat, sauté the onions and garlic in the oil, stirring, until soft and golden, about 4 to 5 minutes. Add salt and pepper.

2. Turn heat down to simmer. Stir in potatoes, chilies, and jalapeño peppers and cook for 5 minutes more. Stir in some of the chili juice to keep the mixture moist.

3. Add peas, beans, and mock crabmeat, stirring to combine well. Cover and cook for 5 minutes more.

4. Turn heat down to low and stir in sour cream. If the mixture seems dry, add remaining chili juice. Heat through and serve.

Sour cream separates and curdles if heat is too high. Heat should be no higher than a gentle simmer. Sour cream also soothes the heat from the jalapeños. If you like the sting, add another jalapeño or to taste.

1 can (10 ounces) canned
  cannellini beans, drained
  and rinsed
¾ pound mock crabmeat, broken
  into bite-sized pieces
1 cup sour cream

SCALLOPS WITH ORANGE BEAN SAUCE

SERVES 4

1 pound bay scallops, calicoes
  (Florida scallops), or sea
  scallops (if large, sliced in half
  or quartered)
3 tablespoons unsalted butter
¼ teaspoon salt
2 scallions (both green and white
  parts), sliced thin
5 tablespoons ruby port
½ cup orange juice
1 teaspoon ground coriander
  (cilantro)
¼ cup heavy cream
1 can (19 ounces) cannellini
  beans, drained and rinsed
1 large navel orange, peeled,
  wedges separated and cut
  into ½-inch pieces

1. In a large skillet or sauté pan over moderately high heat sauté the scallops in the butter, tossing, until they are just opaque, about 3 minutes.

2. Remove the scallops from the heat and with a slotted spoon transfer them to an oval serving platter. Cover loosely with foil to keep warm.

3. Add the scallions, port, orange juice, and coriander to the skillet. Turn heat to high and cook, stirring frequently, until reduced by almost half, about 3 minutes. Add the cream and stir until it is slightly thickened, about 2 minutes.

4. Turn the heat down to simmer, add the beans, and stir gently until the beans are heated through, about 3 minutes more.

5. Arrange the scallops and orange pieces down the center of the platter and pour the hot bean sauce over and around them.

COLD CURRIED RED SNAPPER WITH PINK BEANS AND GINGERED CARROTS

SERVES 4 TO 6

½ stick plus 2 tablespoons unsalted butter

1 teaspoon minced garlic

2 large red snapper fillets (about 1½ pounds total), skinned, lightly salted if desired

1 teaspoon *garam masala* or curry powder, preferably Madras

½ teaspoon ground cumin

½ teaspoon turmeric

¼ cup slivered blanched almonds

¼ cup sesame seeds, toasted

1 Granny Smith apple, peeled and diced

¼ cup golden raisins

1 cup thin-sliced cooked carrots

¼ cup bottled ginger marmalade
Salt, if desired
Freshly ground pepper

1 cup canned pink beans, drained and rinsed

1. Melt the 2 tablespoons butter over moderate heat in a sauté pan large enough to hold the fish fillets comfortably. Add the garlic and sauté until lightly golden. Add the fish fillets and sauté until fish is just opaque. Remove from pan and set aside to cool.

2. Melt the ½ stick butter in the same sauté pan over low heat. Stir in the *garam masala*, cumin, turmeric, almonds, sesame seeds, apple, raisins, carrots, and ginger marmalade and cook until just heated through. Season with salt and pepper. Remove from heat and cool.

3. With two forks, pull the fillets apart into bite-sized pieces.

4. Combine the curried mixture with the beans and the fish. Toss lightly and chill for ½ hour or serve at room temperature. Garnish with 1 tablespoon shredded unsweetened coconut, if desired.

THE BEANS THAT SATISFIED THE PHARAOHS

Well, maybe not the pharaohs, because this is actually a peasant dish. But it does date back to the time of the pharaohs. *Ful medames*—Egyptian fava beans—are eaten today in great restaurants, in mud huts, penthouses, and in the hand from street corner vendors. This particular version is almost a "national dish," served for centuries in this same manner seasoned with oil, garlic, and lemon and showered with chopped parsley, salt and pepper, with a hard-boiled egg partially submerged in the beans.

SERVES 6

3 cups *peeled* dried fava beans, soaked, rinsed, and cooked until tender, about 2 hours, then drained (peeled dried fava beans are available at many Middle Eastern and Italian markets and at specialty food stores)

1 tablespoon minced garlic

6 hard-boiled eggs (simmered over a very low flame for 10 minutes)

2 tablespoons chopped parsley

Light Tuscan olive oil to taste

Salt to taste

Freshly ground black pepper to taste

3 lemons, quartered

1. While the drained beans are still hot, add the garlic and stir through.

2. Divide the beans among six warm soup bowls, bury a hard-boiled egg in each mound, and sprinkle liberally with parsley. Drizzle a little olive oil over each bowl and pass more at the table along with salt and pepper and the quartered lemons.

3. Diners should add salt and pepper, olive oil to taste, and plenty of lemon juice—then crush the egg with its creamy interior into the beans. More garlic may also be passed at the table. This dish is hearty enough to stand on its own but marries well with buttered rice.

GREEN CHILIES STUFFED WITH REFRIED BEANS OR CHILIES RELLENOS DE FRIJOLES

SERVES 6

6 *chiles poblanos* (California, Anaheim, or *Güero*—the blond chili)
3 cups Mexican Refried Beans (p. 148)
2 eggs, separated
Peanut, corn, or safflower oil for deep frying
½ cup plus 2 tablespoons all-purpose flour
2 tablespoons unsalted butter
1½ cups milk
Salt and white pepper to taste
½ cup grated white cheddar or Monterey Jack cheese

1. Impale a chili on a fork and hold it over a gas flame or electric burner until skin blackens and blisters. Repeat with each chili. Place the chilies in a damp cloth or in a plastic storage bag or brown paper bag; close the bag and allow chilies to cool for 30 minutes. Peel the chilies; the thin skin should slip off easily.

2. Slit each skinned chili lengthwise and remove stem, seeds, and veins.

3. Stuff the prepared chilies with the refried beans.

4. Beat egg yolks well. Beat whites separately until they are glossy and hold stiff peaks. Fold the whites into the yolks. Set aside.

5. Heat the oil in a deep fryer or saucepan to between 360° and 375° on a deep-fry thermometer.

6. Mound the ½ cup flour on a sheet of waxed paper or in a shallow dish. Dip each chili in turn into the flour, coating well, then into the egg. Fry in the hot oil two at a time until golden brown. Drain on paper towels while heating oven and preparing sauce.

7. Preheat oven to 350°.

8. Melt the butter in a saucepan over moderate heat. Gradually stir in milk and continue stirring until sauce boils and thickens. Stir in salt and pepper to taste, add the cheese, and continue stirring until the cheese melts and is incorporated.

9. Arrange the stuffed chilies in an ovenproof baking dish and pour the cheese sauce evenly over them. Bake, uncovered,

for about 15 minutes or until heated through. Serve from baking dish.

The chilies may be garnished with slivered, toasted almonds, fresh pomegranate seeds, or pumpkin seeds.

WARM WHITE BEANS WITH BASIL, TOMATOES, AND CHEESE

SERVES 4 TO 6

4 medium red, ripe tomatoes, peeled, seeded, and chopped coarse

2 teaspoons minced garlic

¾ cup chopped fresh basil

1 teaspoon salt

½ teaspoon freshly ground pepper or more to taste

1 small jalapeño or hot red pepper, seeded, deveined, and chopped fine

½ cup light Tuscan olive oil

2 cans (15 ounces each) cannellini beans, undrained

½ cup grated Parmesan cheese

½ pound Italian fontina cheese, diced fine

1. In a bowl combine the tomatoes, garlic, basil, salt, pepper, chopped jalapeño, and olive oil. Allow to stand at room temperature, mixing occasionally, for 2 to 3 hours.

2. Pour the beans and their liquid into a saucepan, add ½ cup water, and slowly heat through, covered, over moderately low heat.

3. Drain beans and rinse under hot running water. Transfer to a serving bowl. Add the two cheeses and toss gently until cheeses begin to melt. Add the tomato mixture and mix through. Serve warm or at room temperature instead of pasta.

VEGETARIAN BLACK BEAN CHILI SPIKED WITH BOURBON

SERVES 8

1 tablespoon cumin seed
1 tablespoon dried oregano
2 tablespoons paprika
½ teaspoon cayenne pepper
1 small fresh *pasilla* chili, seeded, deveined, and pulverized in a blender or food processor (available at Hispanic food stores and some supermarkets)
3 tablespoons corn oil
1 large onion, chopped
2 teaspoons salt or to taste
1 dried *chipotle* chili, halved, seeded, and deveined (available at Hispanic food stores and some supermarkets)
1 sweet green pepper, seeded, deveined, and chopped
1 can (35 ounces) Italian plum tomatoes with liquid
2 cups dried black beans, soaked
3 cups water
½ cup bourbon or corn whiskey
½ cup chopped fresh coriander leaves (cilantro)
1 cup grated Parmesan cheese
1 cup sour cream

1. In a small dry skillet toast the cumin seeds, the oregano, the paprika, and the cayenne over medium heat, stirring for 2 or 3 minutes or until the paprika turns very dark. Transfer to a small bowl and add the *pasilla* chili.

2. In a large saucepan heat the corn oil over moderate heat until hot but not smoking and sauté the onion for 5 minutes or until wilted. Add 1 teaspoon of the salt, the reserved spice mixture, the *chipotle* chili, the pepper, the garlic, and the tomatoes and simmer for 15 minutes more.

3. Add the black beans, the bourbon, 3 cups of water, and the bay leaf and cook, partially covered, over low heat for 2½ hours or until beans are tender, adding more water if necessary to keep the beans covered.

4. Stir in the coriander and remaining 1 teaspoon salt.

5. Ladle the chili into bowls, sprinkle with Parmesan, and add a large dollop of sour cream. Pass more Parmesan at the table.

SUGGESTION: Serve with additional chopped onion, tostaditas (tortilla chips), shredded romaine lettuce, and chopped fresh ripe tomatoes, if you wish.

Whenever working with hot peppers wear rubber gloves and/or wash hands thoroughly with soap and water after handling. By no means touch your eyes or other sensitive skin areas while working bare-handed with hot peppers. There will be no permanent damage but the temporary burning sensation is terribly uncomfortable. If *pasilla* and *chipotle* peppers are unavailable in your area, substitute 2 or 3 fresh jalapeño peppers, chopped. The smoky flavor of the *chipotle* will be missing, however.

SALADS

GARLICKED WHITE BEAN AND MATJES HERRING SALAD

SERVES 4 TO 6

1 pound Great Northern or other dried white beans, cooked and drained
1½ cups Garlic Vinaigrette Dressing (recipe follows)
1 medium purple onion, sliced very thin
1 cup chopped parsley
1 tablespoon snipped fresh dill
1 cup matjes herring cut in ½-inch dice
1 teaspoon freshly ground pepper
1 cup chopped sweet red pepper

1. Transfer drained beans to a mixing bowl. Pour 1 cup of the dressing over hot beans. Allow to cool.

2. Add onions, parsley, dill, and herring. Toss and season to taste with pepper. Toss again. Cover and refrigerate.

3. To serve, remove from refrigerator ½ hour before serving. Toss with chopped red pepper. Correct seasoning, adding more dressing and more pepper, if you like. Serve as a first course or as a main dish at lunch or supper with black bread, good sweet butter, and a glass of beer.

GARLIC VINAIGRETTE DRESSING

MAKES 3 CUPS

1 whole egg
⅓ cup Dijon mustard
⅔ cup red wine vinegar
Salt to taste
Freshly ground pepper
1 tablespoon garlic, chopped
2 cups light Tuscan olive oil

1. In a food processor or blender, process egg, mustard, and vinegar for 1 minute. Season with salt and pepper.

2. With the motor running, drop the garlic through the feed tube, then slowly add oil in a steady stream. When oil is incorporated, stop processor, taste, and correct seasoning.

3. Transfer to jar or plastic container and refrigerate until ½ hour before using. Dressing will last for two weeks in the refrigerator.

SUGGESTION: Maybe we're just used to it, but a dressing that does not contain several drops of Maggi Seasoning doesn't taste finished to us. Try it. A great Swiss cook we know got us to use it years ago, and it has become addictive.

SAVORY CHICKEN, CHUTNEY, AND WHITE BEAN SALAD

SERVES 4 TO 6

1 cup dried Great Northern or other white beans, cooked and drained

4 slices bacon, cooked and crumbled

3 tablespoons light Tuscan olive oil

2 tablespoons white vinegar

1 tablespoon Dijon mustard

1 small onion, finely chopped

1 whole chicken breast, poached, skinned, boned, and cut into ½-inch cubes

½ teaspoon salt or to taste

½ teaspoon white pepper

3 tablespoons chopped fresh parsley

2 romaine lettuce leaves, shredded

3 tablespoons walnuts or cashews, chopped fine

1 tablespoon minced fresh coriander leaves (cilantro)

3 tablespoons chutney (mixed fruit or mango) or more to taste

1. Transfer beans to a glass or ceramic serving bowl and let them cool, if just cooked.

2. Add remaining ingredients to the cooled beans and toss to combine.

3. Chill, covered, for at least an hour before serving.

BEADS FOR BEANS

*A*merican Indian tribes were great traders and one of the things they traded was their indigenous bean. Consequently American beans were spread throughout much of the U.S., the Caribbean Islands, Central and South America long before the European discoveries. Just which Indian groups grew which beans originally remains somewhat of a mystery but the preferences of different regions of the Western Hemisphere for a particular bean may be continuations of ancient traditions. The Southwest likes the Pinto and Mexican Red. Brazilians and the Caribbeans are partial to Black Beans. Boston likes Pea or Navy Beans. The Indians had a hand in all these preferences and more.

SOPHISTICATED SALMON SALAD WITH WHITE BEANS AND FENNEL

SERVES 4 TO 6

1 15½-ounce can pink salmon, drained, skin discarded

1 16-ounce can cannellini beans, rinsed and drained

20 pitted canned black olives, sliced thin

1 medium fennel bulb (about 1 pound), sliced thin

4 scallions (both white and green parts), sliced thin

6 red radishes, sliced thin

2 tablespoons minced fresh parsley leaves
Salt and freshly ground black pepper

THE DRESSING

½ teaspoon fennel seeds

1 teaspoon minced garlic

4 tablespoons white wine vinegar

3 dashes Maggi Seasoning

2 tablespoons Dijon mustard

¾ cup peanut, corn, or safflower oil

OPTIONAL GARNISH

Fresh lemon juice to taste
Chopped pimento

1. Flake the salmon into a large serving bowl and combine with beans, olives, fennel, scallions, radishes, parsley, salt, and pepper.

2. Make the dressing in a food processor or blender by combining the fennel seeds, garlic, vinegar, Maggi Seasoning, and mustard. With the motor running add the oil in a slow stream until the dressing is combined and emulsified. Pour over salmon mixture and toss gently to combine. Drizzle lemon juice over salad and sprinkle pimento around the edges.

HURRIED SALMON AND CHICK-PEA SALAD

SERVES 4 TO 6

3 cups canned chick-peas,
   drained and rinsed
1 medium onion, chopped
1 celery stalk, chopped fine
1 teaspoon minced garlic
4 tablespoons chopped fresh
   parsley
4 tablespoons snipped fresh dill
3 tablespoons red wine vinegar
½ cup light Tuscan olive oil
   Salt to taste
1 teaspoon freshly ground pepper
   or to taste
2 cups canned salmon, drained
   (15½ ounce can)
2 ripe tomatoes, peeled, seeded,
   and cubed
2 tablespoons capers

1. In a serving bowl combine the chick-peas, onion, celery, garlic, parsley, and dill.

2. Add vinegar, oil, salt, and a generous amount of pepper. Toss.

3. Remove any pieces of skin from salmon and discard. Add salmon and tomatoes to chick-pea mixture and toss again.

4. Chill in the refrigerator for about ½ hour. Before serving, sprinkle capers evenly over salad.

We've had a good deal of success with this recipe using leftover fish or raw tuna. When using raw tuna, cut into ½-inch dice, toss with 1 teaspoon Japanese horseradish powder softened with 2 tablespoons soy sauce, and add to salad.

PILOYES OR SALAD OF CHICKEN WITH PIQUANT KIDNEY BEANS

SERVES 4 TO 6

2 cups dried kidney beans
3 bay leaves
1 teaspoon dried thyme
⅔ cup cider vinegar
1 whole chicken breast, poached, skinned, boned, and cut into ½-inch cubes
½ cup chicken stock from poaching breast
1 medium onion, sliced thin
1 large ripe tomato, seeded and chopped
½ red sweet pepper, seeded, deveined, and cut into ½-inch dice
2 fresh jalapeño peppers, seeded, deveined, and chopped
2 tablespoons chopped fresh coriander leaves (cilantro)
2 tablespoons light Tuscan olive oil
Salt to taste
Freshly ground pepper
1 bunch watercress
Freshly grated Parmesan cheese

1. Pick through, wash, and in a large saucepan, soak the beans with the bay leaves and thyme in water to cover by 2 or 3 inches for 4 hours or overnight. Or use Quick Soaking Method (p. 22).

2. Drain and add fresh water to cover well. Add ⅓ cup vinegar to beans and bring to the boil over high heat. Reduce heat and simmer, partially covered, for about 30 minutes or until the beans are just tender.

3. Drain the beans, reserving ½ cup of the cooking liquid. Cool.

4. Add the remaining ⅓ cup of vinegar and the stock to the reserved cooking liquid. Pour over beans.

5. Combine the chicken, onion, tomato, pepper, jalapeños, coriander, oil, salt, and pepper with the beans. Stir well and chill for 2 hours, covered.

6. Line a salad bowl with the watercress and transfer salad with a slotted spoon to the bowl. Sprinkle with some of the Parmesan and pass more at the table.

CHILLED GREEN BEANS IN WALNUT SAUCE

SERVES 6

1 cup coarsely broken walnut
   pieces
1 teaspoon chopped garlic
1 small onion, chopped
3 tablespoons chopped fresh
   coriander (cilantro) or 1
   teaspoon ground coriander—
   the flavor is completely
   different, however
1½ teaspoons hot paprika
   Salt to taste
¼ cup red wine vinegar
¼ cup or more chicken stock,
   homemade or canned, or
   water
1 pound green beans, trimmed
   and cut in half
1 tablespoon minced parsley

1. In a food processor or blender puree the walnuts, garlic, onion, coriander, paprika, salt, vinegar, and enough chicken stock to result in a smooth paste.

2. In a saucepan over moderately high heat, cook the green beans for 8 to 10 minutes, or until just crisp-tender. Drain, transfer to a serving bowl, and add the walnut sauce. Toss gently but thoroughly, cover with foil or plastic wrap, and refrigerate for 1 hour or until chilled. Sprinkle with parsley and serve.

Green beans were called string beans by the year 1759. The name derived from the long fiber down the side of the pod. Some called them snap beans from the sound the pod makes when broken. Burpee developed "the stringless bean" by 1894 but the old name stuck despite its new meaninglessness. Food processors' public relations people like to call them green beans, the color seemingly more edible than strings. The yellow version got its own name of wax bean by 1900; until then it had been merely a yellow string bean.

WINTER SALAD OF WARM RED LENTILS

SERVES 6

1 cup dried red lentils
1 medium onion, chopped
1 medium carrot, pared and chopped
1 bay leaf
¼ teaspoon thyme
4 slices bacon, cooked crisp, drained, crumbled, 1 tablespoon drippings reserved
3 tablespoons light Tuscan olive oil
1 tablespoon white wine vinegar
1 tablespoon Dijon mustard
1 teaspoon minced garlic
½ teaspoon salt or to taste
¼ teaspoon cumin
½ teaspoon freshly ground pepper
1 cucumber, peeled, seeded, and cut into ½-inch dice
3 scallions (both white and green parts), sliced thin
6 romaine lettuce leaves
¼ cup shredded Jarlsberg cheese
1 tablespoon chopped fresh parsley

1. In a saucepan over moderately high heat bring 4 cups of water, the lentils, onion, carrot, bay leaf, and thyme to the boil. Skim off any foam that rises to surface. Turn down heat to simmer and cook gently, uncovered, for about 15 minutes, or just until lentils are tender but still firm. Remove from heat, drain, and discard bay leaf.

2. In a saucepan over moderate heat whisk reserved bacon drippings, oil, vinegar, mustard, garlic, salt, cumin, and pepper together. Bring to the boil and cook 1 minute.

3. Transfer warm lentils to a heatproof serving bowl. Add cucumbers and scallions and pour hot dressing over them. Toss well to coat.

4. Arrange lettuce leaves on individual serving plates and spoon out lentil salad, dividing evenly. Sprinkle with Jarlsberg and parsley and serve while still warm.

BROWN RICE AND LENTIL SALAD WITH FENNEL AND PEPPERONI

SERVES 4 TO 6

1 cup long-grain brown rice
1 cup lentils, cooked
1 cup pepperoni, casing removed, sliced thin and chopped (about ¼ pound)
1 small fennel bulb, chopped
4 scallions (both white and green parts), sliced thin
4 large garlic cloves, boiled for 10 minutes, drained and peeled
¼ cup red wine vinegar
1 tablespoon Dijon mustard
Salt and freshly ground pepper to taste
⅓ cup peanut, corn, or safflower oil

1. Sprinkle the rice into a large saucepan of rapidly boiling water. Stir and boil for 25 minutes or until tender. Drain in a colander, refresh under cold water, and set aside to drain and cool.

2. Combine the cooled rice and cooked lentils in a bowl along with the pepperoni, fennel, and scallions.

3. In a food processor or blender puree the garlic with the vinegar, mustard, and salt and pepper to taste. With the motor running add the oil in a stream until the dressing is combined and emulsified. Pour over the salad and toss well. Taste for seasoning. May be made a day in advance and refrigerated. Remove from refrigerator at least an hour before serving. Serve at room temperature.

TONNO CON FAGIOLI (TUNA SALAD WITH WHITE BEANS)

SERVES 4

1 can (6½ ounces) solid white tuna packed in oil, drained
1 can (16 ounces) cannellini beans, drained and rinsed
1 medium onion, chopped fine
1 tablespoon chopped parsley, flat-leaf Italian, preferably
½ teaspoon oregano
1 tablespoon light Tuscan olive oil
2 tablespoons fresh squeezed lemon juice
Salt to taste
½ teaspoon freshly ground pepper

1. In a bowl flake the tuna with a fork.

2. Add the rest of the ingredients and toss gently to blend well. Serve at room temperature.

Plain old Tuna Salad American style (a 6½-ounce can of white meat tuna, flaked; a medium onion chopped; plenty of freshly ground pepper; and good quality commercial mayonnaise in quantity) benefits from the addition of a 10-ounce can, drained and rinsed, of cannellini beans mixed in. It also stretches the tuna to feed a couple of more mouths.

CHILI COLESLAW WITH BEANS AND PEANUTS

SERVES 6 TO 8

1 pound cabbage, cored and shredded

1 cup cooked or canned black-eyed peas, drained and rinsed

½ cup dry roasted peanuts, chopped

2 pickled jalapeño peppers, seeded, deveined, and minced

4 tablespoons white wine vinegar

2 tablespoons soy sauce

3 tablespoons peeled and grated fresh gingerroot

2 tablespoons sesame oil

6 tablespoons peanut, corn, or safflower oil

Salt and pepper to taste

1. Combine the cabbage, black-eyed peas, peanuts, and minced jalapeños in a large bowl.

2. In a small bowl whisk together the vinegar, soy sauce, gingerroot, and sesame oil. Add the peanut oil in a thin stream, whisking until the dressing is combined and emulsified.

3. Pour dressing over coleslaw and toss well to coat. Cover and refrigerate to cool. Toss again before serving.

USING THE OLD BEAN

Some legumes have been cultivated for so long now that they can't be found anywhere in their wild state. This is probably why there is such an active interest and trade in "Heirloom Beans," especially for breeding purposes. Some of these antique beans are used by bean breeders for their adaptability to specific topographical and climatic conditions and others for their distinctive cooking qualities. The U.S. Department of Agriculture keeps an extensive seed storage facility for the express purpose of this kind of research—and to preserve beans no longer under cultivation.

SUNOMONO OR GREEN BEANS IN GINGER VINAIGRETTE

SERVES 6 TO 8

1 pound young green beans, trimmed
¼ cup Japanese rice vinegar
¼ cup sugar
1 tablespoon mirin (Japanese rice wine)
1 teaspoon fine-grated fresh gingerroot
1 teaspoon toasted sesame seeds or chopped dry-roasted peanuts
Fresh ginger, julienned very fine

1. In a medium saucepan cook the beans in lightly salted boiling water over moderately high heat until tender, about 7 or 8 minutes. Drain and refresh under cold running water. When cooled, cut beans into 1½-inch lengths and arrange in neat rows on a serving platter. Cover with dampened paper towels and wrap in plastic wrap. Chill in refrigerator up to 24 hours. Remove 30 minutes before serving.

2. Several hours before serving combine the vinegar and sugar in a bowl. Stir or whisk until dissolved and stir in mirin and grated ginger. Cover and allow to stand at room temperature until 10 minutes before serving time.

3. Spoon the dressing over the beans. Garnish with sesame seeds and a sprinkling of julienned ginger.

CHILLED PEA BEAN VINAIGRETTE WITH HAM AND PEANUTS

SERVES 6

1 pound dried pea beans,
   soaked, drained, and rinsed
1 medium onion, chopped coarse
4 garlic cloves, sliced
1 bay leaf
1 tablespoon salt
⅓ cup red wine vinegar
1 teaspoon Maggi Seasoning
1 tablespoon Dijon mustard
½ cup light Tuscan olive oil
6 scallions (both white and green
   parts), sliced thin
¼ pound boiled or smoked
   cooked ham, diced small
½ cup dry-roasted peanuts,
   chopped

1. Pour the soaked beans into a large saucepan and add enough cold water to cover them by 2 inches. Add onion, garlic, and bay leaf. Bring to the boil, then lower heat and simmer, partially covered, for 1 hour and 30 minutes. Test for tenderness. If tender, add salt and simmer 5 minutes more. Drain the beans and discard the bay leaf.

2. In a small bowl whisk together the vinegar, Maggi Seasoning, mustard, and salt and pepper to taste. Add the oil in a stream, whisking until the dressing is combined and emulsified.

3. Transfer the beans to a large serving bowl and pour over the dressing. Add the scallions, ham, and peanuts. Toss gently to mix through. Chill, covered, for 2 hours or more and serve.

WHITE BEAN AND SNOW PEA SALAD WITH SARDINE DRESSING

SERVES 8

THE SALAD

 2 cans (1 pound each) cannellini
    beans, drained and rinsed
 ½ pound snow peas, stringed,
    cut in thirds
 1 red onion, chopped fine
    Salt and pepper to taste

THE DRESSING

 1 can skinless and boneless
    sardines, with their oil
 1 large egg
 ¼ cup fresh lemon juice
 2 tablespoons Dijon mustard
 ⅔ cup vegetable, corn, or
    safflower oil

1. Gently combine beans, snow peas, and onion in serving bowl with salt and freshly ground black pepper to taste.

2. In a food processor or blender, puree the sardines, egg, lemon juice, and mustard. With the motor running add the oil in a stream and blend until smooth.

3. Pour the dressing over the bean mixture and toss carefully to combine.

The dressing may be made 1 day in advance and refrigerated in a covered container. Do not assemble salad until at least 2 hours before serving.

SALT COD AND BEAN SALAD WITH TOMATO AND ONION

SERVES 6 TO 8

¾ pound pure white salt cod
1 large onion, chopped coarse
1 sweet red pepper, cored, seeded, and cut into ¼-inch strips
12 Kalamata black olives or other oil-cured black olives, cut in half and pitted
2 cups cooked Great Northern beans, rinsed
1 cup light Tuscan olive oil or vegetable oil
¼ cup red wine vinegar
1 teaspoon dry mustard
1 teaspoon salt
Freshly ground pepper
1 teaspoon Maggi Seasoning
1 fresh ripe tomato, diced

1. In a large bowl soak salt cod in plenty of water and place in the refrigerator for 36 hours or more or until most of the salt has been leached out and the fish is pliable. Change the water often, whenever you think of it, during soaking.

2. Soak onion in salted water for 1 hour, drain.

3. Drain cod and flake with fingers into a serving bowl. Add onion, pepper, olives, and beans, stirring gently to combine.

4. In a small bowl or covered jar, combine the oil, vinegar, mustard, salt, pepper, and Maggi Seasoning. Whisk or shake. Pour dressing over salad, add tomato, and toss gently. Refrigerate several hours before serving.

LENTIL, TOMATO, AND SCALLION SALAD VINAIGRETTE

SERVES 4 TO 6

⅔ cup lentils, cooked and drained, cooled
2 large tomatoes, skinned, seeded, and chopped coarse
½ cup scallions (both white and green parts), sliced
⅓ cup chopped fresh parsley
½ teaspoon oregano
3 tablespoons light Tuscan olive oil
2 teaspoons fresh lemon juice
2 teaspoons red wine vinegar
Salt and freshly ground pepper

1. In a large serving bowl gently toss the lentils with the tomatoes, scallions, ¼ cup of the parsley, and oregano.

2. Drizzle the olive oil, lemon juice, and wine vinegar over the mixture, season with salt and pepper to taste and toss. Serve at room temperature or chilled, garnished with the remaining parsley.

Lima beans weren't called lima beans originally. They were called butter beans, and still are called that in England. They come from Peru whose capital is Lima, so it was Lima with a capital "L" at first—at first being not until the 1850's. The capital has long since been dropped to lower case and the pronunciation changed from lee-mah to lye-mah.

LIMA BEAN SALAD WITH PROSCIUTTO AND ARUGULA

SERVES 4

1 tablespoon Dijon mustard
1½ tablespoons fresh lemon juice
¼ cup light Tuscan olive oil
1 10-ounce package frozen baby lima beans
2 ounces prosciutto or Westphalian ham, sliced thin, cut into ½-inch pieces
1 small red onion, chopped fine
2½ teaspoons minced fresh tarragon leaves or 1 teaspoon dried
1 cup chopped arugula leaves
Salt and freshly ground pepper to taste

1. In a serving bowl whisk together the mustard, lemon juice, and salt and pepper to taste. Add the oil in a slow stream, whisking the dressing until it is combined and emulsified.

2. In a saucepan of boiling water boil the lima beans for 2 minutes or until just tender. Drain well.

3. While still warm, toss the beans with the dressing, ham, onion, tarragon, arugula, and salt and pepper to taste. Serve warm or at room temperature.

SUGAR SNAP PEA SALAD WITH WALNUT GINGER VINAIGRETTE

SERVES 4

1 pound sugar snap peas or snow peas, stringed
1½ tablespoons lime juice
2 teaspoons *tamari* or soy sauce
⅓ cup walnut oil
1 tablespoon minced fresh gingerroot
3 scallions (both white and green parts), sliced thin diagonally

1. In a large saucepan of boiling water blanch the peas for about 45 seconds or until they begin to puff and turn bright green. Drain immediately and refresh under cold running water. Transfer to serving bowl. Pat dry with paper towels, if necessary.

2. In a small bowl whisk the lime juice, *tamari*, and walnut oil until well blended. Add the gingerroot and scallions and stir well. Pour over snap peas and toss until well coated. Chill, covered, for at least 30 minutes, but not longer than 2 hours or peas will lose their crunch.

CHICK-PEA AND CHORIZO SALAD

SERVES 4

1 19-ounce can chick-peas, rinsed and drained
¾ pound chorizo sausage, cut into ¼-inch slices, cooked in a dry pan to render out most of fat and drained on paper towels
⅓ cup red wine vinegar
1 cup light Tuscan olive oil
1½ tablespoons Dijon mustard
1 teaspoon paprika
1 teaspoon ground cumin
  Salt and freshly ground pepper to taste
6 scallions (both white and green parts), sliced thin
3 or 4 dashes Maggi Seasoning

1. In a serving bowl combine the chick-peas and the sausage. Drizzle 2 tablespoons vinegar and ¼ cup of oil over the mixture and toss well.

2. In a small bowl whisk together the remaining vinegar, the mustard, paprika, cumin, and salt and pepper to taste. Add the remaining oil in a slow stream, whisking until the dressing is combined and emulsified.

3. Pour the dressing over the salad, add the scallions and Maggi Seasoning, and toss well. Serve at room temperature. (May be made 1 day in advance and refrigerated, covered. Let come to room temperature for 1 hour before serving.)

GREEN BEAN AND RADISH SALAD

SERVES 6

1 pound green beans, trimmed,
  cut into 2-inch lengths
3 tablespoons light Tuscan olive
  oil
1 tablespoon tarragon vinegar
½ teaspoon dried tarragon
¾ teaspoon salt or to taste
¼ teaspoon freshly ground pepper
1 cup diced (⅛ inch) red
  radishes
1 scallion (both white and green
  parts), sliced very thin

1. Over high heat bring a large saucepan of water to the boil. Add green beans, return to boil, and cook until just crisp-tender, about 4 minutes. Drain immediately and refresh under cold running water, drain well, and transfer to serving bowl.

2. In a small bowl whisk together oil, vinegar, tarragon, and salt and pepper. Add dressing and radishes to beans and toss well. Let stand at room temperature no longer than 30 minutes, tossing occasionally, or beans will lose their bright color. Sprinkle with scallion and serve.

CHICK-PEA AND FETA SALAD

SERVES 6

2 cans (19 ounces each)
  chick-peas, drained and
  rinsed

2 large fresh ripe tomatoes, cut
  into ½-inch dice

6 ounces feta cheese, cut into
  ½-inch dice

3 scallions (both white and green
  parts), sliced thin

6 Kalamata olives, pitted and
  quartered

2 tablespoons chopped fresh
  parsley

½ cup light Tuscan olive oil

1 tablespoon red wine vinegar or
  more to taste

1 teaspoon oregano

½ teaspoon freshly ground pepper
  or more to taste

1. Combine chick-peas, tomatoes, cheese, scallions, olives, and parsley in a serving bowl.

2. Whisk together oil, vinegar, oregano, and pepper in a small bowl or shake in a jar or bottle with a tight-fitting lid. Pour over salad and toss gently to coat. Serve at room temperature.

HOOF & VINE

*T*he bean family seems to have had its beginnings in the wild state in the world's tropical zone. So adaptable were these ancient beans that early human agriculturalists extended their growth into sub-tropic and temperate areas which allowed them not only the growth of forage for their animals but the cultivation of fresh edible beans which when dried could see whole tribes through harsh northern winters. So beans let them take along their proteins both on the hoof and on the vine. Beans also allowed men to live and thrive in previously inhospitable areas. Thus beans accounted in part for the migration of cultures, and, sometimes because of crop failures, forced the emigration of peoples as well.

WARM GREEN LENTIL SALAD

SERVES 6 TO 8

1 pound dried green lentils
1 medium onion, stuck with 3 cloves
1 teaspoon chopped garlic
1 bay leaf
2 tablespoons red wine vinegar
6 tablespoons light Tuscan olive oil
Salt and freshly ground pepper to taste
½ teaspoon dry mustard or 1 teaspoon Dijon mustard

1. Put lentils, onion, garlic, and bay leaf in a saucepan and cover by 1 inch with water. Turn heat to high and bring to the boil. Turn heat immediately to low and simmer, covered, about 30 minutes or until lentils are just tender. Check a few times to see that there is enough water. (Tip the pot slightly; if you can see liquid, do not add more—in any case don't add more than ¼ cup. Liquid should all be absorbed by end of cooking time.)

2. Remove from heat, discard onion and bay leaf, and drain, if necessary.

3. Whisk together the vinegar, oil, salt, pepper, and mustard in a small bowl. Pour over hot lentils and toss to coat thoroughly. Taste for seasoning. Do not chill. Serve warm.

ADZUKI BEAN AND HONEYDEW SALAD WITH YOGURT-CARDAMOM DRESSING

This is almost a dessert—a sweet salad—like fruit salad or cranberry sauce. And like cranberry sauce, it can be served with turkey, roasts, and game. Or it can be served on its own like fruit salad. The adzuki beans are tiny, dark-coated, nutty-tasting Japanese beans that are underutilized in this country.

SERVES 4

½ cup plain yogurt
½ teaspoon ground cardamom
1 tablespoon maple syrup or to taste
¼ cup fresh lime juice or to taste
1 cup cooked adzuki beans, drained and rinsed
1 small honeydew scooped into balls with a melon-ball scoop or cut into 1-inch chunks

1. In a serving bowl combine the yogurt, cardamom, maple syrup, and lime juice and whisk till smooth.

2. Add the adzuki beans, stir, and allow to marinate in the refrigerator for 1 hour.

3. Add the honeydew balls and stir gently until combined well.

WHITE BEAN SALAD WITH ROSEMARY AND ROQUEFORT

SERVES 4

2 cups cooked white kidney beans or 1 can (19 ounces) cannellini beans, drained and rinsed under hot running water

1 small onion, chopped fine

2 red, ripe tomatoes, peeled, seeded, and cut into ½-inch dice

¼ cup plus 1 tablespoon white wine vinegar

2 tablespoons minced fresh rosemary leaves or 2 teaspoons crumbled dried rosemary

1 tablespoon Dijon mustard
Salt and freshly ground pepper to taste

½ cup light Tuscan olive oil

¼ pound Roquefort cheese, crumbled

1. Place the drained, hot beans in a serving bowl and toss gently with onion, tomatoes, ¼ cup vinegar, and the rosemary. Allow to cool.

2. In a small bowl whisk the remaining 1 tablespoon vinegar, mustard, salt, and pepper to taste, and still whisking, add the oil in a slow stream until the dressing is combined and emulsified.

3. Add the dressing and Roquefort to the salad and toss gently to combine well. Serve at room temperature or chill for 1 hour in the refrigerator.

If you find Roquefort too pungent, substitute shredded white cheddar or shredded Monterey Jack.

POTATO AND
SUGAR SNAP PEA SALAD

SERVES 4

1½ pounds red boiling potatoes,
quartered lengthwise and cut
into ½-inch pieces
3 tablespoons fresh lemon juice
Salt and freshly ground pepper
to taste
½ pound sugar snap peas,
stringed, pods halved
diagonally
1 tablespoon grainy Dijon
mustard
⅓ cup olive oil
1 tablespoon minced fresh
parsley

1. Steam the potatoes in a colander or steamer set over rapidly boiling water, covered, for 8 to 12 minutes, or until just tender. Transfer to serving bowl and toss with 1 tablespoon of the lemon juice and salt and pepper to taste. Allow to cool.

2. Blanch the snap peas in a saucepan of boiling water for 5 seconds. Drain and refresh under cold running water.

3. Whisk together the remaining 2 tablespoons lemon juice and the mustard. Add the oil in a slow stream, whisking until combined and emulsified.

4. Add the snap peas to the potatoes, sprinkle with parsley, and stir in the dressing, tossing salad gently. This salad is best served at room temperature.

BEAN AND POTATO SALAD WITH SOUR CREAM AND CUCUMBERS

SERVES 6 TO 8

2 cups sliced (¼ inch) pared boiling potatoes

2 cups cooked pink, pinto, or cannellini beans or 1 can (16 ounces), drained and rinsed

1 cup sour cream

½ cup mayonnaise or more to taste

¼ cup snipped fresh dill

1 cup chopped, seeded, unpared cucumber*

1 small onion, chopped fine

1½ teaspoons salt or to taste

½ teaspoon freshly ground pepper

*If the cucumber is waxed, peel it—the long skinny European cucumbers are never waxed and work well in this salad.

1. In a saucepan of salted boiling water, cook the potatoes, uncovered, for 10 minutes or until firm-tender.

2. Place the beans in a colander and pour the hot potatoes and their liquid over them.

3. Whisk sour cream, mayonnaise, and dill in a bowl until smooth. Stir in cucumber, onion, salt, and pepper.

4. Transfer warm potatoes and beans to a serving bowl and pour dressing over them. Toss gently until well combined. Refrigerate, covered, until well chilled.

*B*ostonians, because of baked beans, have been called bean eaters since 1800, a somewhat derogatory appellation. The city itself was known as Beantown, still is. Because baked beans took long, slow oven baking often the local baker popped a family's bean pot into his oven overnight and returned it hot with a loaf of his freshly baked brown bread, thus the further tradition of baked beans and brown bread.

SAUCES
AND PUREES

COLD EGYPTIAN FAVA BEAN PUREE WITH HERBS

SERVES 6 TO 8

2 cups *peeled* dried fava beans, soaked and rinsed (the peeled beans are available at many Middle Eastern and Italian markets and at specialty food stores)

1 large onion, chopped coarse

1 celery stalk with leaves, cut into 2-inch lengths

½ cup chopped fresh parsley

½ cup snipped fresh dill

1 teaspoon crushed caraway seeds

1 tablespoon dried mint

1 teaspoon salt or to taste

½ teaspoon freshly ground pepper

2 tablespoons peanut, corn, or safflower oil

2 medium onions, chopped

1 teaspoon minced garlic

1. Place beans in a saucepan with water to cover by 1 inch. Add the onion and celery and bring to the boil over high heat. Turn heat to simmer and cook, covered, about 2 hours or until beans are very soft. Add water, if necessary, to keep beans covered.

2. Drain beans, reserving about a cup of cooking liquid.

3. In a food processor, working in batches, process the beans with a little cooking liquid to a thick puree. Return each batch of puree to saucepan. To the last batch of beans add the parsley, dill, caraway seeds, mint, and salt and pepper. Process well. Combine with rest of bean puree, stirring to blend.

4. In a skillet over moderate heat bring the oil to rippling and stir in the onions and garlic. Sauté, stirring frequently, until golden brown, about 7 minutes.

5. Stir half the onion-garlic mixture into the puree and blend well. Transfer the puree to a serving bowl and spread remaining onion-garlic mixture on top. Cover with foil or plastic wrap and refrigerate for about 2 hours or until puree firms up. Remove from refrigerator at least ½ hour before serving. Serve cold or at room temperature as a side dish.

BEAN ROUILLE (GARLIC AND PEPPER SAUCE)

To serve with fish or seafood.

MAKES ABOUT 1½ CUPS

1 cup canned or cooked cannellini beans, drained and rinsed

4 large garlic cloves, crushed

1 6-ounce jar roasted sweet red peppers, drained and patted dry

2 teaspoons tomato paste

½ teaspoon cayenne or to taste

½ teaspoon paprika

¼ cup light Tuscan olive oil

1. In a blender or food processor puree the beans, garlic, red peppers, tomato paste, cayenne, and paprika until a smooth paste is formed.

2. With the motor running add the oil in a stream until it is combined. Thin the sauce with 1 or 2 tablespoons of water, if it is too thick (it should have the consistency of heavy cream). Prepare up to 8 hours ahead, cover, and refrigerate.

SAVORY COUNTRY-STYLE LENTIL PUREE

SERVES 10

1 pound lentils, rinsed and picked over
2 medium onions
4 whole cloves
2 garlic cloves, sliced thin
2 medium carrots, halved lengthwise, cut into ¼-inch semicircles
1 parsnip, peeled, quartered lengthwise, and cut into ¼-inch pieces
1 celery stalk, sliced thin
1 bay leaf
½ teaspoon thyme
3 tablespoons chopped fresh parsley
½ teaspoon freshly ground pepper
2 teaspoons salt or to taste
4 tablespoons unsalted butter

1. Place the lentils in a large saucepan. Stud the onions with 2 cloves each and bury them in the lentils. Add the garlic, carrots, parsnip, celery, bay leaf, thyme, and pepper.

2. Cover beans and vegetables with 1 inch of water and bring to the boil. Turn heat to moderately low and simmer, covered, for 30 minutes. Add the salt and continue cooking 20 minutes more, stirring occasionally, until lentils are very tender but not mushy.

3. Drain the lentils, reserving the liquid. Remove and discard the cloves and bay leaf.

4. Puree the lentils and vegetables in a food processor, food mill, or blender, in batches, if necessary. If the puree is stiff and dry, add up to 1 cup of reserved cooking liquid.

5. For a silken texture force the puree through a fine sieve to remove any bits of skin (if a food mill is used this may not be necessary).

6. To reheat the puree place it in a double boiler or in a covered saucepan set in a larger pan of boiling water reaching halfway up the sides of the saucepan. Stir or whisk occasionally until hot. Whisk in the butter, 1 tablespoon at a time. Taste and adjust seasoning. Serve with roast turkey, duck, fresh ham, or other roasted or grilled meats.

To serve as a vegetable without pureeing, drain, reserving liquid, remove and discard cloves and bay leaf. Remove onion and chop or crush with a potato masher and return to lentils. Reheat briefly, if necessary, with a little of the cooking liquid.

PUREED FAVA BEANS
WITH CREAM AND SAVORY

SERVES 4 TO 6

2 pounds fresh young fava beans,
shelled and boiled for 15
minutes or 1 can (19 ounces)
favas, drained and rinsed
½ cup heavy cream
1 teaspoon crumbled dried
savory
Salt and freshly ground pepper
to taste

1. In a food processor or blender puree the beans with the cream until satiny smooth. Add savory, salt and pepper, and process briefly to combine.

2. In a saucepan over low heat, cook the puree gently, stirring occasionally, until heated through.

If using mature fresh beans, shell, drop into rapidly boiling water to cover and cook for 20 minutes, or until tender. Drain, pat dry, and peel off outer seed coat. Proceed as above.

ALL IN THE FAMILY

*O*f the flowering plants, only orchids and daisies can boast larger families than the legumes. But neither of them can say that they are the second most important contributor to the human diet. Grasses—rice, wheat among them— are first. But in spite of being second, beans offer more nutrients to our diets than the grains. They're more versatile as well. Some are eaten pod and all, some just the seed, some fresh, some dried, some offer the whole plant for consumption, roots, stems, leaves, pods, and seeds.

What protein legumes do not offer us directly we get a good percentage of after it is processed into meat through the digestive systems of animals and fowl. Legumes are widely grown for feed, you see. Alfalfa, clover, the lespedezas, and the vetches are all in the family.

PIQUANT WHITE BEAN PUREE

SERVES 6

¼ cup peanut, corn, or safflower oil
1 medium onion, chopped fine
1 tablespoon minced garlic
½ teaspoon cumin
⅛ teaspoon cayenne or more to taste
3 cups cooked Great Northern or white kidney beans or canned cannellini beans, drained and rinsed
¼ cup chicken stock, homemade or canned, for thinning puree
3 tablespoons minced fresh parsley
Salt to taste

1. In a skillet heat the oil until rippling, add the onion and garlic and cook, stirring, until onion is soft and translucent. Stir in cumin and cayenne and cook mixture, stirring, for 30 seconds, until well combined.

2. In a food processor or blender puree the beans with enough chicken stock to thin the puree to the consistency of sour cream. Add the onion mixture and the parsley, salt to taste, and pulse until combined well.

3. Heat the puree in a saucepan over moderate heat, stirring, until heated through.

SUGGESTION: Serve with grilled meats, fish, or poultry. Serve in place of mashed potatoes or plain rice to accompany anything with gravy.

Leftover bean puree makes a wonderful sandwich spread. Try it slathered thickly on pumpernickel with thin slices of raw onion and lots of freshly ground pepper.

ITALIAN BEAN PUREE WITH GARLIC

This is a side dish that can become a soup in minutes. We often double the recipe for this very reason. It keeps well for several days in the refrigerator or freezes for use weeks or months later. All you do is add water or stock to the puree to thin it into a soup—a little Parmesan sprinkled on top and some hot Italian bread, a green salad, and there's a light but filling dinner for a cold winter's night.

SERVES 6 TO 8

1 tablespoon chopped garlic
½ cup light Tuscan olive oil
2 tablespoons chopped flat-leaf Italian parsley
2 cups dried white kidney beans (cannellini) or white navy beans, Great Northerns, or other white beans cooked and drained—or 2 20-ounce cans of cannellini beans, drained and rinsed
Salt to taste
½ teaspoon freshly ground pepper (or more to taste)
1 cup beef or chicken stock, homemade or canned

1. In a soup pot sauté the garlic in the oil over medium heat, stirring until just golden. Add parsley and stir to combine. Add the cooked beans, salt to taste, and the pepper.

2. Turn the heat to simmer, cover the pot, and cook for about 5 to 7 minutes. Puree the beans in batches in a food processor or blender—or put through a food mill—adding a little stock with each batch.

3. Return puree to pot with any remaining stock and simmer for another 5 to 7 minutes. Taste for seasoning and serve.

SPICY DIPPING SAUCE OF BEANS AND SOUR CREAM

MAKES 4 CUPS

3 cups cooked and drained Great Northern, white kidney beans, red kidney beans, or pinto beans—or 3 cups canned, drained, and rinsed
1 cup sour cream
1 teaspoon chopped garlic
1 scallion (both white and green parts), chopped
2 tablespoons minced fresh coriander leaves (cilantro)
2 tablespoons soy sauce
½ cup fresh lemon juice
1 tablespoon Dijon mustard
⅓ cup vegetable, corn, or safflower oil
½ teaspoon freshly ground pepper
½ teaspoon ground cumin

1. In a food processor or blender puree the beans together with the sour cream, garlic, scallion, coriander, soy sauce, lemon juice, and mustard until very smooth.

2. With the motor running add the oil in a slow stream until combined well with the puree. Add the pepper and cumin and pulse once or twice to blend.

3. Transfer to a serving bowl and chill covered, for 2 hours or more. Serve with raw vegetables, potato chips, or tortilla chips.

FRESHLY MINTED CHICK-PEA YOGURT DIPPING SAUCE

MAKES 3 CUPS

2 cups canned chick-peas, drained and rinsed
1 cup plain yogurt
2 tablespoons freshly squeezed lemon juice
2 tablespoons chopped fresh mint leaves, or 1 tablespoon dried
3 cloves garlic, minced
¼ teaspoon sweet paprika
¼ teaspoon freshly ground pepper
½ teaspoon salt, if desired, or to taste

1. Remove and discard any loose skins from chick-peas. Place in a food processor or blender and process with on-and-off motions until a smooth puree, stopping machine and scraping down sides if necessary.

2. Over a bowl, press puree through sieve with back of spoon to remove any remaining skins—or put through food mill.

3. Stir in yogurt, lemon juice, mint, garlic, paprika, pepper, and salt. Taste and correct seasoning.

4. Blend well and refrigerate, covered, for at least an hour. Remove from refrigerator ½ hour before serving. Transfer to serving bowl and serve as a dip for lightly blanched cold vegetables or as a sauce for cold poached fish.

When mint leaves are not available, try substituting snipped fresh dill or minced fresh basil.

SUGGESTION: Serve with quartered, small-sized pita breads, toasted in the oven, as an appetizer or with drinks.

DESSERTS

FROZEN BLUSHING BEAN SOUFFLE WITH RASPBERRY SAUCE

SERVES 6 TO 8

1½ cups confectioners' sugar, sifted
6 large egg yolks
2 cups milk, scalded
2 cups heavy cream, chilled
2 cups adzuki bean puree
1 package (10 ounces) frozen raspberries, thawed

1. In the bowl of an electric mixer beat the sugar and the egg yolks until very light and add the scalded milk in a stream, beating at slow speed.

2. Transfer custard mixture to a heavy saucepan and cook over moderate heat, stirring, until thickened. Strain through a fine sieve into a metal bowl set in a bowl of ice cubes and allow to cool, stirring occasionally, for 1 hour.

3. In a chilled bowl beat the cream until it forms soft peaks. Fold one-third the cream into the bean puree to lighten it, then gently fold in the rest of the cream just to combine thoroughly.

4. Fold the custard into the bean mixture and freeze in an ice-cream freezer according to the manufacturer's instructions.

5. Fit a 1½ quart soufflé dish with a collar of doubled foil or waxed paper extending 3 inches above the rim of the dish. Spoon the frozen mixture into the dish, smoothing the top. Freeze the soufflé, covered with plastic wrap, in the freezer for 24 hours.

6. Remove from freezer, strip off collar, and allow soufflé to stand in refrigerator for 30 minutes. Serve with the raspberries spooned over.

RESERVATION PUDDING À LA MODE

Butter for greasing baking dish
2 whole eggs
¾ cup dark unsulphured molasses
⅓ cup firmly packed dark brown sugar
1 teaspoon ground cinnamon
1 tablespoon minced fresh gingerroot or 1 teaspoon ground ginger
½ teaspoon salt
¼ teaspoon baking soda
4 cups milk
1 cup canned cannellini beans or chick-peas, drained and pureed in a blender or food processor
½ cup raisins plumped in a jigger of sherry or rum
3 tablespoons unsalted butter
Vanilla ice cream

1. Preheat oven to 350°.

2. Butter a deep 1½ quart baking dish.

3. In a saucepan combine eggs, molasses, brown sugar, cinnamon, ginger, salt, baking soda, and 2½ cups of the milk. Whisk until blended.

4. Stir in pureed beans and cook over moderate heat, stirring constantly, until mixture bubbles and becomes thick.

5. Remove from heat, add raisins and soaking liquor, butter, and remaining 1½ cups milk. Stir until smooth.

6. Turn into baking dish and bake 1¼ hours or until pudding is still slightly soft in the center. Allow to cool and firm up for 15 minutes before serving.

7. Serve warm with vanilla ice cream.

PINK SPANISH CREAM

SERVES 8

1 cup pink bean puree (or
   adzuki bean puree)
1 quart milk
1 cup plus 8 teaspoons sugar
   Zest of 1 lemon cut in strips
1 3-inch cinnamon stick
9 large egg yolks
5 tablespoons cornstarch

1. Whisk the bean puree and 3 cups of the milk in a heavy saucepan and add the lemon zest and cinnamon stick.

2. In a bowl whisk the egg yolks, the cornstarch, and the remaining cup of milk. Pour the mixture through a sieve into the milk-bean mixture and bring to a boil. Turn heat down to moderate and stir with a wooden spoon until it starts to thicken. Simmer for 2 minutes, whisking, until smooth and thick. Discard the cinnamon stick and lemon zest.

3. Divide the custard among 8 heatproof 1-cup custard cups and sprinkle the top of each with 1 of the remaining 8 teaspoons of sugar. Set the cups in a baking pan and broil about 4 inches from the heat for about 2 minutes or until the sugar caramelizes. Serve warm or refrigerate and serve cold.

FRANGELICO-SPIKED ADZUKI BEAN MOUSSE

SERVES 6

1 envelope plus 1¼ teaspoons
  unflavored gelatin
6 tablespoons water
1 cup sieved adzuki bean puree
  (or red kidney bean puree)
6 egg yolks
½ cup plus 1 tablespoon sugar
½ teaspoon vanilla
1½ cups heavy whipping cream
1 jigger (1 ounce) plus 1
  tablespoon Frangelico (hazelnut)
  liqueur
¼ cup chopped hazelnuts

1. Sprinkle gelatin over water in small saucepan; allow to stand until softened. Cook over low heat, stirring constantly, until gelatin is dissolved. Remove from heat. Stir in adzuki puree and combine thoroughly.

2. Beat egg yolks in the bowl of an electric mixer. Gradually beat in ½ cup of the sugar until light and fluffy. Beat in vanilla and the gelatin mixture until smooth.

3. Beat 1 cup of the heavy cream until stiff peaks form. Add jigger of Frangelico and beat until combined, than fold into gelatin mixture. Pour into lightly oiled 4- or 5-cup mold. Refrigerate until set, about 4 hours.

4. Beat remaining ½ cup cream with 1 tablespoon Frangelico and 1 tablespoon sugar until stiff peaks form. To serve, unmold mousse and garnish with whipped cream and chopped hazelnuts.

*N*avy beans *are called that because in the mid-nineteenth century the Navy used a lot of them.*

Pinto beans, *of course, get their name from the Spanish word for* painted. *The beans are streaked with color. But it wasn't until 1916 that they were given the name—the horse of the same color was called* pinto *by Southwesterners long before, since 1860.*

TIRAMI SU ALLA CECI

V enice's favorite dessert has hit our shores like a tidal wave. The name means "pick-me-up" yet it is so rich it could "lay-one-low." Venetians often use *savoiardi*, a type of stale ladyfinger, as the base, or, in more elegant homes and restaurants, a *genoise*. We've adapted the original using our chick-pea cake for a chewier, more hearty confection.

4-LAYER CAKE SERVING 12

2 recipes Garbanzo Bean Cake (p. 262–63)

2 pounds mascarpone (see note below)

6 eggs at room temperature, separated

½ cup sugar

6 ounces semisweet chocolate, chopped fine

2 cups strong brewed espresso coffee at room temperature, sweetened with 2 tablespoons sugar and 2 ounces coffee liqueur or brandy

⅓ cup unsweetened cocoa powder, preferably Dutch process

1. Divide each cake into two layers. Set aside.

2. In a large bowl, stir the mascarpone with a wooden spoon until smooth. Add egg yolks and ½ cup sugar, stirring vigorously until very smooth. Stir in the chopped chocolate.

3. Beat the egg whites until stiff peaks form. Stir ¼ of the whites into the mascarpone mixture to lighten, then gently fold in the remaining whites.

4. Place one cake layer cut side up on a round cake plate with a raised lip. Moisten cake thoroughly by brushing or pouring ¼ of the espresso over it. Spread ¼ of the mascarpone mixture evenly on top. Repeat with remaining layers ending with the mascarpone spread smoothly and evenly.

5. Sift cocoa powder over the top and refrigerate, covered, for 24 hours before serving.

Mascarpone is like a buttery cream cheese, available in Italian markets and some specialty food stores. If unavailable mix 2 cups heavy cream with 1 pound ricotta cheese in a food processor until smooth and unlumpy. Refrigerate until ready to use.

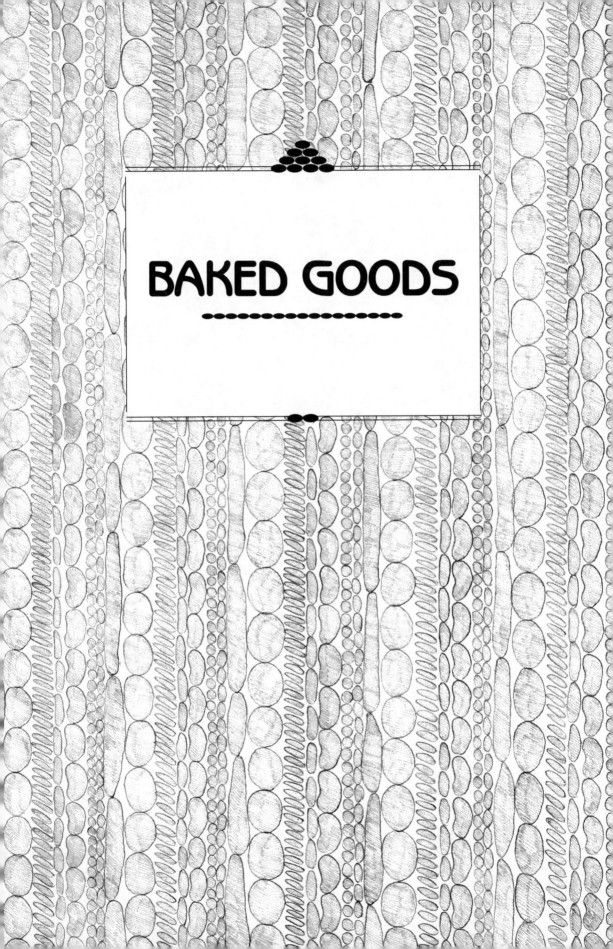

BAKED GOODS

Why bake with beans when flour produces a product by which all—or most—standards are set? Besides, beans are limited. Even bean flours don't bake into flaky pie crusts or combine with yeast to make traditional breads.

But beans do offer at least two guarantees over white flour and whole wheat flour baking. The product will be more nutritious, containing fiber, protein and other healthful components that are milled away in white flour production. The product is also moister than that produced by white or whole wheat flours.

Bean baking does take patience, however. Bean purees contain a good deal of water and so baking times are longer. But if you like moist, almost creamy-textured cakes, beans are beautiful.

We use bean purees made from beans cooked in water until soft, with no other flavorings. They are drained and then processed until very smooth in a food processor. That's it. We use either home-cooked beans or canned. The canned varieties must be well rinsed and drained to remove as much of the salt as possible as well as the oligosaccharides.

Bean purees make excellent tortes alone or in combination with nuts, and because they come in an assortment of colors they often can add a subtle taste-bud-tingling extra. The use of black bean puree when making chocolate tortes or cakes, for instance, makes them *look* more chocolatey and seem to taste more intensely chocolate, as well.

Try a few of the recipes here and get the feel of baking with beans. Experiment with your own favorite cakes and tortes. Just remember that baking times must be extended, measurements of liquid such as milk should be cut back, and that the final texture may be different—finer-grained and more tender, almost velvety.

The bean, one of the kitchen's humblest ingredients, reaches new heights of brilliance when combined with eggs, nuts, cream, chocolate, butter, and other traditional friends of flour. Not as versatile in the bake oven as flour, the bean, nevertheless, should take its rightful place as one of the brightest stars in the celestial confectionery. If we can increase its radiance, if we can help launch a new culinary career for one of the oldest of man's sustainers, we will know "how sweet it is!"

SOIL FOOD

Botanically classed in the plant family as Leguminosae, meaning pod-bearing, beans and peas are similar to other legumes like alfalfa and the vetches in their unique ability to capture nitrogen from the air and use it to aid their growth—and not incidentally, enrich the soil they grow in rather than rob it of nutrients. Even the earliest agricultural accounts recognized the value of growing legumes to maintain the fertility of the soil.

GINGERED BEAN
AND CARROT CAKE

2 cups sugar

4 eggs

1½ cups corn oil

2 cups pink bean or cannellini
bean puree

2 teaspoons baking soda

½ teaspoon salt

2 teaspoons cinnamon

2 tablespoons minced fresh
gingerroot

½ teaspoon nutmeg, preferably
freshly grated

1 cup chopped pecans

2 cups grated carrots

½ cup raisins or currants

1. Preheat oven to 350°. Butter a 12-inch round cake pan.

2. In the large bowl of an electric mixer, beat the eggs, one at a time, into the sugar, incorporating each one thoroughly before adding the next.

3. Beat the oil into the egg mixture and add the bean puree, baking soda, salt, cinnamon, ginger, and nutmeg. Incorporate thoroughly.

4. With a spatula fold in the nuts and raisins, then fold in the carrots until well combined.

5. Bake in center of the oven for 1 hour and 10 minutes. Cool on a wire rack before frosting.

CREAM CHEESE FROSTING

8 ounces cream cheese, softened

½ stick unsalted butter, softened

1 cup confectioner's sugar

2 teaspoons vanilla extract

12 pecan halves

1. Beat all ingredients together until smooth. Frost top and sides of cake. Decorate edge with pecan halves.

BLACK BEAN BROWNIES

These are moist, fudgy, creamy-textured brownies, the kind we like best. If you like a drier brownie, bake 5 to 10 minutes more.

4 squares unsweetened chocolate
½ pound unsalted butter
2 cups sugar
4 eggs
1 cup black bean puree
2 tablespoons instant espresso coffee powder
1 cup chopped walnuts

1. Preheat oven to 350°. Butter a 9-by-13-by-2-inch pan.

2. In a small saucepan over lowest heat possible melt the chocolate with the butter. Set aside.

3. With an electric mixer beat the eggs, one at a time, into the sugar. Add the chocolate mixture and beat until well combined.

4. Beat in the bean puree and the instant espresso powder.

5. With a spatula fold in the walnuts. Pour and scrape the batter into the pan, smooth the top and bake for 45 minutes.

6. Allow to cool completely in pan before cutting into 1½-inch-by-2-inch bars.

THE NEW ALCHEMY—FOOD INTO GOLD

When Cortez and his army of adventurers invaded and conquered Mexico, they brought the horse, which completely amazed the Indians who thought the men and the beasts they were riding were all of a piece. But the Indians confronted Cortez & Co. with marvels which would completely transform the way of life Spain and its neighbors in Europe had lived until that moment.

Cortez was looking for gold (which he found, of course) but he returned to Spain with items of much more value: cotton, tobacco, rubber, corn, chocolate, tomatoes, peanuts, vanilla, chili, avocado, turkeys, pineapple and other foods and products unfamiliar to the Spanish. This fantastic variety of then exotic foods made up the rich and varied diet of the Indians but none of them was known to the Europeans—even the bean of Mexico in all its varieties was new, lusher tasting, and more versatile than the broad bean common to the old world. Beans—along with most of the other foods just mentioned—were eaten out of necessity by the Spanish conquistadores but with enormous enthusiasm and immediately shipped off to Spain for cultivation and eventual introduction to the rest of the world.

BATHSHEBA OR BLACK BEAN CHOCOLATE TORTE

This torte is so rich and fudgy-textured that it needs no icing, but a dollop of whipped cream won't do any harm.

SERVES 6 TO 8

4 ounces (4 squares) semisweet chocolate melted with 2 tablespoons coffee
¼ pound unsalted butter
¾ cup plus 1 tablespoon sugar
3 eggs, separated
⅓ cup ground walnuts
1 tablespoon vanilla extract
1 cup black bean puree
Confectioner's sugar

1. Preheat oven to 350°.
2. Butter an 8-inch round cake pan.
3. In a small saucepan over lowest possible heat melt the chocolate with the coffee. Set aside to cool.
4. In a large bowl of an electric mixer, cream butter and sugar together until well combined and pale yellow in color.
5. Beat in egg yolks one at a time.
6. Add the cooled chocolate, nuts, vanilla, and bean puree to the egg mixture on low speed and mix until just blended.
7. In a separate bowl beat egg whites until soft peaks form. Add the remaining tablespoon sugar and continue beating until stiff peaks form.
8. With a rubber spatula fold one-third of the egg whites into the batter to lighten, incorporating thoroughly. Gently fold in remaining two-thirds of the egg whites until they are completely blended in.
9. Turn the batter into the cake pan, smoothing the top with the spatula, pushing it to the rim of the pan. Bake in the center of the oven for 1 hour. The middle of the torte may move slightly when the pan is shaken. It is meant to be quite moist.
10. Cool in the pan on a wire rack for 10 minutes. Run a sharp knife around the edge and reverse cake onto the rack. Allow to cool completely. Transfer to serving plate. Dust top with confectioner's sugar and serve.

SPICED PINTO BEAN CAKE WITH FRUITS AND NUTS

SERVES 10

Butter for cake pan
2 cups cooked pinto beans
1 egg, beaten
¼ cup (½ stick) melted unsalted butter
1 cup all-purpose flour
1 teaspoon baking soda
¼ teaspoon salt
1 teaspoon cinnamon
1 teaspoon allspice
½ teaspoon ground cloves
2 cups chopped apples
½ cup chopped walnuts
1 cup raisins or currants
2 teaspoons vanilla extract
Confectioners' sugar
8 walnut halves

1. Preheat oven to 375°. Generously butter a 10-inch tube pan.

2. In a food processor puree the beans, egg, and melted butter.

3. Add the flour, baking soda, salt, cinnamon, allspice, and ground cloves. Blend dry ingredients into bean mixture with several on and off motions until well combined.

4. Scrape batter into a mixing bowl and add apples, chopped walnuts, raisins, and vanilla. Stir until well blended.

5. Pour into tube pan and bake in center of the oven for 45 minutes to 1 hour. Turn out onto wire rack to cool. Dust with confectioners' sugar and decorate with walnut halves.

CITRUS CREAM BEAN CAKE

SERVES 8

THE SYRUP
- ⅓ cup sugar
- 3 tablespoons grated orange zest
- ⅓ cup water

THE CUSTARD
- 2¼ cups milk
- 1 4-inch vanilla bean
- 5 large egg yolks
- ½ cup sugar
- 3 tablespoons cornstarch
- 2 tablespoons grated lemon zest
- 1 tablespoon fresh lemon juice
- ½ cup very cold heavy whipping cream

THE CAKE
- 1 recipe Garbanzo Bean cake (p. 263), baked and cooled

1. To make the syrup combine the sugar, orange zest, and water in a small saucepan and bring to the boil, stirring. Lower heat and simmer for 5 minutes. Remove from heat and allow mixture to cool, then strain through a sieve, pressing hard on the zest. Reserve the zest in a separate bowl.

2. To make the custard scald the milk with the vanilla bean in a saucepan. Discard the vanilla bean. In a bowl whisk the yolks then whisk in the sugar and cornstarch. Add the milk in a slow stream whisking as you do so (this may be done with an electric mixer, but since the ingredients are not beaten, just well-combined, the hand method is adequate). Pour the mixture into the saucepan and cook, stirring, over moderate heat until it thickens. Simmer the custard for 10 minutes, stirring occasionally, and stir in the lemon zest and juice. Remove from heat and allow to cool, covered with a round of waxed paper, then chill for 1 hour.

3. To assemble the cake, slice it horizontally into 2 layers. Brush the cut sides generously with the syrup. Set the bottom layer on a serving plate cut side up and spread with ¾ cup of the custard. Set the second layer, cut side down, on the custard.

4. Beat the cream in a chilled bowl until it holds stiff peaks, then fold it into the remaining custard. Spread the top and sides of the cake with the cream mixture. Decorate the edge of the cake with the reserved orange zest. Chill for at least 2 hours or overnight before serving.

CHOCOLATE MIDNIGHT BEAN TORTE

SERVES 8 TO 10
ONE 9-INCH CAKE

Unsalted butter and all-purpose
flour for cake pan
2 cups black bean puree
½ cup Cognac or brandy
⅓ cup heavy cream
¾ cup sugar
6 tablespoons unsalted butter,
softened
1 pound semisweet chocolate,
broken into small pieces
5 eggs, at room temperature
2 egg yolks, at room temperature
2 tablespoons cornstarch
Chocolate icing

1. Butter and flour a 9-inch round cake pan.

2. Whisk bean puree, Cognac, and heavy cream in large bowl until just smooth. *Do not overbeat or cream will curdle.* Whisk in sugar and butter.

3. Melt chocolate in top of double boiler over simmering water, stirring occasionally until smooth. Stir into bean mixture. Whisk the eggs and egg yolks into the bean mixture, one at a time, beating well after each addition. Sift cornstarch over batter and fold in.

4. Pour batter into prepared pan. Place in unheated oven then turn oven to 300°. Bake until a toothpick inserted in center of cake withdraws *almost*, but not quite, clean, about 1 hour and 10 minutes. (Check after 1 hour because ovens vary and temperature may not be true.) Cool on wire rack 15 minutes. Invert on serving plate and remove pan. Allow to stand, covered in plastic, at room temperature, overnight.

5. Spread top and sides of cake evenly with the icing. Serve in small slices—this is a rich, dense cake.

CHOCOLATE ICING

4 ounces semisweet chocolate
2 tablespoons unsalted butter
1 tablespoon espresso or strong
brewed coffee
1 tablespoon Cognac, brandy, or
coffee liqueur

1. Melt chocolate and butter in top of double boiler over simmering water (or in small saucepan over very low heat), stirring constantly until smooth.

2. Stir in coffee and Cognac, remove from heat, and cool to room temperature before spreading on cake.

RUM CASHEW RED BEAN CREAM PIE

SERVES 6 TO 8

FOR THE PIE SHELL

1⅔ cups graham cracker crumbs
¼ cup sugar
¾ stick unsalted butter, melted and cooled

FOR THE FILLING

3-ounce package cream cheese
1 cup confectioners' sugar, sifted
¼ cup milk
1 cup sieved (to remove bits of skin) red kidney bean puree
2 teaspoons vanilla extract
½ cup plus 3 tablespoons chopped rum cashews (available at specialty stores and fine candy shops)
1½ cups well-chilled heavy whipping cream

1. Preheat the oven to 425°. To make the pie shell, combine well the crumbs, sugar, and melted butter in a bowl and press the mixture into a 9-inch glass pie plate. Bake the shell for about 10 minutes or until it darkens slightly. Remove and let cool.

2. To make the filling, in the bowl of an electric mixer beat the cream cheese with the confectioners' sugar until light and fluffy, beat in the milk, the bean puree, vanilla, and ½ cup rum cashews.

3. In a chilled bowl beat the heavy cream until it holds stiff peaks. Stir ⅓ of it into the bean mixture, then fold in the remaining cream gently but thoroughly. Mound the filling in the shell and sprinkle with remaining rum cashews. Chill, covered, for at least 4 hours or overnight.

VARIATION: Substitute an equal amount of rum-soaked currants, drained, for the cashews.

CHOCOLATE RED BEAN CAKE WITH COCOA ICING

SERVES 6 TO 8

Butter for coating pans
2 ounces unsweetened chocolate
3 cups red kidney bean puree
¾ teaspoon baking powder
½ teaspoon baking soda
½ teaspoon salt
3 large eggs, lightly beaten
1½ cups sugar
1 teaspoon instant espresso powder
¾ cup vegetable oil
½ cup chopped walnuts

1. Line 2 buttered 8-inch round cake pans with waxed paper; butter paper and dust with flour.

2. In a double boiler melt the chocolate over hot water.

3. Preheat oven to 350°.

4. In a food processor combine the bean puree, baking powder, baking soda, salt, eggs, and chocolate. Process until well blended. Add the sugar, espresso powder, and oil and process to combine well. Pulse in the walnuts until just distributed.

5. Divide the batter between the two pans and bake the layers on the center rack of the oven for 35 to 45 minutes or until a knife inserted in the center comes out dry.

6. Set pans on wire racks to cool for 15 minutes, then turn out onto racks and remove waxed paper. Allow layers to cool completely.

THE ICING
8-ounce package cream cheese, softened
¼ pound unsalted butter, softened
1 pound confectioners' sugar, sifted
1 tablespoon coffee flavored liqueur or 1 teaspoon vanilla
⅔ cups Dutch-process cocoa powder

TO MAKE THE ICING AND ASSEMBLE

1. In the large bowl of an electric mixer beat the cream cheese and butter until the mixture is smooth.

2. Beat in the confectioners' sugar a little at a time until incorporated. Beat in the coffee liqueur and cocoa.

3. Place one layer of the cake on a serving platter, spread it with the icing, and place the second layer over it. Spread the top and sides of the cake with the remaining icing and chill the cake for at least an hour or overnight. Remove from refrigerator ½ hour before serving.

MUHAMMAD ALI'S FAVORITE WHITE BEAN DESSERT PIE

We don't remember where we heard that this southern-based pie was a favorite of Muhammad Ali or who passed the recipe on to us. But to taste it is to understand—if indeed it is his (the heavyweight champion's) favorite—exactly why. We must admit we've beefed up the spices in the filling and changed the pastry recipe to our tastes.

SERVES 6

1 recipe *pâte brisé* (recipe follows)

3 cups cooked Great Northern or white kidney beans or 3 cups canned cannellini beans, drained and rinsed

1 cup heavy whipping cream

¼ teaspoon freshly grated nutmeg or ½ teaspoon powdered

¼ teaspoon powdered ginger

¼ teaspoon cinnamon

¼ teaspoon mace

¾ cup sugar

3 large egg yolks

1 tablespoon dark rum

Pinch of salt

½ cup chopped pecans (optional)

1. Roll out dough ⅛ inch thick and fit it into a 9-inch pie tin. Crimp the edges with your fingers or fold a double thickness of dough around the edge and press with the tines of a fork or ruffled pastry wheel.

2. Prick the shell with a fork and refrigerate for ½ hour.

3. Preheat oven to 425°.

4. Set another 9-inch pie tin inside the lined tin and fill with dried beans or raw rice to weight it. Bake the shell for 10 minutes, remove the pie tin with the beans or rice and bake for 5 minutes more. Cool on rack.

5. Turn up oven heat to 450°.

6. In a food processor fitted with the steel blade or a blender, puree the cooked beans with the cream, nutmeg, ginger, cinnamon, and mace until smooth. Add sugar, egg yolks, rum, and a pinch of salt and process until combined well.

7. Pour mixture into baked pie shell, place on baking sheet, and bake at 450° for 10 minutes.

8. Reduce oven to 350° and bake for 25 minutes more or until well set.

9. Cool to room temperature, cover loosely with plastic wrap, and chill for at least 3 hours.

While pie is still hot from the oven we like to sprinkle chopped pecans over the filling.

PÂTE BRISÉ OR BROWN BUTTER PASTRY FOR PIE SHELL

1¼ cups all-purpose flour
¾ stick (6 tablespoons) cold
   unsalted butter, browned
   lightly, and resolidified in
   refrigerator or freezer, cut
   into small pieces
2 tablespoons cold solid vegetable
   shortening
¼ teaspoon salt
3 tablespoons ice water

1. In a large, chilled bowl blend the flour, browned butter, shortening, and salt until the mixture resembles coarse meal.

2. Add 3 tablespoons ice water and toss the mixture with two forks until the water is incorporated.

3. Quickly form the dough into a ball and knead it on a cool, flat surface for a few seconds to distribute the butter and shortening evenly. Reform into a ball. (The first 3 steps in this recipe may be done in a food processor fitted with the steel blade.)

4. Dust the dough with flour, wrap in waxed paper, and chill for at least 1 hour before rolling out.

The browned butter in this *pâte brisé* recipe gives the crust a nutty, even more buttery taste.

FAVA FEVER

*T*he fava or broad bean is almost never seen on the tables of this country but it was practically the only bean known to Europe until Columbus opened up a new world of food. Egyptians, Greeks, and Romans cultivated and ate fava beans (one of the most illustrious Roman families derived its name from the bean: Fabius).

The Romans ate them but at the same time considered fava beans unlucky. Maybe because they were used in elections—the white beans meaning "for," the black "against." Pythagoras, the philosopher, would not allow his disciples and followers to eat favas. Superstitious as he was brilliant, he evidently believed that beans contained the souls of the dead. This belief may have derived from the Roman funeral tradition of offering up beans to the dead at wakes. The Roman aristocracy preferred chick-peas to fava beans, demoting the latter to food for the lower classes. That peas and beans have, throughout history, been food for the masses may have been started by these Romans. Why not? They certainly originated a lot of other things—good as well as bad. Egyptians as far back as 500 B.C. thought favas unclean, causing insomnia and nightmares. Silly, perhaps, but they can cause favism in some Mediterranean peoples genetically susceptible—a severe anemic condition from eating undercooked favas or breathing their pollen.

LEMONY GARBANZO BEAN CAKE

A moist, tight-textured Mexican cake to serve with fresh fruit or ice cream.

SERVES 6 TO 8

2 cups canned chick-peas, drained and rinsed, any loose skins discarded
4 eggs
1 cup sugar
½ teaspoon baking powder
Grated zest of 1 lemon
Juice of 1 lemon
Confectioners' sugar

1. Place drained beans in the work bowl of a food processor and puree.

2. Add the eggs, sugar, baking powder, and lemon zest to the puree and pulse processor a few times just to combine ingredients well.

3. Preheat oven to 350°.

4. Butter a 9-inch cake pan. Cut a round of waxed paper to fit bottom of pan, set it in place, and butter top side. Pour in batter.

5. Bake on center rack of oven for 45 minutes or until a knife inserted in the center comes out dry.

6. Set on wire rack to cool for 15 minutes, then remove cake from pan and allow to cool to room temperature.

7. Before serving, squeeze lemon juice over the cake and sprinkle generously with confectioners' sugar.

GARBANZO BEAN CAKE II

For a lighter cake with more volume, try this variation.

½ cup evaporated milk
2 cups canned chick-peas, drained and rinsed, any loose skins discarded
4 eggs
1 cup sugar
½ teaspoon baking powder
Grated zest of 1 lemon
Juice of 1 lemon
Confectioners' sugar

1. Add ½ cup evaporated milk when pureeing the beans.

2. Separate eggs.

3. Add the yolks, sugar, baking powder, and lemon zest to the puree. Pulse to combine.

4. Beat egg whites until soft peaks form.

5. Fold batter gently into whites.

6. Pour into an angel food cake pan and bake in a 350° oven for 1 hour and 10 minutes. Test with knife before removing from oven to rack to cool.

7. Remove cake from pan and before serving, squeeze lemon juice over the cake and sprinkle generously with confectioners' sugar.

SUGGESTION: Add a cup of raisins, glacéed fruits, or nuts to the batter.

Or: add ½ to 1 cup of chocolate bits to the batter, eliminating the lemon zest and juice. Sprinkle with cinnamon-sugar instead of confectioners' sugar after unmolding still-warm cake.

Or: add ½ cup crushed lemon-flavored sour balls to batter.

INDEX